BASIC

# English Grammar

## FOURTH EDITION

**VOLUME A with Essential Online Resources**

*Betty S. Azar*
*Stacy A. Hagen*

**Basic English Grammar, Fourth Edition**
**Volume A**

Azar Associates: Shelley Hartle, Editor, and Sue Van Etten, Manager

Pearson Education, 221 River Street, Hoboken, NJ 07030

Staff credits: The people who made up the *Basic English Grammar, Fourth Edition, Volume A* team, representing editorial, production, design, and manufacturing, are, Dave Dickey, Nancy Flaggman, Amy McCormick, Robert Ruvo, and Marian Wassner.

Text composition: S4Carlisle Publishing Services

Illustrations: Don Martinetti—pages 5, 6, 8, 9, 17, 18, 19, 21, 22, 26, 29, 31, 33, 34, 36, 40, 41, 45, 46, 47, 48, 50, 51, 52, 53, 54, 59, 61, 63, 64, 69, 71, 74, 77, 78, 79, 81, 85, 89, 90, 91, 99, 101, 103, 106, 112, 114, 117, 125, 126, 129, 130, 133, 135, 139, 142, 143, 144, 146, 147, 153, 154, 155, 156, 162, 164, 171, 172, 173, 180, 184, 187, 188, 191, 192, 193, 197, 200, 202, 203, 204, 206, 207, 208, 210, 211, 212, 213, 214, 216, 217, 219, 220, 221, 222, 223, 228, 229, 230, 234, 237, 256, 258, 260, 262

Chris Pavely—pages 1, 3, 13, 14, 15, 16, 21, 32, 35, 38, 39, 43, 44, 49, 52, 62, 67, 68, 75, 79, 81, 88, 92, 95, 96, 98, 102, 103, 104, 105, 107, 108, 109, 120, 124, 148, 149, 151, 158, 161, 169, 173, 174, 175, 178, 181, 185, 189, 216, 236, 241, 247, 250, 252, 255, 259

Printed in the United States of America

ISBN 10: 0-13-466016-1
ISBN 13: 978-0-13-466016-5

2 2019

*To Shelley Hartle*

*For her watchful eye, her vast expertise,
her indefatigable good cheer*

# Contents

# Preface to the Fourth Edition

*Basic English Grammar* is a developmental skills text for beginning English language learners. It uses a grammar-based approach integrated with communicative methodologies to promote the development of all language skills in a variety of ways. Starting from a foundation of understanding form and meaning, students engage in meaningful communication about real actions, real things, and their own lives in the classroom context. Grammar tasks are designed to encourage both fluency and accuracy.

The eclectic approach and abundant variety of exercise material remain the same as in the earlier editions, but this fourth edition incorporates new ways and means. In particular:

- **CORPUS-INFORMED CONTENT**

  Based on corpus research, grammar content has been added, deleted, or modified to reflect discourse patterns. New information highlighting differences between spoken and written English has been added to the charts, and students practice more frequently used structures. We have been careful to keep the information manageable for beginning students.

- **PRESENTATION OF KEY GRAMMAR**

  Chapter 15 (in earlier editions of *BEG*) has been moved to Chapter 6 of this edition in order to teach possessive forms earlier and present all pronouns together.

- **WARM-UP EXERCISES FOR THE GRAMMAR CHARTS**

  Newly created for the fourth edition, these innovative exercises precede the grammar charts and introduce the point(s) to be taught. They have been carefully crafted to help students *discover* the target grammar as they progress through each warm-up exercise. The warm-up exercises can help the teacher assess how much explanation and practice students will need.

- **MICRO-PRACTICE**

  At the beginning level, a single grammar structure (e.g. basic pronouns and possessives) sometimes needs to be presented in several steps. Additional exercises have been created to give students more incremental practice.

- **LISTENING PRACTICE**

  Recent research highlights the importance of helping students at all levels understand authentic spoken English. New as well as revised exercises introduce students to relaxed, reduced speech. The student text audio is available on Essential Online Resources, and a full audio script can be found in the back of the book.

- **READINGS**

  This fourth edition now has a wide selection of readings for students to read and respond to. The content is carefully controlled so that the vocabulary is accessible to beginning students and the grammar structures appropriate to the chapter(s) studied.

- **WRITING TASKS**

  New writing tasks help students naturally produce the target grammar structures in extended discourse. These end-of-chapter activities include writing models for students to follow. Editing checklists draw students' attention to the grammar focus and help them develop proofreading skills.

*Components of Basic English Grammar*, Fourth Edition:

- **Student Book with Essential Online Resources** includes the access code for the audio, video, self-assessments, and teacher resources with the Student Book answer key.
- **Student Book with MyEnglishLab** that includes the access code to MyEnglishLab, an easy-to-use online learning management system that delivers rich online practice to engage and motivate students.
- A comprehensive *Workbook*, consisting of self-study exercises for independent work.
- An all-new *Teacher's Guide*, with step-by-step teaching suggestions for each chart, notes to the teacher on key grammar structures, vocabulary lists, and expansion activities.
- An expanded *Test Bank*, with additional quizzes, chapter tests, mid-terms, and final exams.
- *ExamView* software that allows teachers to customize their own tests using quizzes and tests from the *Test Bank*.
- *AzarGrammar.com*, a website that provides a variety of supplementary classroom materials, *PowerPoint* presentations for all chapters, and a place where teachers can support each other by sharing their knowledge and experience.

The Student Book answer key is available in the Teacher Resource Folder on Essential Online Resources. Teachers can choose to make the answer key available to their students. Homework can be corrected as a class or, if appropriate, students can correct it at home with the answer key and bring questions to class. In some cases, the teacher may want to collect the assignments written on a separate piece of paper, correct them, and then highlight common problems in class.

# MyEnglishLab

MyEnglishLab provides a range of interactive activities that help motivate and engage students. MyEnglishLab for *Basic English Grammar*, Fourth Edition includes:

- Rich online practice for all skill areas: grammar, reading, writing, speaking, and listening
- Instant feedback on incorrect answers
- Remediation activities
- Grammar Coach videos
- Robust assessments that include diagnostic tests, chapter review tests, mid- and end-of-term review tests, and final exams
- Gradebook and diagnostic tools that allow teachers to monitor student progress and analyze data to determine steps for remediation and support
- Student Book answer key in the Teacher Resource Folder

The Azar-Hagen Grammar Series consists of

- *Understanding and Using English Grammar* (blue cover), for upper-level students.
- *Fundamentals of English Grammar* (black cover), for mid-level students.
- *Basic English Grammar* (red cover), for lower or beginning levels.

# Tips for Using the New Features in this Text

## WARM-UPS

The *Warm-Up* exercises are a brief pre-teaching tool for the charts. They highlight the key point(s) that will be introduced in the chart directly following the *Warm-Up* exercise. Before beginning the task, teachers will want to familiarize themselves with the material in the chart. Then, with the teacher's guidance, students can discover many or all of the new patterns while completing the *Warm-Up* activity. After students finish the exercise, teachers may find that no further explanation is necessary, and the charts can then serve as a useful reference.

## LISTENING

The *Listening* exercises have been designed to help students understand American English as it is actually spoken. As such, they include reductions and other phenomena that are part of the natural, relaxed speech of everyday English. Because the pace of speech in the audio may be faster than what students are used to, they may need to hear sentences two or three times as they complete a task.

The *Listening* exercises do not encourage immediate pronunciation (unless they are linked to a specific pronunciation task). Receptive skills precede productive ones, and it is essential that students gain receptive familiarity with the speech patterns before they begin using them in their own speech.

Students are encouraged to listen to conversations the first time without looking at their text. Teachers can explain any vocabulary that has not already been clarified. During the second listening, students complete the assigned task. Teachers will want to pause the audio appropriately. Depending on the level of the class, pauses may be needed after every sentence, or even within a sentence.

It is inevitable that sound representations in the text will at times differ from the instructor's speech, whether due to register or regional variation. A general guideline is that if the instructor expects students will *hear* a variation, or if students themselves raise questions, alternate representations can be presented.

A *Listening Script* is included in the back of the book.

## READING

The *Readings* give students an opportunity to work with the grammar structures in extended contexts. Vocabulary that may be new to students is presented on yellow notes for teachers to introduce. One approach to the reading is to have students read the passage independently the first time through. Then they work in small groups or as a class to clarify vocabulary questions that didn't come up in the notes. A second reading may be necessary. Varied reading tasks allow students to check their comprehension, use the target structures, and expand upon the topic in speaking or writing.

## WRITING

As students gain confidence in using the target structures, they are encouraged to express their ideas in longer writing tasks. Model paragraphs accompany assignments, and question-prompts help students develop their ideas.

Editing checklists provide guidance for self- or peer-editing. One suggested technique is to pair students, have them exchange papers, and then have the *partner* read the paragraph aloud. The writer can *hear* if the content is what he or she intended. This also keeps the writer from automatically self-correcting while reading aloud. The partner can then offer comments and complete the checklist.

For classes that have not had much experience with writing, the teacher may want students to complete the task in small groups. The group composes a paragraph together, which the teacher then collects and marks by calling attention to beginning-level errors, but not correcting them. The teacher makes a copy for each group member, and each student makes the corrections *individually*.

### LET'S TALK

Each *Let's Talk* activity is set up as one of the following: **Pairwork, Small Group, Class Activity, Interview,** or **Game**. Language learning is a social activity, and these tasks encourage students to speak with others about their ideas, their everyday lives, and the world around them. Students speak more easily and freely when they can connect language to their own knowledge and experiences.

### CHECK YOUR KNOWLEDGE

Toward the end of the chapter, students can practice sentence-level editing skills by correcting errors common to this level. They can work on the sentences for homework or in small groups in class.

This task can easily be set up as a game. The teacher calls out an item number at random. Students work in teams to correct the sentence, and the first team to correctly edit it wins a point.

Please see the *Teacher's Guide* for detailed information about teaching from this book, including expansion activities and step-by-step instructions.

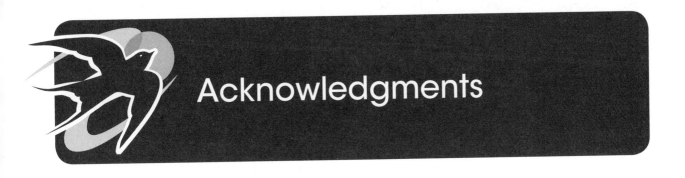

# Acknowledgments

Our revision began with extensive reviews from many talented professionals. We are grateful for the expertise of the following teachers: Susan Boland, Tidewater Community College; Lee Chen, Palomar College; Gene Hahn, University of Wisconsin, Stevens Point; Kathleen Keeble, Illinois Institute of Art, Chicago; Steven Lasswell, Santa Barbara City College; Michael Pitts, Los Angeles Southwest College; Carla Reible, Riverside City College; Alison Rice, Hunter College; Maria S. Roche, Housatonic Community College; Nelky Rodriguez, Riverside Community College; John Stasinopoulos, College of DuPage; Hallie Wallack, International Language Institute; Robert L. Woods, Central Washington University.

We were assisted throughout the process by a skilled and dedicated editorial staff. We would like to thank Shelley Hartle, managing editor, for her passion for the series and gifted editing and layout skills; Amy McCormick, editorial director, for guiding the project with exceptional judgment, attentiveness, and foresight; Marian Wassner, senior development editor (and grammar master), for her superb editing and thoughtful responses; Robert Ruvo, production manager, for his deft project management, keen eye for design, and unfailing good humor; Janice Baillie, copy-editor, for her stellar editing and remarkable ability to track all manner of detail; Sue Van Etten, business and website manager, for her expert and dedicated counsel.

We'd also like to express our appreciation to the writers of the supplementary texts: Kelly Roberts Weibel, *Test Bank* and Martha Hall, *Teacher's Guide*. Their creative and fresh ideas greatly enrich the series.

Finally, our thanks to our committed leadership team at Pearson Education who oversaw the entire revision: Pietro Alongi, Rhea Banker, and Paula Van Ells.

We are grateful for the artistic talents of Don Martinetti and Chris Pavely — their colorful work brightens every chapter.

Our families, as always, support and encourage our work. They truly inspire us every day.

Betty S. Azar
Stacy A. Hagen

# Chapter 1
## Using Be

❏ **Exercise 1. Let's talk: class activity.** (Chart 1-1)
Introduce yourself to six classmates. Use this model.

Hi, I am _____.
　　　　　　(name)

I am from _____.
　　　　　　(country or city)

I speak _____.
　　　　　(language)

Write down information about six classmates you talk to.

| FIRST NAME | COUNTRY OR CITY | LANGUAGE |
|---|---|---|
|  |  |  |
|  |  |  |
|  |  |  |
|  |  |  |
|  |  |  |
|  |  |  |

❏ **Exercise 2. Warm-up.** (Chart 1-1)
Read the sentences and circle *yes* or *no*.

1. He is happy.　　　　　　yes　　no
2. She is sad.　　　　　　　yes　　no
3. I am happy.　　　　　　 yes　　no

**1**

## 1-1 Singular Pronouns + *Be*

| | PRONOUN + | *BE* | | Singular means "one." |
|---|---|---|---|---|
| (a) | *I* | *am* | late. | |
| (b) | *You* | *are* | late. | *I, you, she, he,* and *it* in (a)—(e) refer to one person. |
| (c) | *She* | *is* | late. | |
| (d) | *He* | *is* | late. | *am, are, is* = forms of *be* |
| (e) | *It* | *is* | late. | |

| | | |
|---|---|---|
| (f) | *Maria* is late. <br> ↓ <br> *She* is late. | Pronouns refer to nouns. <br><br> In (f): *She* (feminine) = Maria |
| (g) | *Tom* is late. <br> ↓ <br> *He* is late. | In (g): *He* (masculine) = Tom |
| (h) | *Bus 10* is late. <br> ↓ <br> *It* is late. | In (h): *It* = Bus 10 |

❑ **Exercise 3. Looking at grammar.** (Chart 1-1)
Write the correct pronoun: *he, she,* or *it*.  Some items have two answers.

1. Mary ____*she*____

2. David _____

3. Mr. Smith _____

4. Canada _____

5. Dr. Jones _____

6. Ms. Wilson _____

7. Professor Lee _____

8. English _____

9. Robert _____

10. Miss Allen _____

❑ **Exercise 4. Looking at grammar.** (Chart 1-1)
Complete the sentences with *am, is,* or *are*.

1. He _____*is*_____ here.

2. You _____ late.

3. It _____ ready.

4. She _____ early.

5. I _____ hot.

6. He _____ cold.

### Exercise 5. Let's talk. (Chart 1-1)

*Part I.* Check (✓) all the words that are true for you right now.

*I am . . .*

1. ____ happy.     6. ____ sad.

2. ____ hot.     7. ____ cold.

3. ____ nice.     8. ____ nervous.

4. ____ hungry.     9. ____ sick.

5. ____ tired.     10. ____ funny.

She is nervous.

He is hungry.

She is tired.

*Part II.* Share some sentences with a partner: "I am ____."

*Part III.* Tell the class a few things about your partner: "He is ____." OR "She is ____."

❑ ### Exercise 6. Warm-up. (Chart 1-2)

Circle the correct answer. One sentence has two answers.

*How many people?*

1. We are ready.        one     two, three, or more

2. You are ready.        one     two, three, or more

3. They are ready.       one     two, three, or more

## 1-2 Plural Pronouns + Be

| PRONOUN + BE | Plural means "two, three, or more." |
|---|---|
| (a) **We** **are** here. <br> (b) **You** **are** here. <br> (c) **They** **are** here. | **We**, **you**, and **they** in (a)—(c) refer to two, three, or more persons. |
| (d) ⌐Sam and I ⌐ are here. <br> ↓ <br> **We** are here. | In (d): **We** = Sam and I |
| (e) ⌐Sam and you ⌐ are here. <br> ↓ <br> **You** are here. | In (e): **You** = Sam and you <br> NOTE: **You** can be singular or plural. |
| (f) ⌐Sam and Lisa ⌐ are here. <br> ↓ <br> **They** are here. | In (f): **They** = Sam and Lisa |

❏ **Exercise 7. Looking at grammar.** (Chart 1-2)
Choose the correct pronoun.

1. Lee and Bill      (they)    we
2. Alice and I      they    we
3. Mr. and Mrs. Martin and I      they    we
4. you and Dr. Taher      they    you
5. Tony and she      they    we
6. Tony and you      they    you

❏ **Exercise 8. Looking at grammar.** (Charts 1-1 and 1-2)
Complete the sentences with **am**, **is**, or **are**.

1. We ___are___ ready.

2. I ___am___ late.

3. He ___is___ happy.

4. They ___are___ sick.

5. She ___is___ homesick.

6. Abdul and Taka ___are___ homesick.

7. You (one person) ___are___ funny.

8. You (two persons) ___are___ early.

9. You and I ___are___ ready.

10. It ___is___ hot.

11. Sara and I ___are___ late.

12. You and Emily ___are___ tired.

□ **Exercise 9. Looking at grammar.** (Charts 1-1 and 1-2)
Make complete sentences.

1. He \ here _He is here._

2. They \ absent _They are present_

3. She \ sick _She is sick_

4. I \ homesick _I am homesick_

5. You and I \ homesick _You & I are homesick_

6. We \ late _We are late_

7. Jack \ hungry _Jack is hungry_

8. You (one person) \ early _You are early._

9. You (two persons) \ early _You are early_

10. Mr. and Mrs. Nelson \ late _Mr & Mrs Nelson are late._

11. Amy and I \ late _Amy & I are late._

□ **Exercise 10. Warm-up.** (Chart 1-3)
Read the sentences and circle *yes* or *no*.

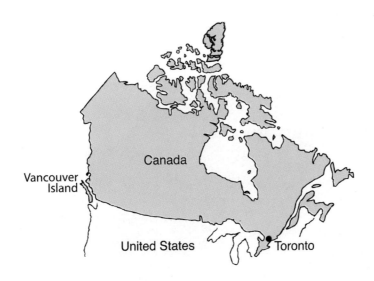

1. Canada is a country.                    yes     no

2. Toronto is a city.                       yes     no

3. Vancouver is an island.                  yes     no

## 1-3 Singular Nouns + Be

| | |
|---|---|
| NOUN + *IS* + NOUN<br><br>(a) **Canada** **is** **a country.**<br><br>INCORRECT: *Canada is country.* | In (a): **Canada** = a singular noun<br>　　　 **is** = a singular verb<br>　　　 **country** = a singular noun<br><br>**A** frequently comes in front of singular nouns.<br>In (a): **a** comes in front of the singular noun **country**.<br>**A** is called an "article." |
| (b) Bali is **an** island.<br><br>INCORRECT: *Bali is island.*<br><br><br><br>an island | **A** and **an** have the same meaning. They are both articles.<br>**A** is used in front of words that begin with consonants:<br>*b, c, d, f, g, etc.*<br>　　Examples: *a bed, a cat, a dog, a friend, a girl*<br><br>**An** is used in front of words that begin with the vowels<br>*a, e, i,* and *o.* *<br>　　Examples: *an animal, an ear, an island, an office*<br><br><br>an ear |

* **An** is sometimes used in front of words that begin with *u*. See Chart 7-2, p. 196.
　Vowels = a, e, i, o, u
　Consonants = b, c, d, f, g, h, j, k, l, m, n, p, q, r, s, t, v, w, x, y, z

❏ **Exercise 11. Looking at grammar.** (Chart 1-3)
　Write **a** or **an**.

1. ___*a*___ town

2. _____ city

3. _____ island

4. _____ place

5. _____ street

6. _____ avenue

7. _____ ocean

8. _____ continent

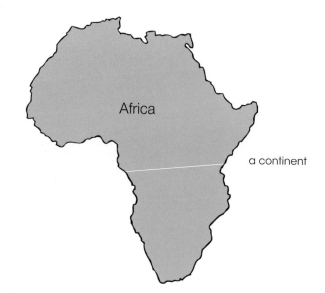

a continent

❏ **Exercise 12. Vocabulary and grammar.** (Chart 1-3)

*Part I.* Put the words from the box in the correct column. Some words go in two places.

| | | | | | |
|---|---|---|---|---|---|
| ✓ Arabic | Cuba | Hawaii | Mexico | Russia | Spanish |
| ✓ Beijing | France | Japanese | Moscow | Russian | Taiwan |
| Chinese | French | Lima | Paris | Saudi Arabia | Tokyo |

| COUNTRY | LANGUAGE | CITY | ISLAND |
|---|---|---|---|
| | *Arabic* | *Beijing* | |
| | | | |
| | | | |
| | | | |
| | | | |
| | | | |

*Part II.* Work in small groups. Check your answers. Finish the chart with your own choices. Your teacher will help you. Take turns making sentences. Share some of your sentences with the class.

*Example:* France, Japanese
STUDENT A: France is a country.
STUDENT B: Japanese is a language.

❏ **Exercise 13. Warm-up.** (Chart 1-4)

Complete the sentences with *a book* or *books*. What do you notice about the verbs in red?

1. A dictionary is _____.

2. Textbooks are _____.

3. Dictionaries and textbooks are _____.

## 1-4  Plural Nouns + *Be*

| | |
|---|---|
| NOUN + *ARE* + NOUN<br>(a) **Cats**   **are**   **animals**. | **Cats** = a plural noun<br>**are** = a plural verb<br>**animals** = a plural noun |
| (b) SINGULAR:  a cat, an animal<br>PLURAL:   *cats, animals* | Plural nouns end in **-s**.<br>**A** and **an** are used only with singular nouns. |
| (c) SINGULAR:  a city, a country<br>PLURAL:   cit*ies*, countr*ies* | Some singular nouns that end in **-y** have a special plural form: They omit the **-y** and add **-ies**.* |
| NOUN  and  NOUN + *ARE* +  NOUN<br>(d) **Canada and China**   **are**   **countries**.<br>(e) **Dogs**   **and cats**   **are**   **animals**. | Two nouns connected by **and** are followed by **are**.<br>In (d): **Canada** is a singular noun. **China** is a singular noun. They are connected by **and**. Together they are plural, i.e., "more than one." |

*See Chart 3-5, p. 69, for more information about adding **-s/-es** to words that end in **-y**.

❑  **Exercise 14. Looking at grammar.** (Charts 1-3 and 1-4)
Look at each noun.  Is it singular or plural?  Choose the correct answer.

| | | | |
|---|---|---|---|
| 1. | animals | one | two or more |
| 2. | a dog | one | two or more |
| 3. | a city | one | two or more |
| 4. | cities | one | two or more |
| 5. | an island | one | two or more |
| 6. | languages | one | two or more |
| 7. | a country | one | two or more |

❑  **Exercise 15. Looking at grammar.** (Charts 1-3 and 1-4)
Write the plural form.

1. a book         *books*              4. an eraser    _____

2. a textbook  _____          5. a pen        _____

3. a pencil     _____          6. a dictionary _____

a pencil                an eraser

❏ **Exercise 16. Looking at grammar.** (Charts 1-3 and 1-4)
Complete the sentences. Use **a** or **an** and the words from the box.

| | | |
|---|---|---|
| animal | country | language |
| city | island | sport |

1. A bird is ____*an animal*____ .  Birds and cats are ____*animals*____ .
2. Tennis is ____*a sport*____ .  Tennis and soccer are ____*sports*____ .
3. Chicago is ____*a city*____ .  Chicago and Berlin are ____*cities*____ .
4. Spanish is ____*a language*____  Spanish and Italian are ____*languages*____
5. Mexico is ____*a country*____ .  Mexico and Brazil are ____*countries*____ .
6. A cow is ____*an animal*____ .  Cows and horses are ____*animals*____ .
7. Hawaii is ____*a country*____ .  Hawaii and Taiwan are ____*countries*____ .

❏ **Exercise 17. Looking at grammar.** (Charts 1-3 and 1-4)
Change the singular sentences to plural sentences.

SINGULAR                                        PLURAL

1. A chicken is an animal.  →  ____*Chickens are animals.*____

a chicken                                        a pea

2. A pea is a vegetable.  →  _____

3. A dictionary is a book.  →  _____

4. An airplane is a machine.  →  _____

5. June is a month.
   July is a month.  →  _____

6. Winter is a season.
   Summer is a season.  →  _____

7. Egypt is a country.
   Indonesia is a country.  →  _____

❑ **Exercise 18. Game.** (Charts 1-3 and 1-4)
Work in teams. Your teacher will say the beginning of a sentence. As a team, finish the sentence and write it down. The team with the most correct sentences wins the game. Close your book for this activity.

*Example:*
TEACHER: Spanish . . .
TEAM A:    Spanish is a language.

1. A dog . . .
2. Arabic . . .
3. London . . .
4. Summer . . .
5. September and October . . .

6. Mexico and Canada . . .
7. An airplane . . .
8. Winter and summer . . .
9. Peas . . .
10. A car . . .

❑ **Exercise 19. Let's talk: pairwork.** (Charts 1-3 and 1-4)
Your partner will ask you to name something. Answer in a complete sentence. You can look at your book before you speak. When you speak, look at your partner.

*Example:*

| PARTNER A | PARTNER B |
|---|---|
| 1. a country | 1. two countries |

PARTNER A: Name a country.
PARTNER B: Brazil is a country.
PARTNER A: Good. Brazil is a country.
            Your turn now.

PARTNER B: Name two countries.
PARTNER A: Italy and China are countries.
PARTNER B: Right. Italy and China are countries.
            Your turn now.

*Remember:* You can look at your book before you speak. When you speak, look at your partner.

| PARTNER A | PARTNER B |
|---|---|
| 1. a language | 1. two cities |
| 2. two languages | 2. an island |
| 3. a machine | 3. two countries in Asia |
| 4. an animal | 4. a vegetable |
| 5. two seasons | 5. a street in this city |

Listen to the conversation.  Notice the words in red.  Do you know the long form for them?

A: Hi.  My name is Mrs. Smith.  I'm the substitute teacher.

B: Hi.  I'm Franco.

C: Hi.  I'm Lisa.  We're in your class.

A: It's nice to meet you.

B: We're glad to meet you too.

## 1-5 Contractions with *Be*

| | PRONOUN + *BE* → CONTRACTION | | | | |
|---|---|---|---|---|---|
| AM | *I* | + *am* → | **I'm** | (a) **I'm** a student. | When people speak, they often push two words together.  *A contraction* = two words that are pushed together |
| IS | *she* | + *is* → | **she's** | (b) **She's** a student. | |
| | *he* | + *is* → | **he's** | (c) **He's** a student. | Contractions of a *subject pronoun* + *be* are used in both speaking and writing. |
| | *it* | + *is* → | **it's** | (d) **It's** a city. | |
| ARE | *you* | + *are* → | **you're** | (e) **You're** a student. | PUNCTUATION:  The mark in the middle of a contraction is called an "apostrophe" (').* |
| | *we* | + *are* → | **we're** | (f) **We're** students. | |
| | *they* | + *are* → | **they're** | (g) **They're** students. | |

*NOTE: Write an apostrophe above the line.  Do not write an apostrophe on the line.

CORRECT: ___*I'm a student*___ .

INCORRECT: ___*I,m a student*___ .

❑ **Exercise 21. Looking at grammar.** (Chart 1-5)

Write the contractions.

1. I am ___*I'm*___        5. it is _____

2. she is _____        6. they are _____

3. you are _____        7. he is _____

4. we are _____

❑ **Exercise 22. Looking at grammar.** (Chart 1-5)

Write the long form for each contraction.

1. They're sick. ___*They are*___ sick.

2. He's absent. _____ absent.

3. It's hot. _____ hot.

4. I'm late. _____ late.

5. She's hungry. _____ hungry.

6. We're students. _____ students.

7. You're here. _____ here.

❑ **Exercise 23. Looking at grammar.** (Chart 1-5)

Complete the sentences with pronouns. Use contractions.

1. *Sara* is a student. _____*She's*_____ in my class.

2. *James* is a student. _____ in my class.

3. *I* am at school. _____ in the cafeteria.

4. *Yuri and Anna* are absent. _____ at home.

5. *Anna* is from Russia. _____ nice.

6. *Ali and I* are in the same class. _____ friends.

7. *Yuri, Ali, and Anna* are friends. _____ funny.


❑ **Exercise 24. Listening.** (Chart 1-5)

*Part I.* Listen to the conversation. Write the contractions.

A: Hello. ___*I'm*___ Mrs. Brown. _____ the substitute teacher.
　　　　　　 1　　　　　　　　　　2

B: Hi. _____ Paulo, and this is Marie. _____ in your class.
　　　　　 3　　　　　　　　　　　　　　　　　 4

A: _____ nice to meet you.
　　 5

B: _____ happy to meet you too.
　　　　 6

A: _____ time for class. Please take a seat.
　　 7


*Part II.* Listen to the conversation again and check your answers.


❑ **Exercise 25. Warm-up: pairwork.** (Chart 1-6)

Work with a partner. Complete the sentences with <u>all</u> the words from the box that are true. Share a few of your answers with the class.

| | | |
|---|---|---|
| a baby | a husband | a teacher |
| a bird | a student | a wife |

1. I'm not _____.

2. You're not _____.

## 1-6 Negative with *Be*

|  | CONTRACTIONS |  |
|---|---|---|
| (a) I *am not* a teacher. | I'*m not* | **Not** makes a sentence negative. |
| (b) You *are not* a teacher. | you'*re not* / you *aren't* | CONTRACTIONS |
| (c) She *is not* a teacher. | she'*s not* / she *isn't* | **Be** and **not** can be contracted. |
| (d) He *is not* a teacher. | he'*s not* / he *isn't* | Note that "I am" has only one |
| (e) It *is not* a city. | it'*s not* / it *isn't* | contraction with **be**, as in (a), but |
| ( f ) We *are not* teachers. | we'*re not* / we *aren't* | there are two contractions with **be** |
| (g) You *are not* teachers. | you'*re not* / you *aren't* | for (b)—(h). |
| (h) They *are not* teachers. | they'*re not* / they *aren't* | |

❑ **Exercise 26. Looking at grammar.** (Chart 1-6)
Complete the sentences with the negative form of **be**.

an astronaut

FULL FORM                                        CONTRACTION

1. I _____*am not*_____ an astronaut.    I _*'m not*_____ an astronaut.

2. He __*is not*__ an astronaut.    He __*isn't*____ an astronaut.  OR

    He _____ an astronaut.

3. They __*are not*__ astronauts.    They _*aren't*_____ astronauts.  OR

    They _____ astronauts.

4. You __*are not*__ an astronaut.    You _*aren't*_____ an astronaut.  OR

    You _____ an astronaut.

5. She __*is not*__ an astronaut.    She _*isn't*____ an astronaut.  OR

    She _____ an astronaut.

6. We __*are not*__ astronauts.    We _*aren't*_____ astronauts.  OR

    We _____ astronauts.

**Exercise 27. Looking at grammar.** (Charts 1-5 and 1-6)
Make sentences with *is*, *isn't*, *are*, and *aren't*.

*Examples:* Africa \ city . . . It \ continent
<u>Africa isn't a city. It's a continent.</u>

Baghdad and Chicago \ city . . . They \ continent
<u>Baghdad and Chicago are cities. They aren't continents.</u>

1. Canada \ country . . . It \ city
<u>Canada is a country. It isn't city.</u>

2. Argentina \ city . . . It \ country
<u>Argentina isn't city. It is a Country.</u>

3. Beijing and London \ city . . . They \ country
<u>Beijing & london aren't city. They are country.</u>

4. Asia \ country . . . It \ continent
<u>Asia is a Continent. It isn't country.</u>

5. Asia and South America \ continent . . . They \ country
<u>Asia & South America are Continent. They aren't Countries.</u>

❑ **Exercise 28. Vocabulary and listening.** (Charts 1-3 and 1-6)
*Part I.* Write *a* or *an*.

**Peterson Family Tree**

Marie + Andrew     Isabelle + David
Billy     Janey

1. <u> a </u> mother      8. _____ son

2. _____ mom      9. _____ aunt

3. _____ father      10. _____ uncle

4. _____ dad      11. _____ parent

5. _____ sister      12. _____ adult

6. _____ brother      13. _____ child

7. _____ daughter

*Part II.* Listen to the sentences. Choose the correct answer. *Note:* in spoken English, the "t" in negative contractions may be hard to hear.

| 1. is   isn't | 3. is   isn't | 5. are   aren't | 7. are   aren't |
| 2. is   isn't | 4. is   isn't | 6. are   aren't | 8. are   aren't |

❏ **Exercise 29. Looking at grammar.** (Charts 1-5 and 1-6)

Paul Cox

Gloria Perez

Nurse Lars Jensen

Rick Hayes

Jennifer Evans

Dr. Sana Gupta

Omar Khan

Joe Davis

***Part I.*** Write the name of the person next to the job.

1. plumber _____*Paul*_____     5. police officer _____

2. bus driver _____     6. doctor _____

3. nurse _____     7. auto mechanic _____

4. gardener _____     8. construction worker _____

***Part II.*** Complete the sentences. Items may vary in items 3–7.

1. Jennifer _____*isn't*_____ a gardener. She *'s a police officer* _____.

2. Lars _____*is*_____ a nurse. He _____ a doctor.

3. Omar _____ an auto mechanic. He isn't _____.

4. Paul _____ a construction worker. He _____.

5. Sana _____. _____.

6. Gloria _____. _____.

7. I'm not a _____. I'm _____.

❏ **Exercise 30. Warm-up.** (Chart 1-7)
Complete each sentence with a word from the box.

| short | tall | young | old |

1. Bill is _____.

2. He is also _____.

3. Sam is _____ and _____.

Bill        Sam

---

## 1-7 *Be* + Adjective

| | NOUN | + | *BE* | + | ADJECTIVE | | round ⎫ |
|---|---|---|---|---|---|---|---|
| (a) | A ball | | is | | **round**. | | intelligent |
| (b) | Balls | | are | | **round**. | | hungry ⎬ = adjectives |
| (c) | Mary | | is | | **intelligent**. | | young |
| (d) | Mary and Tom | | are | | **intelligent**. | | happy ⎭ |

| | PRONOUN | + | *BE* | + | ADJECTIVE |
|---|---|---|---|---|---|
| (e) | I | | am | | **hungry**. |
| (f) | She | | is | | **young**. |
| (g) | They | | are | | **happy**. |

Adjectives often follow a form of **be** *(am, is, are).*

In (a)—(g), the adjectives give information about a noun or pronoun that comes at the beginning of a sentence.★

★The noun or pronoun that comes at the beginning of a sentence is called a "subject."  See Chart 6-1, p. 159.

---

❏ **Exercise 31. Grammar and vocabulary.** (Charts 1-5 and 1-7)
Find the adjective in the first sentence.  Then complete the second sentence with **be** + *an adjective* with an opposite meaning.  Use an adjective from the box.  Write the contracted form of **be**.

| beautiful | expensive | noisy | short |
|---|---|---|---|
| clean | fast | old | tall |
| easy | ✓ happy | poor | |

1. I'm not sad.  I _'m happy_____.

2. Mr. Thomas isn't rich.  He _____.

3. My hair isn't long.  It _____.

4. My clothes aren't dirty.  They _____.

5. Flowers aren't ugly.  They _____.

6. Cars aren't cheap. They _____.

7. Airplanes aren't slow. They _____.

8. Grammar isn't difficult. It _____.

9. My sister isn't short. She _____.

10. My grandparents aren't young. They _____.

11. The classroom isn't quiet. It _____.

❑ **Exercise 32. Grammar and vocabulary.** (Charts 1-3, 1-4, and 1-7)
Complete each sentence with *is* or *are* and an adjective from the box.

| | | | | |
|---|---|---|---|---|
| cold | flat | important | small/little | sweet |
| dangerous | funny | large/big | sour | wet |
| dry | ✓ hot | round | square | |

1. Fire ____*is hot*____.

2. Ice and snow _____.

3. A box _____.

4. Balls and oranges _____.

5. Sugar _____.

6. An elephant _____, but
   a mouse _____.

7. A rain forest _____, but
   a desert _____.

8. A joke _____.

9. Good health _____.

10. Guns aren't safe. They _____.

11. A coin _____ small, round, and _____.

12. A lemon _____.

an elephant

a mouse

a lemon    sugar    water    lemonade

❑ **Exercise 33. Let's talk: game.** (Chart 1-7)

Work in teams. Your teacher will ask you to name things. Your team will make a list. Share your list with the class. The group with the longest list gets a point. The group with the most points at the end of the game is the winner. Close your book for this activity.

*Example:* round

TEACHER: Name round things.
TEAM A's LIST: a ball, an orange, a clock
TEAM B's LIST: a baseball, a basketball, a soccer ball
TEAM C's LIST: a ball, a head, an orange, a coin, a ring, a planet

Group C wins a point.

| | | |
|---|---|---|
| 1. hot | 4. free | 7. beautiful |
| 2. difficult | 5. little | 8. expensive |
| 3. sweet | 6. important | 9. cheap |

❑ **Exercise 34. Let's talk: pairwork.** (Charts 1-5 → 1-7)

Work with a partner. Take turns making two sentences for each picture. Use the given adjectives. You can look at your book before you speak. When you speak, look at your partner.

*Example:* The girl . . . happy/sad
PARTNER A: The girl isn't happy. She's sad.
Your turn now.

*Example:* The flower . . . beautiful/ugly
PARTNER B: The flower is beautiful. It isn't ugly.
Your turn now.

| PARTNER A | PARTNER B |
|---|---|
| 1. The table . . . clean/dirty. | 1. The man . . . friendly/unfriendly. |
| 2. The boy . . . sick/well. | 2. The coffee . . . cold/hot. |

$$x^2 + 5 + 4 = (x + 4)(x + 1)$$

3. The algebra problem . . . easy/difficult.

3. The woman . . . tall/short.

4. The cars . . . old/new.

4. Katie . . . old/young.

❏ **Exercise 35. Grammar and vocabulary.** (Charts 1-5 → 1-7)
Complete the sentences with *is* or *are* and the correct pronoun. Use contractions. Some sentences are negative.

1. A pea _____*is*_____ green. _____*It isn't*_____ red.

2. Carrots _____*aren't*_____ blue. _____*They're*_____ orange.

3. An onion _____ orange. _____
   brown, white, or green.

4. A strawberry _____ black. _____ red.

5. Bananas _____ yellow. _____ white.

6. A banana _____ yellow. _____ white.

7. An orange _____ orange. _____
   brown.

8. Apples _____ red or green. _____
   purple.

9. A tomato _____ blue. _____
   red or green.

❑ **Exercise 36. Let's talk: game.** (Charts 1-5 → 1-7)
**Part I.** Check (✓) all the words you know. Your teacher will explain the words you don't know.

| | | | |
|---|---|---|---|
| 1. ____ hungry | | 11. ____ angry |
| 2. ____ thirsty | | 12. ____ nervous |
| 3. ____ sleepy | | 13. ____ friendly |
| 4. ____ tired | | 14. ____ lazy |
| 5. ____ old | | 15. ____ hardworking |
| 6. ____ young | | 16. ____ famous |
| 7. ____ happy | | 17. ____ sick |
| 8. ____ homesick | | 18. ____ healthy |
| 9. ____ married | | 19. ____ unfriendly |
| 10. ____ single | | 20. ____ shy |

**Part II.** Sit in a circle. Student A makes a sentence using "I" and the first word. Student B repeats the information about Student A and makes a new sentence using the second word. Continue around the circle until everyone in class has spoken. The teacher is the last person to speak and must repeat the information about everyone in the class.

*Example:*
STUDENT A: I'm not hungry.
STUDENT B: He's not hungry. I'm thirsty.
STUDENT C: He's not hungry. She's thirsty. I'm sleepy.

❑ **Exercise 37. Let's talk: pairwork.** (Charts 1-5 → 1-7)
Work with a partner. Check (✓) each adjective that describes this city/town (the city or town where you are studying now). When you finish, compare your work with a partner. Do you and your partner have the same answers? Tell the class about some of your differences.

| | | | |
|---|---|---|---|
| 1. ____ big | | 11. ____ noisy |
| 2. ____ small | | 12. ____ quiet |
| 3. ____ clean | | 13. ____ crowded |
| 4. ____ dirty | | 14. ____ not crowded |
| 5. ____ friendly | | 15. ____ hot |
| 6. ____ unfriendly | | 16. ____ cold |
| 7. ____ safe | | 17. ____ warm |
| 8. ____ dangerous | | 18. ____ cool |
| 9. ____ beautiful | | 19. ____ expensive |
| 10. ____ ugly | | 20. ____ inexpensive/cheap |

❑ **Exercise 38. Warm-up.** (Chart 1-8)
Read the sentences and choose *yes* or *no*.

1. The cat is next to the mousetrap.        yes        no

2. The mouse is under the chair.        yes        no

3. The mouse is behind the cat.        yes        no

---

## 1-8 *Be* + a Place

| | |
|---|---|
| (a) Maria is **here**. <br><br> (b) Bob is **at the library**. | In (a): *here* = a place. <br> In (b): *at the library* = a place. <br> **Be** is often followed by *a place*. |
| (c) Maria is { *here.* <br> *there.* <br> *downstairs.* <br> *upstairs.* <br> *inside.* <br> *outside.* <br> *downtown.* } | A place may be one word, as in the examples in (c). |
| (d) Bob is { PREPOSITION + NOUN <br> *at* — *the library.* <br> *on* — *the bus.* <br> *in* — *his room.* <br> *at* — *work.* <br> *next to* — *Maria.* } | A place may be a prepositional phrase (*preposition + noun*), as in (d). |

ON

IN

NEXT TO

ABOVE

BEHIND

UNDER

SOME COMMON PREPOSITIONS

| above | behind | from | next to | under |
|---|---|---|---|---|
| at | between | in | on | |

□ **Exercise 39. Looking at grammar.** (Chart 1-8)
Complete each sentence with a preposition from the box.

> above      between      next to      under
> behind      ✓ in      on

1. The cat is _____*in*_____ the desk.

2. The cat is _____ the desk.

3. The cat is _____ the desk.

4. The cat is _____ the desk.

5. The cat is _____ the desk.

6. The cat is _____ the desk.

7. The cat is _____ the desks.

**Exercise 40. Let's talk: pairwork.** (Chart 1-8)
Work with a partner. Follow your partner's instructions.

*Example:*
PARTNER A: Put your hand under your chair.
PARTNER B: (*Partner B performs the action.*)

| PARTNER A | PARTNER B |
|---|---|
| *Put your pen . . .* | *Put a piece of paper . . .* |
| 1. on your book. | 1. behind your back. |
| 2. in your hand. | 2. between two fingers. |
| 3. next to your thumb. | 3. next to your thumb. |
| 4. under your desk. | 4. in the air. |

❑ **Exercise 41. Listening.** (Charts 1-1 → 1-8)
Listen to the sentences. Write the words you hear. Some answers have contractions.

### The First Day of Class

Paulo ___*is a student*___ from Brazil. Marie _____ student
                    1                                        2
from France. _____ the classroom. Today _____ exciting day.
                   3                                    4
_____ the first day of school, but they _____ nervous.
       5                                                6
_____ to be here. Mrs. Brown _____ the teacher. She
        7                                    8
_____ in the classroom right now. _____ late today.
     9                                          10

❑ **Exercise 42. Reading and writing.** (Charts 1-1 → 1-8)
Read the paragraph. Then complete the sentences with true answers. Several answers are possible for each item.

### A Substitute Teacher

   Today is Monday. It is the first day of English class. Mr. Anderson is an English teacher, but he isn't in class today. He is at home in bed. Mrs. Anderson is in the classroom today. Mrs. and Mr. Anderson are husband and wife. Mrs. Anderson is a good teacher. The students are a little nervous, but they're happy. Mrs. Anderson is very funny, and her explanations are clear. It's a good class.

1. Mr. Anderson is ___*an English teacher, sick, etc.*_____.

2. Mrs. Anderson is not _____.

3. Mr. and Mrs. Anderson are _____.

4. The students are _____.

5. The English class is _____.

## 1-9 Summary: Basic Sentence Patterns with *Be*

| | | |
|---|---|---|
| (a) | SUBJECT + BE + NOUN<br>I    am    *a student.* | The noun or pronoun that comes at the beginning of a sentence is called the "subject." |
| (b) | SUBJECT + BE + ADJECTIVE<br>He    is    *intelligent.* | **Be** is a "verb." Almost all English sentences have a subject and a verb. |
| (c)<br>(d) | SUBJECT + BE + A PLACE<br>We    are    *in class.*<br>She    is    *upstairs.* | Notice in the examples: There are three basic completions for sentences that begin with a *subject + the verb be:*<br>• *a noun,* as in (a)<br>• *an adjective,* as in (b)<br>• *an expression of place,*\* as in (c) and (d) |

\*An expression of place can be a *preposition + noun,* or it can be one word: *upstairs.*

❑ **Exercise 43. Looking at grammar.** (Chart 1-9)
Write the form of *be* (*am, is,* or *are*) that is used in each sentence. Then write the grammar structure that follows *be*.

|  | BE | + | COMPLETION |
|---|---|---|---|
| 1. We're students. | *are* | + | *noun* |
| 2. Anna is in Rome. | *is* | + | *place* |
| 3. I'm hungry. | *am* | + | *adjective* |
| 4. Dogs are animals. | _____ | + | _____ |
| 5. Jack is at home. | _____ | + | _____ |
| 6. He's sick. | _____ | + | _____ |
| 7. They're in class. | _____ | + | _____ |
| 8. I'm a mechanic. | _____ | + | _____ |
| 9. Gina is upstairs. | _____ | + | _____ |
| 10. The peas are good. | _____ | + | _____ |
| 11. Dan and I are nurses. | _____ | + | _____ |
| 12. Nora is downstairs. | _____ | + | _____ |
| 13. We aren't homesick. | _____ | + | _____ |
| 14. They are astronauts. | _____ | + | _____ |

❑ **Exercise 44. Listening.** (Chapter 1)

*Is* and *are* are often contracted with nouns in spoken English.  Listen to the sentences.
Practice saying them yourself.  *Note:* *'s* and *'re* can be hard to hear.

1. Grammar is easy. → Grammar's easy.
2. My name is Josh.
3. My books are on the table.
4. My brother is 21 years old.
5. The weather is cold today.
6. The windows are open.
7. My money is in my wallet.
8. Mr. Smith is a teacher.
9. My parents are at work now.
10. The food is good.
11. Tom is sick today.
12. My roommates are from Chicago.
13. My sister is a student in high school.

❑ **Exercise 45. Looking at grammar.** (Chapter 1)

Choose the correct completion.

*Example:*  My friend _____ from South Korea.
    a.  he   (b.) 's   c.  Ø⋆

1. The test _____ easy.
    a.  are     b.  is       c.  Ø

2. My notebook _____ on the table.
    a.  is      b.  are     c.  Ø

3. My notebooks _____ on the table.
    a.  is      b.  are     c.  Ø

4. Sue _____ a student.
    a.  is      b.  she    c.  Ø

5. The weather _____ warm today.
    a.  is      b.  it      c.  Ø

6. My friends _____ from Cuba.
    a.  are     b.  is      c.  Ø

7. My book _____ on my desk.
    a.  it      b.  is      c.  Ø

8. The teachers _____ in class.
    a.  is      b.  are     c.  Ø

9. The teacher _____ nice.
    a.  's      b.  are     c.  Ø

10. Dinner _____ ready.
    a.  it      b.  is      c.  Ø

⋆Ø = nothing

❏ **Exercise 46. Reading and writing.** (Chapter 1)

*Part I.* Read the paragraph. Look at new vocabulary with your teacher first.

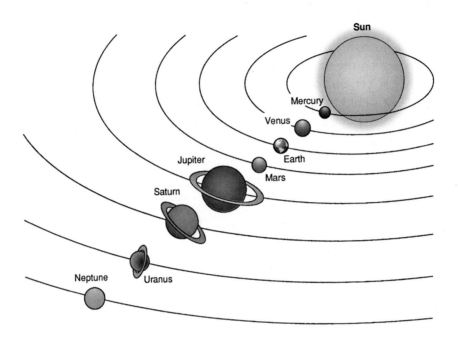

### Venus

Venus is the second planet from the sun. It isn't big and it isn't small. It is between Earth and Mercury. It is an interesting planet. It is very bright at night. It is rocky and dusty. It is also hot. The temperature on Venus is 464 degrees Celsius or 867 degrees Fahrenheit.

*Do you know these words?*

bright
at night
rocky
dusty
temperature

*Part II.* Write a paragraph about Mars. Use the following information.

*Facts:*
- 4th (fourth) planet from the sun
- small
- between Earth and Jupiter
- red

- very rocky
- very dusty
- very cold (-55° C / -67° F)
- interesting?

Before you begin, look at the paragraph format.

**Paragraph Format**

capital letter

period

indent → Venus xxxxxxxxxxxxxxxxxxxxxxxxxxxx sun. It xxxxxxxxxxx

xxxxxxxxxxxxxxxxxxxxxxxxxxxxxxxxxxxxxxxxxxxxxxxxxxxxxx

xxxxxxxxxxxxxxxxxxxxxxxxxxxxxxxxxxxxxxxxxxxxxxxxxx

xxxxxxxxxxxxxxxxxxxxxxxxxxxx

***Part III.*** Editing check: Work individually or change papers with a partner. Check (✓) for the following:

1. \_\_\_\_ capital letter at the beginning of each sentence

2. \_\_\_\_ period at the end of each sentence

3. \_\_\_\_ paragraph indent

4. \_\_\_\_ a verb (for example, ***is*** or ***are***) in every sentence

5. \_\_\_\_ correct spelling (use a dictionary or spell-check)

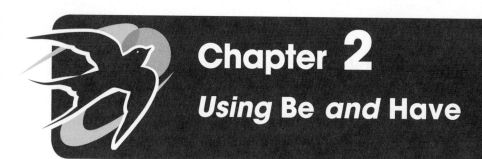

# Chapter 2
## Using Be and Have

❑ **Exercise 1. Warm-up.** (Chart 2-1)
Answer the questions.

1. Is the weather nice today?                                   yes     no
2. Are you in a classroom right now?                            yes     no
3. Are you hungry?                                              yes     no

## 2-1 Yes/No Questions with *Be*

| QUESTION | | | STATEMENT | | | |
|---|---|---|---|---|---|---|
| *BE* | + | SUBJECT | SUBJECT | + | *BE* | In a question, ***be*** comes in front of the subject. |
| (a) **Am** | **I** | early? | **I** | **am** | early. | |
| (b) **Is** | **Ana** | a student? | **Ana** | **is** | a student. | PUNCTUATION A question ends with a question mark (?). |
| (c) **Are** | **they** | at home? | **They** | **are** | at home. | A statement ends with a period (.). |

❑ **Exercise 2. Looking at grammar.** (Chart 2-1)
Complete the questions with *am*, *is*, or *are*.

1. _____ you tired?

2. _____ he late?

3. _____ they here?

4. _____ we early?

5. _____ she at home?

6. _____ I a new student?

7. _____ they new students?

8. _____ you and Bill ready?

9. _____ Mr. Rivera sick?

10. _____ Mr. and Mrs. Rivera sick?

❏ **Exercise 3. Looking at grammar.** (Chart 2-1)
Make questions.

1. A: _____Is Mrs. Han a teacher?_____
   B: Yes, Mrs. Han is a teacher.

2. A: _____
   B: Yes, carrots are vegetables.

3. A: _____
   B: Yes, Mr. Wang is absent today.

4. A: _____
   B: Yes, planets are big.

5. A: _____
   B: Yes, Amy and Mika are here today.

6. A: _____
   B: Yes, English grammar is fun.

7. A: _____
   B: Yes, I am ready for the next exercise.

❏ **Exercise 4. Listening.** (Chart 2-1)
Listen to the sentences. Write the words you hear.

*Example:* You will hear:  A: Elena's absent today.
                           B: Is she sick?
            You will write: B: _____Is_____ she sick?

A: Elena's absent today.
B: _____ she sick?
         1
A: No.
B: _____ her husband sick?
         2
A: No.
B: _____ her children sick?
         3
A: No.
B: _____ she homesick?
         4
A: No.
B: So? What's the matter?
A: Her turtle _____ sick.
                   5
B: Are you serious? That's crazy!

a turtle

**Exercise 5. Warm-up.** (Chart 2-2)

Answer the questions. In b., both answers are possible. Which negative contraction do you prefer?

1. Is the classroom cold?
    a. Yes, it is.              b. No, it isn't. / No, it's not.

2. Are the chairs in the classroom comfortable?
    a. Yes, they are.          b. No, they aren't. / No, they're not.

## 2-2 Short Answers to Yes/No Questions

| QUESTION | SHORT ANSWER | Spoken contractions are not used in short answers that begin with *yes*. |
|---|---|---|
| (a) *Is Kari* a student? → → → | Yes, *she is*. <br> No, *she's not*. <br> No, *she isn't*. | In (a): INCORRECT: *Yes, she's.* |
| (b) *Are they* at home? → → | Yes, *they are*. <br> No, *they aren't*. <br> No, *they're not*. | In (b): INCORRECT: *Yes, they're.* |
| (c) *Are you* ready? → → | Yes, *I am*. <br> No, *I'm not*.★ | In (c): INCORRECT: *Yes, I'm.* |

★*Am* and *not* are not contracted.

❑ **Exercise 6. Looking at grammar.** (Chart 2-2)

Make questions and give short answers.

1. A: _____*Are you tired?*_____
   B: _____*No, I'm not.*_____ (I'm not tired.)

2. A: _____*Is Alma in your class?*_____
   B: _____*Yes, she is.*_____ (Alma is in my class.)

3. A: _____
   B: _____ (I'm not homesick.)

4. A: _____
   B: _____ (Kareem is homesick.)

5. A: _____
   B: _____ (Kara isn't here today.)

6. A: _____
   B: _____ (The students in this class are smart.)

7. A: _____

   B: _____ (The chairs in this room aren't comfortable.)

8. A: _____

   B: _____ (I'm not single.)

9. A: _____

   B: _____ (We're married.)

❏ **Exercise 7. Let's talk: pairwork.** (Chart 2-2)
Work with a partner. Ask and answer questions. You can look at your book before you speak. When you speak, look at your partner.

*Example:* dolphins: intelligent/dumb
PARTNER A: Are dolphins intelligent?
PARTNER B: Yes, they are.
                OR
PARTNER A: Are dolphins dumb?
PARTNER B: No, they aren't.

a dolphin

| PARTNER A | PARTNER B |
|---|---|
| 1. a mouse: big/little | 1. diamonds: expensive/cheap |
| 2. lemons: sweet/sour | 2. your grammar book: light/heavy |
| 3. the world: flat/round | 3. butterflies: beautiful/ugly |
| 4. the weather: cool today/warm today | 4. English grammar: easy/difficult |
| 5. your dictionary: with you/at home | 5. turtles: fast/slow |
| 6. your shoes: comfortable/uncomfortable | 6. the floor in this room: clean/dirty |

❏ **Exercise 8. Looking at grammar.** (Charts 2-1 and 2-2)
Complete the conversations with your own words.

1. A: ____*Are*____ you a student at this school?

   B: Yes, ____*I am*____ .

   A: _____ you from _____?

   B: No, _____ from _____ .

2. A: Are you a/an _____?

   B: No, _____ not. I'm a/an _____ .

3. A: Are _____ expensive?

   B: Yes, _____.

   A: Is _____ expensive?

   B: No, _____.

4. A: _____ Vietnam and Cambodia countries in Asia?

   B: Yes, _____ are.

   A: _____ a country in South America?

   B: Yes, _____ is.

   A: _____ a country in Africa?

   B: No, _____ not.  It's a country in _____.

❏ **Exercise 9. Warm-up.** (Chart 2-3)
Choose the correct answer for each question.

> On your head          No, they aren't

A:  Are my glasses in the kitchen?

B:  _____ .
            ¹

A:  Where are they?

B:  _____ !
          ²

glasses

## 2-3 Questions with *Be:* Using *Where*

*Where* asks about place.  *Where* comes at the beginning of the question, in front of *be*.

| | | QUESTION | | | SHORT ANSWER | (LONG ANSWER) |
|---|---|---|---|---|---|---|
| | | BE | + | SUBJECT | | |
| (a) | | *Is* | | *the book* on the table? | → Yes, *it is*. | (The book is on the table.) |
| (b) | | *Are* | | *the books* on the table? | → Yes, *they are*. | (The books are on the table.) |
| | WHERE + | BE | + | SUBJECT | | |
| (c) | *Where* | *is* | | *the book*? | → On the table. | (The book is on the table.) |
| (d) | *Where* | *are* | | *the books*? | → On the table. | (The books are on the table.) |

## Exercise 10. Looking at grammar. (Chart 2-3)

Choose the correct question for each response.

| Question | Response |
|---|---|
| 1. a. Is Sami absent? <br> b. Where is Sami? | At home. |
| 2. a. Where are the boxes? <br> b. Are the boxes in the closet? | Yes, they are. |
| 3. a. Are you outside? <br> b. Where are you? | No, I'm not. |
| 4. a. Is the mail on the kitchen counter? <br> b. Where is the mail? | On the kitchen counter. |

## Exercise 11. Looking at grammar. (Chart 2-3)

Make questions.

1. A: _____Is Sara at home?_____

   B: Yes, she is. (Sara is at home.)

2. A: _____Where is Sara?_____

   B: At home. (Sara is at home.)

3. A: _____

   B: Yes, it is. (Cairo is in Egypt.)

4. A: _____

   B: In Egypt. (Cairo is in Egypt.)

5. A: _____

   B: Yes, they are. (The students are in class today.)

6. A: _____

   B: In class. (The students are in class today.)

7. A: _____

   B: On Main Street. (The post office is on Main Street.)

8. A: _____

   B: Yes, it is. (The train station is on Grand Avenue.)

9. A: _____

   B: Over there. (The bus stop is over there.)

10. A: _____

    B: At work. (Ali and Jake are at work now.)

❑ **Exercise 12. Let's talk: pairwork.** (Chart 2-3)

Work with a partner. Ask and answer questions. Use ***where***. You can look at your book before you speak. When you speak, look at your partner.

*Example:*
PARTNER A: Where is your pen?
PARTNER B: It's in my hand. (*or any other true answer*)

| PARTNER A | PARTNER B |
|---|---|
| 1. your money | 1. your wallet |
| 2. your books | 2. your glasses or sunglasses |
| 3. your coat | 3. your family |
| 4. your pencil | 4. your apartment |
| 5. (*name of a classmate*) | 5. (*names of two classmates*) |
| 6. your hometown | 6. your hometown |
| 7. (*name of a city in the world*) | 7. (*name of a country in the world*) |

❑ **Exercise 13. Warm-up.** (Chart 2-4)

Check (✓) the true sentences.

1. _____ I have a dictionary on my desk.

2. _____ Many students have backpacks.

3. _____ My teacher has a cell phone.

4. _____ Her cell phone has a case.

5. _____ The classroom has a globe.

a globe

## 2-4 Using *Have* and *Has*

| SINGULAR | | | PLURAL | | | | | |
|---|---|---|---|---|---|---|---|---|
| (a) *I* | *have* | a pen. | (f) *We* | *have* | pens. | I<br>you<br>we<br>they | + | *have* |
| (b) *You* | *have* | a pen. | (g) *You* | *have* | pens. | | | |
| (c) *She* | *has* | a pen. | (h) *They* | *have* | pens. | | | |
| (d) *He* | *has* | a pen. | | | | she<br>he<br>it | + | *has* |
| (e) *It* | *has* | blue ink. | | | | | | |

❏ **Exercise 14. Looking at grammar.** (Chart 2-4)

Complete the sentences with *have* or *has*.

trucks

a van

1. You _____ a bike.

2. I _____ a bike.

3. She _____ a small car.

4. They _____ trucks.

5. We _____ trucks.

6. You and I _____ bikes.

7. The business _____ a van.

8. He _____ a motorcycle.

9. Radek _____ a motorcycle.

10. The Molinas _____ two motorcycles.

❏ **Exercise 15. Looking at grammar.** (Chart 2-4)

Choose the correct answer.

1. We   has /(have)   a daughter.

2. Venita   has / have   two daughters.

3. She   has / have   twin daughters.

4. The Leons are grandparents. They   has / have   one grandchild.

5. Hiro   has / have   an interesting job.  He's a journalist.

6. You   has / have   a good job too.

7. You and I   has / have   good jobs.

8. I   has / have   a laptop computer.
    It   has / have   a small screen.

9. Samir is a website designer.  He
    has / have   a laptop and a desktop.

10. A laptop   has / have   a battery.

11. Laptops   has / have   batteries.

a desktop        a laptop

❑  **Exercise 16. Vocabulary and grammar.** (Chart 2-4)
Complete each sentence with *have* or *has* and words from the box.

backaches          a fever              a sore throat
the chills       ✓ a headache          a stomachache
a cold             high blood pressure  toothaches
coughs

1. Mr. Kasim ___*has a headache*___ .

2. The patients _____ .

3. I _____ .

4. Mrs. Ramirez _____ .

5. You _____ .

6. The workers _____ .

7. Olga _____ .

8. You _____ .

9. Alan _____ .

10. They _____ .

❏ **Exercise 17. Let's talk: pairwork.** (Chart 2-4)
Complete the conversations with a partner. You can look at your book before you speak. When you speak, look at your partner. Use this model.

   Partner A: How _____?

   Partner B: Not so good. _____.

   Partner A: That's too bad.

*Example:* Jamal? . . . a toothache.
PARTNER A: How's Jamal?
PARTNER B: Not so good. He has a toothache.
PARTNER A: That's too bad. Your turn now.

   1. you? . . . a headache.
   2. you? . . . a sore tooth.
   3. your mother? . . . a sore back.
   4. Mr. Park? . . . a backache.

   5. your parents? . . . colds.
   6. the patients? . . . stomachaches.
   7. your little brother? . . . a sore throat.
   8. Mrs. Luna? . . . a fever.

❏ **Exercise 18. Looking at grammar.** (Charts 1-1 and 2-4)
Rewrite the paragraph. Change "I" to "he." You will also need to change the verbs in **bold**.

### Dr. Lee

   I **am** a doctor. I **am** 70 years old, so I **have** many years of experience. I **have** many patients. Some are very sick. I **have** a clinic downtown. I also **have** patients at the hospital. It is hard work, and I **am** often very tired. But I **am** also happy. I help many people.

   _____He is a doctor._____

   _____

   _____

   _____

   _____He helps many people.

❏ **Exercise 19. Looking at grammar.** (Charts 1-1, 1-2, and 2-4)
*Part I.* Complete the sentences with *is* or *has*.

*I have a college roommate, Tia. She . . .*

   1. ____is____ from a small town.
   2. _____ nice.
   3. _____ a motorcycle.
   4. _____ a smart phone.
   5. _____ smart.
   6. _____ homework every night.

   7. _____ homesick.
   8. _____ a large family.
   9. _____ quiet.
   10. _____ a boyfriend.
   11. _____ a pet bird at home.
   12. _____ serious.

***Part II.*** Complete the sentences with ***are*** or ***have***.

*The two students in the room next to us . . .*

1. _____ a TV.
2. _____ two computers.
3. _____ noisy.
4. _____ messy.
5. _____ from a big city.

6. _____ busy.
7. _____ a lot of friends.
8. _____ friendly.
9. _____ parties on weekends.
10. _____ low grades.

❑ **Exercise 20. Warm-up.** (Chart 2-5)
Complete each sentence with a word from the box.

| Her | His | My | Their |
|-----|-----|-----|-------|

1. _____ name is Evita.

2. _____ name is Paulo.

| Her | His | My | Their |

3. _____ name is Natalie.

4. _____ names are Natalie and Paulo.

## 2-5 Using *My, Your, Her, His, Our, Their*

| SINGULAR | PLURAL | SUBJECT FORM | | POSSESSIVE FORM |
|---|---|---|---|---|
| (a) **I** have a book. *My* book is red. | (e) **We** have books. *Our* books are red. | I | → | my |
| | | you | → | your |
| (b) **You** have a book. *Your* book is red. | (f) **You** have books. *Your* books are red. | she | → | her |
| | | he | → | his |
| (c) **She** has a book. *Her* book is red. | (g) **They** have books. *Their* books are red. | we | → | our |
| | | they | → | their |
| (d) **He** has a book. *His* book is red. | | | | |

I *possess* a book. = I *have* a book. = It is *my* book.

*My, your, her, his, our,* and *their* are called "possessive adjectives." They come in front of nouns.

❑ **Exercise 21. Looking at grammar.** (Chart 2-5)
Complete each sentence with a word from the box.

| her | his | my | our | their | your |

1. You're next.  It's _____*your*_____ turn.

2. Susana's next.  It's _____ turn.

| her | his | my | our | their | your |

3. Bruno and Maria are next. It's _____ turn.

4. My aunt is next. It's _____ turn.

5. I'm next. It's _____ turn.

6. The children are next. It's _____ turn.

7. You and Mohamed are next. It's _____ turn.

8. Marcos and I are next. It's _____ turn.

9. Bill's next. It's _____ turn.

10. Mrs. Sung is next. It's _____ turn.

❑ **Exercise 22. Vocabulary and grammar.** (Chart 2-5)
Complete the sentences with the information on the ID cards.

What information do you know about this person from his ID card?

John B. Palmer

1. _____ last name is _____.

2. _____ first name is _____.

3. _____ middle initial is _____.

What information do the ID cards give you about Don and Kathy Johnson?

4. _____ zip code is _____.

5. _____ area code is _____.

Kathy Johnson
10 Broadway
Vista, CA 98301
(888) 555-1573

Don Johnson
10 Broadway
Vista, CA 98301
(888) 555-1573

Dr. Diane Ellen Nelson
4/12/80

What do you know
about Dr. Nelson?

6. _____ birthdate is _____.

7. _____ birthday is _____.

8. _____ middle name is _____.

Write about yourself.

9. _____ first name is _____.

10. _____ last name is _____.

11. _____ middle name is _____.

12. _____ middle initial is _____.

13. _____ area code is _____.

14. _____ phone number is _____.

15. _____ zip code is _____.

16. _____ birthday is _____.

❑ **Exercise 23. Vocabulary: pairwork.** (Chart 2-5)

Work with a partner. Look at the vocabulary. Put a check (✓) beside the words you know. Ask your partner about the ones you don't know. Your teacher can help you. The picture on the next page shows clothes and jewelry.

<table>
<tr><th colspan="3">Vocabulary Checklist</th></tr>
<tr><td>COLORS</td><td>CLOTHES</td><td>JEWELRY</td></tr>
<tr><td>___ black</td><td>___ belt</td><td>___ bracelet</td></tr>
<tr><td>___ blue, dark blue, light blue</td><td>___ blouse</td><td>___ earrings</td></tr>
<tr><td>___ blue green</td><td>___ boots</td><td>___ necklace</td></tr>
<tr><td>___ brown, dark brown, light brown</td><td>___ coat</td><td>___ ring</td></tr>
<tr><td>___ gold</td><td>___ dress</td><td>___ watch</td></tr>
<tr><td>___ gray, dark gray, light gray</td><td>___ gloves</td><td></td></tr>
<tr><td>___ green, dark green, light green</td><td>___ hat</td><td></td></tr>
<tr><td>___ orange</td><td>___ jacket</td><td></td></tr>
<tr><td>___ pink</td><td>___ jeans</td><td></td></tr>
<tr><td>___ purple</td><td>___ pants</td><td></td></tr>
<tr><td>___ red</td><td>___ sandals</td><td></td></tr>
<tr><td>___ silver</td><td>___ shirt</td><td></td></tr>
<tr><td>___ tan, beige</td><td>___ shoes</td><td></td></tr>
<tr><td>___ white</td><td>___ skirt</td><td></td></tr>
<tr><td>___ yellow</td><td>___ socks</td><td></td></tr>
<tr><td></td><td>___ suit</td><td></td></tr>
<tr><td></td><td>___ sweater</td><td></td></tr>
<tr><td></td><td>___ tie, necktie</td><td></td></tr>
<tr><td></td><td>___ T-shirt</td><td></td></tr>
</table>

❑ **Exercise 24. Looking at grammar.** (Chart 2-5)

Complete the sentences with *my, your, her, his, our,* or *their.*

1. Malena has on* a blouse. _____*Her*_____ blouse is light blue.

2. Tomas has on a shirt. _____ shirt is yellow and brown.

3. I have on jeans. _____ jeans are blue.

4. Kiril and Oleg have on boots. _____ boots are brown.

5. Diana and you have on dresses. _____ dresses are red.

_____

* **has on** and **have on** = wear (clothes)

6. Salma and I have on sweaters. _____ sweaters are green.

7. You have on shoes. _____ shoes are dark brown.

8. Nora has on a skirt. _____ skirt is black.

9. Leo has on a belt. _____ belt is white.

10. Sashi and Akira have on socks. _____ socks are gray.

11. Arturo has on pants. _____ pants are dark blue.

12. I have on earrings. _____ earrings are gold.

❏ **Exercise 25. Listening.** (Charts 2-4 and 2-5)

Listen to the sentences. Write the words you hear.

*Example:* You will hear: She has on boots.
You will write: ___*She has*___ on boots.

**Anna's clothes**

1. _____ boots _____ zippers.

2. _____ a raincoat.

3. _____ raincoat _____ buttons.

4. _____ small.

5. _____ sweater _____ long sleeves.

6. _____ earrings on _____ ears.

7. _____ silver.

8. _____ on jeans.

9. _____ jeans _____ pockets.

an earring

a sweater

a raincoat

jeans

boots with
zippers

❏ **Exercise 26. Looking at grammar.** (Charts 2-4 and 2-5)

Complete the sentences. Use **have** or **has** and **my, your, her, his, our,** or **their.**

1. You ___*have*___ a big family. ___*Your*___ family is nice.

2. You and Tina _____ many cousins. _____ cousins are friendly.

3. I _____ a brother. _____ brother is in college.

4. William _____ a sister. _____ sister is a doctor.

5. Lisa _____ a twin sister. _____ sister is disabled.

6. Iman and Amir are married. They _____ a baby. _____ baby is six months old.

7. Anton and I _____ a son. _____ son is seven years old.

8. Pietro and Julieta _____ a daughter. _____ daughter is ten years old.

9. I _____ an adopted brother. _____ brother is thirty.

10. Lidia is single. She _____ a brother. _____ brother is single too.

❑ **Exercise 27. Reading and grammar.** (Chapter 1 and Charts 2-4 and 2-5)
*Part I.* Read the story and answer the questions. Look at new vocabulary with your teacher first.

### One Big Happy Family

Kanai is 13 years old. She has a big family. She has four sisters and five brothers. Kanai and her siblings are adopted. They are from several different countries. She likes her brothers and sisters. They have a good time. They are always busy. Kanai's parents are busy too. Her mother is an airline pilot. She goes away overnight fifteen days a month. Kanai's dad is a stay-at-home father. He has a lot of work, but the older kids are helpful. Kanai's parents love children. They are one big happy family.

*Do you know these words?*

sibling
adopted
pilot
overnight
stay-at-home father

1. Kanai is a girl.                          yes    no
2. Only the girls are adopted.                yes    no
3. Kanai's father is home a lot.              yes    no
4. Her mother is home every night.            yes    no

*Part II.* Complete the sentences with *her*, *his*, or *their*. One sentence has two possible answers.

1. Kanai is adopted. _____ brothers and sisters are adopted too.

2. Her parents are busy. _____ mother is an airline pilot. _____ father is a stay-at-home dad.

3. She has nine siblings. _____ family is very large.

4. Kanai's dad is very busy. _____ children are helpful.

**Part III.** Complete the story with **is, are, has,** or **have.**

### One Big Happy Family

Kanai _____ 13 years old. She _____ a big family. She
                    1                                   2

_____ four sisters and five brothers. Kanai and her siblings are adopted.
      3

They _____ from several different countries. She likes her brothers and
              4

sisters. They _____ a good time. They _____ always busy.
                      5                                        6

Kanai's parents _____ busy too. Her mother _____ an airline pilot.
                             7                                              8

She _____ away overnight fifteen days a month. Kanai's dad _____
                  9                                                                    10

a stay-at-home father. He _____ a lot of work, but the older kids are helpful.
                                    11

Kanai's parents love children. They are one big happy family.

❏ **Exercise 28. Warm-up.** (Chart 2-6)
Match the sentences to the pictures.

Picture A

Picture B

1. This is my wallet. ____          2. That is your wallet. ____

## 2-6 Using *This* and *That*

| | |
|---|---|
| (a) I have a book in my hand. ***This book*** is red.<br>(b) I see a book on your desk. ***That book*** is blue.<br>(c) ***This*** is my book.<br>(d) ***That*** is your book. | *this* book = the book is near me.<br>*that* book = the book is not near me. |
| (e) ***That's*** her book. | CONTRACTION: *that is* = *that's* |
| (f) ***This is*** ("*This's*") her book. | In spoken English, *this is* is usually pronounced as "*this's.*" It is not used in writing. |

Complete the sentences with *this* or *that*.

1.   _This_ is my book.

2.   _That_ is your book.

3.   _____ is a pen.

4.   _____ is a pencil.

5.   _____ is his notebook.

6.   _____ is her notebook.

7.   _____ is my dictionary.

8.   _____ is your dictionary.

9.   _____ is his umbrella.

10.  _____ is our umbrella.

❏ **Exercise 30. Let's talk: pairwork.** (Chart 2-6)

***Part I.*** Work with a partner. Take turns. Make a sentence with ***this*** or ***that*** for each picture.

*Example:*
Partner A: That is a backpack.
　　　　　Your turn.

a backpack

| PARTNER A | PARTNER B |
|---|---|
| 1. a credit card | 2. a wallet |
| 3. a credit card | 4. a checkbook |
| 5. a business card | 6. a computer bag |

***Part II.*** Put items from a school bag, a bookbag, or a purse on a desk or table. Put some near you and some at a distance. Point to them, and your partner will make sentences with ***this*** or ***that***.

❑ **Exercise 31. Warm-up.** (Chart 2-7)
Match the sentences to the pictures.

Picture A

Picture B

1. Those are my keys. ____

2. These are your keys. ____

| 2-7 Using *These* and *Those* | |
|---|---|

| (a) My books are on my desk. ***These*** are my books.<br>(b) Your books are on your desk. ***Those*** are your books. | SINGULAR      PLURAL<br>*this* → *these*<br>*that* → *those* |

❑ **Exercise 32. Looking at grammar.** (Chart 2-7)
Complete the sentences with ***these*** or ***those***.

1. _____ are my books.

2. _____ are your pencils.

3. _____ are his boots.

4. _____ are her shoes.

5. _____ are your hats.

6. _____ are their jackets.

❑ **Exercise 33. Vocabulary and grammar.** (Charts 2-6 and 2-7)

Look at the vocabulary in the picture. Choose the correct verb.

**In our dorm room**

1. This **is**/ are   my pillow.

2. That   is / are   your pillow.

3. Those sheets   is / are   for you.

4. These blankets   is / are   for me.

5. That TV   is / are   broken.

6. This chair   is / are   new.

7. Those mattresses   is / are   soft.

8. This mattress   is / are   uncomfortable.

❑ **Exercise 34. Looking at grammar.** (Charts 2-6 and 2-7)

Complete the sentences. Use the words in parentheses.

1. (*This, These*) _____*This*_____ pencil belongs to Alex.

   (*That, Those*) _____*That*_____ pencil belongs to Olga.

2. (*This, These*) _____ notepads belong to me.

   (*That, Those*) _____ notepad belongs to Kate.

3. (*This, These*) _____ coat is waterproof.

   (*That, Those*) _____ coats are not.

4. (*This, These*) _____ sunglasses belong to me.

   (*That, Those*) _____ sunglasses belong to you.

5. (*This, These*) _____ pillows are soft.

   (*That, Those*) _____ pillows are hard.

6. (*This, These*) _____ exercise is easy.

   (*That, Those*) _____ exercises are hard.

7. (*This, These*) _____ eraser is on my desk.

   (*That, Those*) _____ erasers are on your desk.

❑ **Exercise 35. Let's talk: pairwork.** (Charts 2-6 and 2-7)
Work with a partner. Make a sentence for each picture using ***this***, ***that***, ***these***, or ***those***.
Take turns.

*Examples:*
PARTNER A:  That is a cap.
　　　　　　 Your turn now.

a cap

PARTNER B:  These are caps.
　　　　　　 Your turn now.

caps

| PARTNER A | PARTNER B |
|---|---|
| 1. a debit card | 2. a wallet |
| 3. rulers | 4. paper clips |
| 5. a notepad | 6. checks |
| 7. checkbooks | 8. a folder |
| 9. a stapler | 10. staples |

Listen to the sentences. Write the words you hear.

*Example:* You will hear:   Those are clean dishes.

You will write:   <u>*Those are*</u>   clean dishes.

### In the kitchen

1. _____ my coffee cup.

2. _____ your dessert.

3. _____ our plates.

4. _____ sponges _____ wet.

5. _____ dishcloths _____ dry.

6. _____ frying pan _____ dirty.

7. _____ frying pan _____ clean.

8. _____ salt shaker _____ empty.

sponges

❑ **Exercise 37. Warm-up.** (Chart 2-8)
Answer the questions.

1. What is that? _____

2. Who is that? _____

a beetle                    Tim

| 2-8 | **Asking Questions with *What* and *Who* + *Be*** |
|---|---|

| | | |
|---|---|---|
| (a) ***What is*** this (thing)? | It's a pen. | **What** asks about things. |
| (b) ***Who is*** that (man)? | That's Mr. Lee. | **Who** asks about people. |
| (c) ***What are*** those (things)? | They're pens. | Note: In questions with **what** and **who**, |
| (d) ***Who are*** they? | They're Mr. and Mrs. Lee. | • **is** is followed by a singular word. |
| | | • **are** is followed by a plural word. |
| (e) ***What's*** this? | | CONTRACTIONS: |
| (f) ***Who's*** that man? | | *what is = what's* |
| | | *who is = who's* |

❑ **Exercise 38. Looking at grammar.** (Chart 2-8)
Complete the questions with *what* or *who* and *is* or *are*.

1.  A: _____*Who is*_____ that woman?
    B: She's my sister.  Her name is Sonya.

2.  A: _____ those things?
    B: They're erasers.

3.  A: _____ that?
    B: That's Ms. Walenski.

4.  A: _____ this?
    B: That's my new camera.  It's really small.

5.  A: _____ those people?
    B: I'm not sure, but I think they're new students from Thailand.

6.  A: _____ your name?
    B: Anita.

7.  A: _____ your grammar teacher?
    B: Mr. Walker.

8.  A: _____ your favorite teachers?
    B: Mr. Walker and Ms. Rosenberg.

9.  A: _____ an only child?
    B: It's a child with no brothers or sisters.

10. A: _____ bats?
    B: They're animals with wings.  They fly at night.  They're not birds.

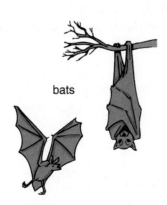

bats

❑ **Exercise 39. Vocabulary and speaking: pairwork.** (Chart 2-8)

***Part I.*** Work with a partner. Write the names of the parts of the body on the pictures below. Use the words from the box.

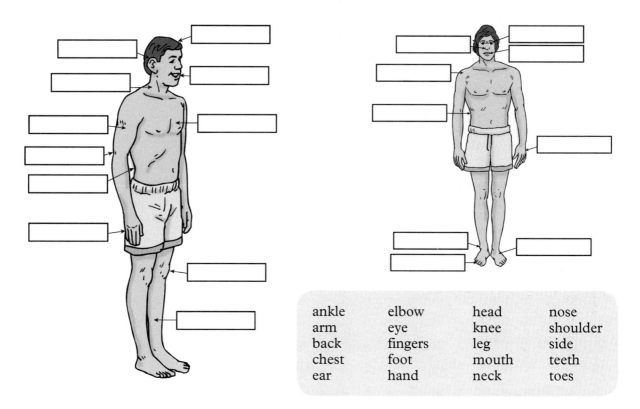

| | | | |
|---|---|---|---|
| ankle | elbow | head | nose |
| arm | eye | knee | shoulder |
| back | fingers | leg | side |
| chest | foot | mouth | teeth |
| ear | hand | neck | toes |

***Part II.*** With your partner, take turns asking questions with ***this, that, these,*** and ***those***. *Note:* Both partners can ask about both pictures.

*Example:*
PARTNER A: What is this?
PARTNER B: This is his leg. (*to Partner A*) What are those?
PARTNER A: Those are his fingers.

❑ **Exercise 40. Let's talk: class activity.** (Chart 2-8)

Your teacher will ask questions. Answer with ***this, that, these,*** and ***those***. Close your book for this activity.

*Example:* hand
TEACHER: What is this? (*The teacher indicates her or his hand.*)
STUDENT: That is your hand.
          OR
TEACHER: What is that? (*The teacher indicates a student's hand.*)
STUDENT: This is my hand.

| | | | | |
|---|---|---|---|---|
| 1. nose | 3. arm | 5. legs | 7. foot | 9. fingers |
| 2. eyes | 4. elbow | 6. knee | 8. shoulder | 10. ears |

❏ **Exercise 41. Check your knowledge.** (Chapter 2)
Correct the mistakes.

*has*
1. She ~~have~~ a headache.

2. What are that?

3. Roberto he is a student in your class?

4. I am have a backache.

5. This is you dictionary.  I my dictionary is at home.

6. Where my keys?

7. I am a sore throat.

8. He's father is from Cuba.

9. This books are expensive.

10. Where is the teachers?

11. A:  Are you tired?

    B:  Yes, I'm.

❏ **Exercise 42. Looking at grammar.** (Chapter 2)
Choose the correct completion.

1. Carla _____ a grammar book.
   a. have                  b. is                  ⓒ has

2. This floor _____.
   a. dirty is              b. dirty               c. is dirty

3. _____ yellow.
   a. A banana are          b. A banana is         c. Bananas is

4. Lucas is _____ engineer.
   a. a                     b. an                  c. Ø

5. _____ books are really expensive.
   a. Those                 b. They                c. This

6. Give this to Kathleen.  It is _____ math book.
   a. she                   b. an                  c. her

7. That is _____.
   a. a mistakes          b. mistakes          c. a mistake

8. PABLO:   _____ is your apartment?
   BLANCA:  It's on Forest Street.
   a. What                b. Where             c. Who

9. YOKO:  _____ these?
   GINA:  My art books.  I'm taking an art history class.
   a. What are            b. Who are           c. What is

10. MALIK: Are you hungry?
    LAYLA: Yes, _____.
    a. I'm                b. I'm not           c. I am

11. TINA: _____ that?
    LUIS:  That's Paul Carter.
    a. Who's              b. What's            c. Where's

12. PAUL: _____ in your class?
    ERIC: No.
    a. Mr. Kim            b. Is Mr. Kim        c. Mr. Kim is he


❑  **Exercise 43. Looking at grammar.** (Chapter 2)
   Complete the sentences with *am*, *is*, or *are*.  Use *not* if necessary.

   1. Apples _____ vegetables.

   2. An apple _____ a kind of fruit.

   3. I _____ from the United States.

   4. We _____ human beings.

   5. Balls _____ square.

   6. Chickens _____ birds, but bats _____ birds.

   7. Lemons _____ sweet.  They _____ sour.

   8. Soccer _____ a sport.

   9. Soccer and basketball _____ sports.

   10. Africa _____ a country.  It _____ a continent.

❑ **Exercise 44. Looking at grammar.** (Chapter 2)
Complete the conversations with any words that make sense.

1. A: Where _____ your book?

   B: Hiroko _____ it.

   A: Where _____ your notebooks?

   B: Nasir and Angela _____ them.

2. A: _____ this?

   B: It _____ a picture of my family.

   A: _____ this?

   B: That's _____ father.

   A: _____ they?

   B: My brother and sister.

3. A: What's _____ ?

   B: I don't know. Ask the teacher.

   A: What's _____ ?

   C: It's _____ .

4. A: Where _____ ?

   B: He's _____ .

   A: Where _____ ?

   B: They're _____ .

❑ **Exercise 45. Grammar and writing.** (Chapter 2)
*Part I.* Complete the sentences in the composition by Carlos.

My name _____*is*_____ Carlos. ___*I am* OR *I'm*___ from Mexico.
          1             2

_____ a student. _____ twenty years old.
     3               4

My family lives in Mexico City. _____ father _____ a
                         5                    6

businessman. _____ fifty-one years old. _____ mother
               7                       8

_____ an accountant. _____ forty-nine years old.
     9               10

I _____ two sisters and one brother. The names of my sisters
     11

_____ Rosa and Patricia. Rosa _____ a teacher.
  12                         13

_____ twenty-eight years old. Patricia _____ a student.
  14                            15

_____ eighteen years old.  My brother _____ an engineer.  His
name _____ Pedro.  He is married.  He _____ two children.

    I live in a dormitory.  _____ a tall building on Pine Street.  My address
_____ 3225 Pine St.  I live with my roommate.  _____ name is
Bob.  _____ from Chicago.  _____ nineteen years old.

    I like my classes.  They _____ interesting.  I like _____
classmates.  _____ friendly.


**Part II.**  Write about yourself.  Follow the style below.  Use your own paper.

PARAGRAPH I:    **Information about you:**
    your name, hometown, age (*optional*)

PARAGRAPH II:    **Information about your parents (if they are alive):**
    their ages, jobs

PARAGRAPH III:    **Information about other family or people in your life:**
    your siblings:  names, ages, jobs OR
    your husband/wife:  name, job OR
    your roommate/partner/friend:  name, job

PARAGRAPH IV:    **Additional information:**
    your home (apartment/dormitory/house):  I live in a/an ____ .
    your classes
    your classmates


**Part III.**  Editing check:  Work individually or change papers with a partner.  Check (✓) for
the following:

1. _____ capital letter at the beginning of each sentence

2. _____ capital letter at the beginning of a person's name

3. _____ period at the end of each sentence

4. _____ paragraph indents

5. _____ a verb in every sentence

6. _____ correct use of **be** and **have**

7. _____ correct spelling (use a dictionary or computer spell-check)

# Chapter 3
## Using the Simple Present

❑ **Exercise 1. Warm-up.** (Chart 3-1)
Read the paragraph. Write the verb forms for *take, post,* and *share.*

    I often take videos of my family and friends. I post them online. I share them with my family and friends. My brother Mario is a science teacher. He takes videos of his students and their experiments. He posts them online. He shares them with his classes.

| *take* | *post* | *share* |
|---|---|---|
| 1. I _____ | 3. I _____ | 5. I _____ |
| 2. Mario _____ | 4. He _____ | 6. He _____ |

## 3-1 Form and Basic Meaning of the Simple Present Tense

| | |
|---|---|
| I *talk.*<br>You *talk.*<br>He *talks.*<br>She *talks.*<br>It *rains.*<br>We *talk.*<br>They *talk.* | The verb after 3rd person singular (**she**, **he**, **it**) has a final **-s**: *talks*.<br><br>                 SINGULAR      PLURAL<br>1st person:   I *talk*       we *talk*<br>2nd person:  you *talk*   you *talk*<br>3rd person:  she *talks*  they *talk*<br>                 he *talks*<br>                 it *rains* |
| (a) I *eat* breakfast **every morning**.<br>(b) Olga *speaks* English **every day**.<br>(c) We *sleep* **every night**.<br>(d) They *go* to the beach **every weekend**. | The simple present tense expresses habits.<br><br>In (a): Eating breakfast is a habit, a usual activity.<br>*Every morning* = Monday morning, Tuesday morning, Wednesday morning, Thursday morning, Friday morning, Saturday morning, and Sunday morning. |
| She wakes up every morning at 7:00. | He shaves every morning. |

❑ **Exercise 2. Looking at grammar.** (Chart 3-1)
Complete the sentences with *speak* or *speaks*.

1. Martin _____ English.

2. I _____ German.

3. Erika _____ several languages.

4. Her husband _____ Thai and Vietnamese.

5. My friends and I _____ a little Persian.

6. My friends _____ Arabic.

7. They _____ Arabic fluently.

8. You _____ Spanish well.

9. You and I _____ Spanish well.

10. We _____ it well.

11. You and Peter _____ it well.

❑ **Exercise 3. Let's talk: pairwork.** (Chart 3-1)
*Part I.* Look at the list of habits. Check (✓) your habits every morning. Put them in order. What do you do first, second, third, etc.? Write them on the lines.

| HABITS | | MY HABITS EVERY MORNING |
|---|---|---|
| ___ eat breakfast | 1. | *I turn off the alarm clock.* |
| ___ go to class | 2. | _____ |
| ___ put on my clothes | 3. | _____ |
| ___ drink a cup of coffee/tea | 4. | _____ |
| ___ shave | 5. | _____ |
| ___ put on my make-up | 6. | _____ |
| ___ take a shower/bath | 7. | _____ |
| ___ get up | 8. | _____ |
| ___ pick up my books | 9. | _____ |
| ___ walk to the bathroom | 10. | _____ |
| ___ watch TV | 11. | _____ |
| ___ look in the mirror | 12. | _____ |
| ✓ turn off the alarm clock | 13. | _____ |
| ___ go to the kitchen/the cafeteria | 14. | _____ |
| ___ brush/comb my hair | 15. | _____ |

_____ say good-bye to someone        16. _____

_____ brush my teeth                 17. _____

_____ do exercises                   18. _____

_____ wash my face                   19. _____

**Part II.** Work with a partner. Talk about your habits every morning. Close your book for this activity.

❏ **Exercise 4. Listening.** (Chart 3-1)

Listen to the sentences. Choose the verbs you hear.

1. (wake)    wakes          6. watch     watches

2. wake      wakes          7. take      takes

3. get       gets           8. take      takes

4. go        goes           9. take      takes

5. do        does          10. talk      talks

❏ **Exercise 5. Looking at grammar.** (Chart 3-1)

Choose the correct completion.

1. My mother and father _____*eat*_____ breakfast at 7:00 every day.
   eat / eats

2. My mother _____ tea with her breakfast.
   drink / drinks

3. I _____ a bath every morning.
   take / takes

4. My sister _____ a shower.
   take / takes

5. I _____ English with my friends.
   study / studies

6. We _____ to school together every morning.
   walk / walks

7. Class _____ at 9:00 every day.
   begin / begins

8. It _____ at 12:00 for lunch.
   stop / stops

9. We _____ in the cafeteria.
   eat / eats

10. You _____ your lunch from home every day.
    bring / brings

11. My friends and I _____ home at 3:00 every afternoon.
    go / goes

12. You and Jamal _____ to the library after school every day.
    go / goes

❑ **Exercise 6. Warm-up.** (Chart 3-2)
Which sentence is true for you?

1. I always do my homework.
2. I usually do my homework.
3. I sometimes do my homework.
4. I never do my homework.

## 3-2 Frequency Adverbs

| 100% | always | (a) Ivan *always* eats breakfast. |
| | usually | (b) Maria *usually* eats breakfast. |
| | often | (c) They *often* watch TV. |
| 50% | sometimes | (d) We *sometimes* watch TV. |
| | seldom | (e) Sam *seldom* drinks milk. |
| | rarely | (f) Rita *rarely* drinks milk. |
| 0% | never | (g) I *never* drink milk. |

$$\text{SUBJECT} + \left\{ \begin{array}{l} always \\ usually \\ often \\ sometimes \\ seldom \\ rarely \\ never \end{array} \right\} + \text{VERB}$$

The words in this list are called "frequency adverbs." They come between the subject and the simple present verb.*

**OTHER FREQUENCY EXPRESSIONS**

(h) I drink tea
$$\left\{ \begin{array}{l} \text{once } a\ day. \\ \text{two times / twice } a\ day. \\ \text{three times } a\ day. \\ \text{four times } a\ day. \\ \text{etc.} \end{array} \right.$$

(i) I see my grandparents **three times** *a week*.
(j) I see my aunt **once** *a month*.
(k) I see my cousin Sam **twice** *a year*.

We can express frequency by saying how many times something happens
**a day**.
**a week**.
**a month**.
**a year**.

(l) I see my doctor **every** *year*.

*Every* is singular. The noun that follows (e.g., *morning*) must be singular.
*INCORRECT:* every mornings

---

\* Some frequency adverbs can also come at the beginning or at the end of a sentence. For example:
  ***Sometimes** I get up at seven.*  *I **sometimes** get up at seven.*  *I get up at seven **sometimes**.*
 Also: See Chart 3-3, for the use of frequency adverbs with **be**.

## Exercise 7. Looking at grammar. (Chart 3-2)

Complete each sentence with a word from the box.

| always | often | never | rarely | sometimes | usually |
|--------|-------|-------|--------|-----------|---------|

|  | SUN. | MON. | TUES. | WED. | THURS. | FRI. | SAT. |
|---|---|---|---|---|---|---|---|
| 1. Ana _____ drinks tea with lunch. | ☕ | ☕ | ☕ | ☕ | ☕ | ☕ | ☕ |
| 2. Kenji _____ drinks tea with lunch. |  | ☕ | ☕ | ☕ | ☕ | ☕ | ☕ |
| 3. Clara _____ drinks tea with lunch. |  |  | ☕ | ☕ | ☕ | ☕ | ☕ |
| 4. Igor _____ drinks tea with lunch. |  |  |  |  | ☕ | ☕ | ☕ |
| 5. Sonya _____ drinks tea with lunch. |  |  |  |  |  |  | ☕ |
| 6. Sami _____ drinks tea with lunch. |  |  |  |  |  |  |  |

## Exercise 8. Looking at grammar. (Chart 3-2)

Write "S" over the subject and "V" over the verb in each sentence. Rewrite the sentences, adding the given frequency adverbs.

1. always     S V<br>
I eat breakfast in the morning.

_____ I always eat breakfast _____ in the morning.

2. never     I eat carrots for breakfast.

_____ for breakfast.

3. seldom     I watch TV in the morning.

_____ in the morning.

4. sometimes   I have dessert after dinner.

_____ after dinner.

5. usually     Kiri eats lunch at the cafeteria.

_____ at the cafeteria.

6. often     We listen to music after dinner.

_____ after dinner.

7. always     The students speak English in class.

_____ in class.

❏ **Exercise 9. Let's talk: class activity.** (Chart 3-2)

Your teacher will ask you to talk about your morning, afternoon, and evening activities. Close your book for this activity.

*Tell me something you...*

1. always do in the morning.
2. never do in the morning.
3. sometimes do in the morning.
4. usually do in the afternoon.
5. seldom do in the afternoon.
6. never do in the afternoon.
7. often do in the evening.
8. sometimes do in the evening.
9. rarely do in the evening.
10. sometimes do on weekends.

❏ **Exercise 10. Looking at grammar.** (Chart 3-2)

Use the information in the chart to complete the sentences.

| | SUN. | MON. | TUES. | WED. | THURS. | FRI. | SAT. |
|---|---|---|---|---|---|---|---|
| Hamid | 🚌 | 🚌 | 🚌 | 🚌 | 🚌 | 🚌 | 🚌 |
| Yoko | | | | | | | 🚌 |
| Victoria | | 🚌 | 🚌 | 🚌 | 🚌 | 🚌 | 🚌 |
| Pavel | | | 🚌 | 🚌 | 🚌 | 🚌 | 🚌 |
| Mr. Wu | | | | | | | |
| Mrs. Cook | | | | | 🚌 | 🚌 | 🚌 |

How often do the people in the chart take the bus during the week?

1. Hamid takes the bus _____ *seven times* _____ a week. That means he

   _____ *always* _____ takes the bus.

2. Yoko takes the bus _____ a week. That means she

   _____ takes the bus.

3. Victoria takes the bus _____ a week. That means she

   _____ takes the bus.

4. Pavel takes the bus _____ a week. That means he

   _____ takes the bus.

5. Mr. Wu _____ takes the bus.

6. Mrs. Cook takes the bus _____ a week. That means she

   _____ takes the bus.

❑ **Exercise 11. Warm-up.** (Chart 3-3)
Choose the correct answer. What do you notice about the placement of the verb and the frequency adverb?

| | | |
|---|---|---|
| 1. It often rains here. | yes | no |
| 2. It sometimes snows. | yes | no |
| 3. It is often cold here. | yes | no |
| 4. It is sometimes hot. | yes | no |

## 3-3 Position of Frequency Adverbs

| | | Frequency adverbs come after the simple present tense forms of **be**: **am**, **is**, and **are**. |
|---|---|---|
| SUBJECT + **BE** + FREQUENCY ADVERB | | |
| I am<br>You are<br>He is<br>She is +<br>It is<br>We are<br>They are | { *always*<br>*usually*<br>*often*<br>*sometimes* } + late.<br>*seldom*<br>*rarely*<br>*never* | |
| SUBJECT + FREQUENCY ADVERB + OTHER SIMPLE PRESENT VERBS | | Frequency adverbs come before all simple present verbs except **be**. |
| Tom + | { *always*<br>*usually*<br>*often*<br>*sometimes* } + *comes* late.<br>*seldom*<br>*rarely*<br>*never* | |

❑ **Exercise 12. Looking at grammar.** (Chart 3-3)
Add the frequency adverbs to the sentences.

1. always     Anita is on time for class. → *Anita is always on time for class.*
2. always     Anita comes to class on time. → *Anita always comes to class on time.*
3. often     Liliana is late for class.
4. often     Liliana comes to class late.
5. never     It snows in my hometown.
6. never     It is very cold in my hometown.
7. usually     Hiroshi is at home in the evening.
8. usually     Hiroshi stays at home in the evening.
9. seldom     Thomas studies at the library in the evening.
10. seldom     His classmates are at the library in the evening.
11. sometimes     I skip breakfast.
12. rarely     I have time for a big breakfast.

❑ **Exercise 13. Let's talk: class activity.** (Chart 3-3)

*Part I.* Check (✓) the boxes to describe your activities after 5:00 P.M.

| | ALWAYS | USUALLY | OFTEN | SOMETIMES | RARELY | NEVER |
|---|---|---|---|---|---|---|
| 1. eat dinner | | | | | | |
| 2. go to a movie | | | | | | |
| 3. go shopping | | | | | | |
| 4. go swimming | | | | | | |
| 5. spend time with friends | | | | | | |
| 6. go to class | | | | | | |
| 7. be at home | | | | | | |
| 8. watch videos or DVDs | | | | | | |
| 9. study English | | | | | | |
| 10. send emails | | | | | | |
| 11. surf the Internet | | | | | | |
| 12. drink coffee after 9:00 | | | | | | |
| 13. be in bed at ten o'clock | | | | | | |
| 14. go to bed late | | | | | | |

*Part II.* Exchange books with a partner. Your partner will tell the class two things about your evening.

*Example:* (Carlos) is usually at home. He sometimes sends emails.
(Olga) sometimes drinks coffee after 9:00 P.M. She usually goes to bed late.

❑ **Exercise 14. Writing.** (Chart 3-3)

Write about a typical day in your life, from the time you get up in the morning until you go to bed. Use the following words to show the order of your activities: ***then, next, at . . . o'clock, after that, later.***

*Writing sample:* I usually get up at 7:30. I shave, brush my teeth, and take a shower. Then I put on my clothes and go to the student cafeteria for breakfast. After that, I go back to my room. I sometimes watch the news on TV. At 8:15, I leave the dormitory. I go to class. My class begins at 8:30. I'm in class from 8:30 to 11:30. After that, I eat lunch. I usually have a sandwich and a cup of tea for lunch. (Continue until you complete your day.)

❑ **Exercise 15. Warm-up: listening.** (Chart 3-4)

Listen to the words. Decide if they have one syllable or two.

| | | | | | | |
|---|---|---|---|---|---|---|
| 1. eat | one | two | 4. pushes | one | two |
| 2. eats | one | two | 5. sleeps | one | two |
| 3. push | one | two | 6. fixes | one | two |

## 3-4 Spelling and Pronunciation of Final -es

| | | | SPELLING | PRONUNCIATION | |
|---|---|---|---|---|---|
| **-sh** | (a) | push → | *pushes* | push/əz/ | Ending of verb: **-sh**, **-ch**, **-ss**, **-x**. |
| **-ch** | (b) | teach → | *teaches* | teach/əz/ | Spelling: add **-es**. |
| **-ss** | (c) | kiss → | *kisses* | kiss/əz/ | Pronunciation: /əz/. |
| **-x** | (d) | fix → | *fixes* | fix/əz/ | |

❑ **Exercise 16. Looking at grammar.** (Chart 3-4)
Use the correct form of the given verbs to complete the sentences.

1. brush        Arianna _____*brushes*_____ her hair every morning.

2. teach        Alex _____ English.

3. fix        Pedro _____ his breakfast every morning.
            He makes eggs and toast.

4. drink        Sonya _____ tea every afternoon.

5. watch        Joon Kee often _____ television at night.

6. kiss        Viktor always _____ his children goodnight.

7. wear        Tina usually _____ jeans to class.

8. wash        Eric seldom _____ dishes.

9. walk        Jenny _____ her dog twice each day.

10. stretch,        When Jack gets up in the morning, he _____
    yawn        and _____.

□ **Exercise 17. Listening.** (Chart 3-4)

Listen to the sentences and choose the verbs you hear.

1. teach   (teaches)
2. teach   teaches
3. fix   fixes
4. fix   fixes
5. watch   watches
6. watch   watches
7. brush   brushes
8. brush   brushes
9. wash   washes
10. wash   washes

□ **Exercise 18. Looking at grammar.** (Charts 3-1 and 3-4)

Complete the sentences. Use the words from the box and add **-s** or **-es**. Practice reading the story aloud. Work with a partner or in small groups.

| brush | get | take | wash |
|-------|-----|------|------|
| cook | ✓ leave | turn | watch |
| fall | read | sit | |

Laura ___leaves___ her office every night at 5:00 and _____ on a
                1                                              2
bus to go home. She has the same schedule every evening. She _____ dinner
                                                                    3
and then _____ down to eat at 6:00. After she _____ the
              4                                          5
dishes, she _____ on the TV. She usually _____ the news and
                6                                     7
then a movie. At 9:00, she _____ a shower. She always _____
                                8                                     9
her teeth after her shower. Then she picks up a book and _____ in bed for a
                                                              10
while. She usually _____ asleep before 10:00.
                        11

□ **Exercise 19. Warm-up.** (Chart 3-5)

What kind of ending does each verb have? Put the verbs from the box in the correct column.

| b**uy** | f**ly** | pl**ay** | stu**dy** |
|---------|---------|----------|-----------|

CONSONANT + **-y**          VOWEL + **-y**

_____          _____

_____          _____

## 3-5 Adding Final -s/-es to Words That End in -y

| | | | |
|---|---|---|---|
| (a) *cry* | → | *cries* | ENDING OF VERB: consonant + **-y** |
| *try* | → | *tries* | SPELLING: change **y** to **i**, add **-es** |
| (b) *pay* | → | *pays* | ENDING OF VERB: vowel + **-y** |
| *enjoy* | → | *enjoys* | SPELLING: add **-s** |

❏ **Exercise 20. Looking at grammar.** (Chart 3-5)
Complete the chart with the correct form of each verb.

| | |
|---|---|
| 1. I try. | He _____*tries*_____ . |
| 2. We study. | She _____ . |
| 3. They say. | It _____ . |
| 4. I enjoy games. | Ann _____ games. |
| 5. You worry a lot. | My mother _____ a lot. |
| 6. We pay bills. | Gina _____ bills. |
| 7. You stay awake. | Paul _____ awake. |
| 8. We fly. | A bird _____ . |
| 9. Students buy books. | My brother _____ books. |
| 10. I play music. ♪♪ | My friend _____ music. |

❏ **Exercise 21. Looking at grammar.** (Chart 3-5)
Complete each sentence with the simple present form of a verb from the box.

| | | | |
|---|---|---|---|
| buy | cry | pay | stay |
| carry | employ | ✓ play | study |

1. Monique likes sports. She _____*plays*_____ tennis and soccer several times a week.

2. The school cafeteria is cheap. Rob _____ his lunch there every day.

3. My company is big. It _____ 2,000 people.

4. Elizabeth is always tired. Her new baby _____ during the night.

5. Mr. Garcia travels every week. He _____ in small hotels.

6. Some airplanes are very big. A large airplane _____ 400 to 500 passengers.

7. I usually pay with a debit card, but my husband _____ in cash.

8. Zara is a medical student. She _____ every night and on weekends.

❏ **Exercise 22. Warm-up.** (Chart 3-6)
Read the information about Milos and complete the chart.

Milos is a college student. He **has** a part-time job. He **does** the breakfast dishes at his dorm. Then he **goes** to class.

| HAVE | DO | GO |
|------|------|------|
| I **have** | I **do** | I **go** |
| you **have** | you **do** | you **go** |
| he _____ | he _____ | he _____ |
| she _____ | she _____ | she _____ |
| it _____ | it _____ | it _____ |
| we **have** | we **do** | we **go** |
| they **have** | they **do** | they **go** |

## 3-6 Irregular Singular Verbs: *Has, Does, Goes*

| | | |
|---|---|---|
| (a) I *have* a book. <br><br> (b) He *has* a book. | she <br> he } + **has** /hæz/ <br> it | **Have**, **do**, and **go** have irregular forms for 3rd person singular: <br><br> have → has <br> do → does <br> go → goes |
| (c) I *do* my work. <br><br> (d) She *does* her work. | she <br> he } + **does** /dəz/ <br> it | |
| (e) They *go* to school. <br><br> (f) She *goes* to school. | she <br> he } + **goes** /gowz/ <br> it | Note that final **-s** is pronounced /z/ in these verbs. |

❏ **Exercise 23. Looking at grammar.** (Chart 3-6)
Use the correct form of the given verbs to complete the sentences.

1. do      Pierre always ___*does*___ his homework.

2. do          We always _____*do*_____ our homework.

3. have         Yoko and Hamid _____ their books.

4. have         Mrs. Chang _____ a car.

5. go           Andy _____ to school every day.

6. do          Sara seldom _____ her homework.

7. do          We _____ exercises in class every day.

8. go, go       Roberto _____ downtown every weekend.  He and his wife

                _____ shopping.

9. play         My friends often _____ volleyball at the beach.

### ❏ Exercise 24. Listening. (Chart 3-6)

Listen to the story.  Complete the sentences with *is, has, does,* or *goes.*

Marco _____*is*_____ a student.  He _____*has*_____ an unusual schedule.  All of his
            1                         2

classes are at night.  His first class _____ at 6:00 P.M. every day.  He takes a break
                                            3

from 7:30 to 8:00.  Then he _____ classes from 8:00 to 10:00.
                                4

He leaves school and _____ home at 10:00.  After he _____ dinner,
                        5                                         6

he watches TV.  Then he _____ his homework from midnight to 3:00 or 4:00 in
                            7

the morning.

Marco _____ his own computer at home.  When he finishes his homework,
            8

he usually goes on the Internet.  He often stays at his computer until the sun comes up.

Then he _____ a few exercises, _____ breakfast, and _____ to
            9                              10                             11

bed.  He sleeps all day.  Marco thinks his schedule _____ great, but his friends
                                                        12

think it _____ strange.
            13

Complete the sentences with the words in parentheses. Use the simple present tense. Pay special attention to singular and plural and to the spelling of final **-s/-es**.

1. The students (*ask, often*) _____ *often ask* _____ questions in class.

2. Pablo (*study, usually*) _____ at the library every evening.

3. Olga (*bite*) _____ her fingernails when she is nervous.

4. Donna (*cash*) _____ a check at the bank once a week.

5. Sometimes I (*worry*) _____ about my grades at school. Sonya

   (*worry, never*) _____ about her grades. She (*study*)

   _____ hard.

6. Ms. Fernandez and Mr. Anderson (*teach*) _____ at the local high school.

   Ms. Fernandez (*teach*) _____ math.

7. Birds (*fly*) _____. They (*have*) _____ wings.

8. A bird (*fly*) _____. It (*have*) _____ wings.

9. Emilio (*do, always*) _____ his homework. He (*go, never*)

   _____ to bed until his homework is finished.

10. Mr. Cook (*say, always*)* _____ hello to his neighbor.

11. Ms. Chu (*pay, always*)* _____ attention in class. She (*answer*)

    _____ questions. She (*listen*) _____ to the

    teacher. She (*ask*) _____ questions.

❏ **Exercise 26. Let's talk: game.** (Charts 3-1 → 3-6)

***Part I.*** Your teacher will assign you a verb from the list. Make a sentence with that verb. Walk around the room. Say your sentence to other students. Listen to other students say their sentences.

| | | | | |
|---|---|---|---|---|
| 1. eat | 4. brush | 7. get up | 10. do | 13. put on |
| 2. go | 5. have | 8. watch | 11. listen to | 14. carry |
| 3. drink | 6. study | 9. speak | 12. wash | 15. kiss |

***Part II.*** Work in teams of five to eight students. Write as many sentences as you can remember. Each team will have one paper. The team with the most correct sentences wins.

___

*Pronunciation of **says** = /sɛz/. Pronunciation of **pays** = /peyz/.

❏ **Exercise 27. Let's talk: pairwork.** (Charts 3-1 → 3-6)
Work with a partner. Use frequency adverbs like *sometimes*, *rarely*, etc.

*Part I.* Yuri, Levi, and Peter do many things in the evening. How often do they do the things in the list? Pay attention to final *-s*.

*Example:* Yuri rarely/seldom does homework.

|  | **YURI** | **LEVI** | **PETER** |
|---|---|---|---|
| DO HOMEWORK | once a week | 6 days a week | every day |
| SURF THE INTERNET | every day | once a week | once a month |
| WATCH TV | 3–4 days a week | 3–4 days a week | 3–4 days a week |
| READ FOR PLEASURE | 5 days a week | 5 days a week | 5 days a week |
| GO TO BED EARLY | once a week | 5–6 nights a week | 6–7 nights a week |

*Part II.* For homework, write ten sentences about the activities of Yuri, Levi, and Peter.

❏ **Exercise 28. Looking at grammar.** (Charts 3-1 → 3-6)
Add *-s* or *-es* where necessary.

### Abdul and Pablo

(1) My friend Abdul live (*s*) in an apartment near school. (2) He walk to school almost every day. (3) Sometimes he catch a bus, especially if it's cold and rainy outside. (4) Abdul share the apartment with Pablo. (5) Pablo come from Venezuela. (6) Abdul and Pablo go to the same school. (7) They take English classes. (8) Abdul speak Arabic as his first language, and Pablo speak Spanish. (9) They communicate in English. (10) Sometimes Abdul try to teach Pablo to speak a little Arabic, and Pablo give Abdul Spanish lessons. (11) They laugh a lot during the Arabic and Spanish lessons. (12) Abdul enjoy his roommate, but he miss his family back in Saudi Arabia.

❏ **Exercise 29. Speaking and writing: pairwork.** (Charts 3-1 → 3-6)
Work with a partner. Tell your partner five to ten things you do every morning. Use the list you made in Exercise 3. Your partner will also give you information about his/her morning. Take notes. Then write a paragraph about your partner's morning activities. Pay special attention to the use of final *-s/-es*. Ask your partner to read your paragraph and to check your use of final *-s/-es*.

❏ **Exercise 30. Warm-up.** (Chart 3-7)
Which sentences are true for you?

1. I like to speak English.                                  yes        no

2. I need to learn English.                                  yes        no

3. I want to speak English fluently.                         yes        no

## 3-7 Like To, Want To, Need To

| | VERB + INFINITIVE | | |
|---|---|---|---|
| (a) | I *like* | *to travel*. It's fun. |
| (b) | I *want* | *to travel*. I have vacation time next month. |
| (c) | I *need* | *to travel* for my job. I have no choice. |

**Like**, **want**, and **need** can be followed by an infinitive.

infinitive = **to** + *the base form of the verb.**

**Need to** is stronger than **want to**. **Need to** = necessary, important.

\* The base form of a verb = a verb without *-s*, *-ed*, or *-ing*. Examples of the base form of a verb: *come, help, answer, write*. Examples of infinitives: *to come, to help, to answer, to write*. The base form is also called the simple form of a verb.

❏ **Exercise 31. Looking at grammar.** (Chart 3-7)
Make complete sentences. Pay attention to the final *-s* ending on singular verbs.

1. Maya \ need \ study ____*Maya needs to study.*____

2. We \ want \ go home _____

3. Bill and I \ like \ eat sweets _____

4. You \ need \ speak more quietly _____

5. She \ like \ talk on the phone _____

6. Her friends \ like \ text _____

7. They \ need \ save money _____

8. He \ want \ travel _____

❏ **Exercise 32. Reading and grammar.** (Charts 3-1 → 3-7)
**Part I.** Read the story.

### A Wonderful Cook

Roberto is a wonderful cook. He often tries new recipes. He likes to cook for friends. He frequently invites my girlfriend and me to dinner. When we arrive, we go to the kitchen. He usually has three or four pots on the stove. He makes a big mess when he cooks. We like to watch him, and he wants to tell us about each recipe. His dinners are delicious. After dinner, he needs to clean the kitchen. We want to help him because we want him to invite us back soon.

**Part II.** Complete each sentence with a word from the box.

| help | invite | is | like | likes to | wash |
|------|--------|-----|------|----------|------|

1. Roberto _____ a great cook.

2. He _____ try new recipes.

3. He likes to _____ friends to dinner.

4. After dinner, he needs to _____ the pots, and his friends

   _____ him.

5. His friends _____ his food.

❏ **Exercise 33. Let's talk: game.** (Chart 3-7)

Work in teams. What do you know about mosquitoes? Choose the correct answer.
The team with the most correct answers wins.*

|   |   |   |   |
|---|---|---|---|
| 1. They like to look for food during the day. | yes | no |
| 2. They like to look for food at night. | yes | no |
| 3. They need to lay their eggs in water. | yes | no |
| 4. They like to travel. | yes | no |
| 5. They need to sleep in water. | yes | no |
| 6. Male mosquitoes need to bite. | yes | no |
| 7. Female mosquitoes need to bite. | yes | no |

❏ **Exercise 34. Warm-up.** (Chart 3-8)

Which sentences are true for you?

1. a. I like vegetables.      b. I don't like vegetables.

2. a. I drink tea.      b. I don't drink tea.

3. a. I eat meat.      b. I don't eat meat.

*See *Let's Talk: Answers,* p. 501.

## 3-8 Simple Present Tense: Negative

| | | | | |
|---|---|---|---|---|
| (a) | I | *do not* | drink coffee. | NEGATIVE: *I, You, We, They* + **do not** + *main verb* |
| | You | *do not* | drink coffee. | |
| | We | *do not* | drink coffee. | |
| | They | *do not* | drink coffee. | |
| | | | | |
| (b) | He | *does not* | drink coffee. | *He, She, It* + **does not** + *main verb* |
| | She | *does not* | drink coffee. | |
| | It | *does not* | drink coffee. | |

**Do** and **does** are called "helping verbs."

Notice in (b): In 3rd person singular, there is no **-s** on the main verb, **drink**; the final **-s** is part of the helping verb, **does**.

INCORRECT: *She does not drinks coffee.*

| | |
|---|---|
| (c) I **don't** drink coffee. | CONTRACTIONS: **do not** = **don't** |
| He **doesn't** drink coffee. | **does not** = **doesn't** |

People usually use contractions when they speak.
People often use contractions when they write.

❏ **Exercise 35. Looking at grammar.** (Chart 3-8)
Choose the correct verb.

1. We        does not / (do not)        have a TV.

2. She       does not / do not        like milk.

3. They      does not / do not        play soccer.

4. I         does not / do not        understand.

5. It        does not / do not        rain much here.

6. You       does not / do not        understand.

7. He        doesn't / don't        work hard.

8. You       doesn't / don't        need help.

9. They      doesn't / don't        live here.

10. She      doesn't / don't        speak English.

11. We       doesn't / don't        have time.

12. I        doesn't / don't        study every day.

❏ **Exercise 36. Looking at grammar.** (Chart 3-8)

Use the given words to make negative sentences. Use contractions.

1. like, not    Ingrid _____*doesn't like*_____ tea.

2. like, not    I _____*don't like*_____ tea.

3. know, not    Mary and Jim are strangers. Mary _____ Jim.

4. speak, not    I _____ French.

5. need, not    It's a nice day today. You _____

   your umbrella.

6. live, not    Dogs _____ long.

7. have, not    A dog _____ a long life.

8. have, not    We _____ class every day.

9. have, not    This city _____ nice weather in the summer.

10. snow, not    It _____ in Bangkok in the winter.

11. rain, not    It _____ every day.

an umbrella

❏ **Exercise 37. Let's talk: pairwork.** (Chart 3-8)

Work with a partner. Make two sentences about each picture.

*Example:*

PARTNER A: Isabel takes showers. She doesn't take baths.
          Your turn now.

PARTNER B: Omar has a dog. He doesn't have a cat.
          Your turn now.

YES                                                    NO

1. (Isabel \ take)
   showers
   baths

2. (Omar \ have)
   a cat
   a dog

Using the Simple Present **77**

| YES | | NO |
|---|---|---|

 YES  NO

3. (I \ drink)
   tea
   coffee

4. (Rob and Ed \ live)
   an apartment
   a house

5. (Julia \ drive)
   a new car
   an old car

6. (I \ play)
   soccer
   tennis

7. (Mr. Ortiz \ teach)
   English
   French

8. (we \ use)
   typewriters
   computers

9. (Inga \ watch)
   news reports
   old movies

10. (Marco \ study)
    history
    physics

❑  **Exercise 38.  Let's talk: game.** (Chart 3-8)
Sit in a circle.  Use any of the verbs from the box.  Make sentences with **not**.

*Example:* like
STUDENT A:  I don't like bananas.
STUDENT B:  (*Student A*) doesn't like bananas.  I don't have a dog.
STUDENT C:  (*Student A*) doesn't like bananas.  (*Student B*) doesn't have a dog.
          I don't play baseball.

| have | like | need | play | read | speak |
|------|------|------|------|------|-------|

Continue around the circle.  Each time, repeat the information of your classmates before you say your sentence.  If you have trouble, your classmates can help you.  Your teacher will be the last one to speak.

❑  **Exercise 39.  Looking at grammar.** (Chart 3-8)
Use verbs from the box to complete the sentences.  Make all of the sentences negative by using **does not** or **do not**.  You can use contractions (**doesn't/don't**).  Some verbs may be used more than one time.

| do | eat | make | shave | speak |
|------|------|------|------|------|
| drink | go | put on | smoke | |

1. Ricardo _____*doesn't go*_____ to school every day.

2. My roommates are from Japan.  They _____ Spanish.

3. Roberto has a beard.  He _____ in the morning.

4. We _____ to class on Sunday.

5. Camilla is healthy.  She _____ cigarettes.

6. Nadia and Anton always have lunch at home.  They _____ in the cafeteria.

7. Sometimes I _____ my homework in the evening.  I watch TV instead.

8. My sister likes tea, but she _____ coffee.

9. Hamid is a careful writer.  He _____ spelling mistakes when he writes.

10. Sometimes Julianna _____ her shoes when she goes outside.  She likes to go barefoot.

**Exercise 40. Looking at grammar.** (Charts 1-6, 1-7, and 3-8)
Complete the chart with the correct form of the given verbs.

| SIMPLE PRESENT: *BE* | SIMPLE PRESENT: *EAT* |
|---|---|
| 1. I _____*am not*_____ hungry. | 1. I _____*do not eat*_____ meat. |
| 2. You _____ hungry. | 2. You _____ meat. |
| 3. She _____ hungry. | 3. She _____ meat. |
| 4. We _____ hungry. | 4. We _____ meat. |
| 5. It _____ hungry. | 5. It _____ meat. |
| 6. They _____ hungry. | 6. They _____ meat. |
| 7. He _____ hungry. | 7. He _____ meat. |
| 8. Raj _____ hungry. | 8. Raj _____ meat. |
| 9. You and I _____ hungry. | 9. You and I _____ meat. |

❑ **Exercise 41. Looking at grammar.** (Charts 1-6, 1-7, and 3-8)
Choose the correct verb.

1. I        am not / do not        late.
2. They     are not / do not       drink coffee.
3. He       is not / does not       do his homework.
4. You      are not / do not        poor.
5. She      is not / does not       do her homework.
6. The key  is not / does not       work.
7. It       is not / does not       in the car.
8. I        am not / do not         like vegetables.
9. We       are not / do not        live here.
10. We      are not / do not        citizens.

❑ **Exercise 42. Let's talk: class activity.** (Charts 1-6, 1-7, and 3-8)
***Part I.*** Use the given words to make true sentences for each pair.

*Example:*  a.  Grass \ be blue.
            b.  Grass \ be green
STUDENT A:  Grass isn't blue.
STUDENT B:  Grass is green.

*Example:* a. Dogs \ have tails
           b. People \ have tails.
STUDENT C: Dogs have tails.
STUDENT D: People★ don't have tails.

1. a. A restaurant \ sell shoes.
    b. A restaurant \ serve food.

2. a. People \ wear clothes.
    b. Animals \ wear clothes.

3. a. A child \ need love, food, and care.
    b. A child \ need a driver's license.

4. a. Refrigerators \ be hot inside.
    b. Refrigerators \ be cold inside.

5. a. A cat \ have whiskers.
    b. A bird \ have whiskers.

whiskers

*Part II.* Make true sentences.

6. Doctors in my country \ be expensive.
7. A bus \ carry people from one place to another.
8. It \ be cold today.
9. English \ be an easy language to learn.
10. People in this city \ be friendly.
11. It \ rain a lot in this city.

❑ **Exercise 43. Warm-up.** (Chart 3-9)
What do you notice about the questions with *have* and *need?*

Are you okay?
Are you sick?
Do you have a fever?
Do you need a doctor?

---

★*People* is a plural noun. It takes a plural verb.

## 3-9 Simple Present Tense: Yes/No Questions

| DO/DOES + SUBJECT + MAIN VERB | QUESTION FORMS, SIMPLE PRESENT |
|---|---|
| (a) **Do** *I* **work?** | **Do I** |
| (b) **Do** *you* **work?** | **Do you** |
| (c) **Does** *he* **work?** | **Does he** |
| (d) **Does** *she* **work?** | **Does she** } + *main verb* (base form) |
| (e) **Does** *it* **work?** | **Does it** |
| (f) **Do** *we* **work?** | **Do we** |
| (g) **Do** *they* **work?** | **Do they** |

Notice in (c), (d), and (e): The main verb in the question does not have a final **-s**. The final **-s** is part of **does**.

*INCORRECT:* Does she works?

| | |
|---|---|
| (h) **Am I** late? | When the main verb is a form of **be**, do is NOT used. See Chart 2-1, p. 28, for question forms with **be**. |
| (i) **Are you** ready? | |
| (j) **Is he** a teacher? | |
| (k) **Are we** early? | |
| (l) **Are they** at home? | |
| (m) **Are you** a student? | |
| *INCORRECT:* Do you be a student? | |

| QUESTION | SHORT ANSWER | |
|---|---|---|
| (n) **Do** you *like* fish? → | Yes, I **do**. <br> No, I **don't**. | **Do**, **don't**, **does**, and **doesn't** are used in the short answers to yes/no questions in the simple present. |
| (o) **Does** Liam *like* fish? → | Yes, he **does**. <br> No, he **doesn't**. | |

| | |
|---|---|
| (p) Brad **does** his homework. | Note that **do** can also be a main verb, as in (p) and (q). |
| (q) **Does** Brad **do** his homework? | |

❏ **Exercise 44. Looking at grammar.** (Chart 3-9)
Make questions. Choose the correct answer.

1. A: *like \ you \ tea* _____*Do you like tea?*_____
   B: ⓐ Yes, I do.
      b. Yes, I like.

2. A: *speak \ Anita \ Italian* _____
   B: a. Yes, she does.
      b. Yes, she speaks.

3. A: *speak \ Thomas and Sierra \ Arabic* _____
   B: a. No, they don't.
      b. No, they don't speak.

4. A: *rain \ it \ in April* _____
   B: a. Yes, it does.
      b. Yes, it rains.

5. A: *do \ he \ his homework* _____
   B: a. No, he doesn't.
      b. No, he doesn't do.

6. A: *do \ you \ your homework* _____
   B: a. No, I don't.
      b. No, I don't do.

7. A: *have \ they \ enough money* _____
   B: a. Yes, they do.
      b. Yes, they have.

❏ **Exercise 45. Speaking and grammar: pairwork.** (Charts 2-1, 2-2, and 3-9)

*Part I.* Work with a partner. Take turns making questions and giving short answers. Use the names of your classmates in the questions. *Note: Part I is speaking practice.* Do not write the answers until *Part II.*

*Example:*
PARTNER A: _____
PARTNER B: _____ (He is in class today.)
PARTNER A: Is Ali in class today?
PARTNER B: Yes, he is.

*Example:*
PARTNER B: _____
PARTNER A: _____ (She doesn't speak Spanish.)
PARTNER B: Does Akiko speak Spanish?
PARTNER A: No, she doesn't.

1. PARTNER A: _____
   PARTNER B: _____ (He speaks English in class every day.)

2. PARTNER B: _____
   PARTNER A: _____ (She comes to class every day.)

3. PARTNER A: _____
   PARTNER B: _____ (They're in class today.)

4. PARTNER B: _____
   PARTNER A: _____ (He wears jeans every day.)

5. PARTNER A: _____
   PARTNER B: _____ (They aren't from Australia.)

6. PARTNER B: _____

    PARTNER A: _____ (They don't have dictionaries on their desks.)

7. PARTNER A: _____

    PARTNER B: _____ (They speak English.)

*Part II*. Now write the questions and answers in your book.

❑ **Exercise 46. Vocabulary and speaking.** (Chart 3-9)
*Part I*. Check (✓) the activities you do at least once a week.

| | | |
|---|---|---|
| 1. ____ take a nap | 6. ____ make breakfast | 11. ____ do my homework |
| 2. ____ take a break | 7. ____ make lunch | 12. ____ do the dishes |
| 3. ____ take a shower | 8. ____ make dinner | 13. ____ do the laundry |
| 4. ____ take a bath | 9. ____ make a snack | |
| 5. ____ take a bus/train/taxi | 10. ____ make my bed | |

*Part II*. Walk around the room. Ask questions using these phrases. For each question, find someone who can answer *yes*. *Note:* Remember to change *my* to *your*.

*Example:*
To STUDENT A:  Do you take a nap in the afternoon?
    STUDENT A:  No.
To STUDENT B:  Do you take a nap in the afternoon?
    STUDENT B:  Yes.
To STUDENT C:  Do you make your bed every day?
    STUDENT C:  Yes.

❑ **Exercise 47. Looking at grammar.** (Chapters 1 and 2; Charts 3-1 and 3-7 → 3-9)
Complete each sentence with the correct form of the given verb. Use the full form or contractions for the negative.

*Part I*. Statement Forms

| *LIVE* | *BE* |
|---|---|
| 1. I _____*live*_____ here. | I _____*am*_____ here. |
| 2. They _____ here. | They _____ here. |
| 3. He _____ here. | He _____ here. |
| 4. You _____ here. | You _____ here. |
| 5. She _____ here. | She _____ here. |
| 6. We _____ here. | We _____ here. |

***Part II.*** Negative Forms

7. They _____do not / don't live_____ here.    They _____are not / aren't_____ here.

8. I _____ here.    I _____ here.

9. She _____ here.    She _____ here.

10. You _____ here.    You _____ here.

11. He _____ here.    He _____ here.

12. We _____ here.    We _____ here.

***Part III.*** Question Forms

13. _____Do_____ you _____live_____ here?    _____Are_____ you here?

14. _____ they _____ here?    _____ they here?

15. _____ he _____ here?    _____ he here?

16. _____ we _____ here?    _____ we here?

17. _____ she _____ here?    _____ she here?

❑ **Exercise 48. Let's talk: game.** (Charts 2-1 and 3-9)
Work in teams. Complete the sentences with ***is***, ***are***, ***do***, or ***does***. Answer the questions with *yes* or *no*. The team with the most correct answers wins.

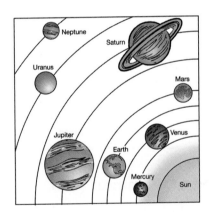

1. _____Does_____    the moon go around the Earth?    (yes)    no

2. _____    the sun go around the Earth?    yes    no

3. _____    the planets go around the sun?    yes    no

4. _____    the sun a planet?    yes    no

5. _____    stars planets?    yes    no

6. _____    Venus hot?    yes    no

7. _____    Neptune easy to see?    yes    no

| 8. | _____ | Jupiter windy? | yes | no |
| 9. | _____ | Venus and Mercury go around the sun? | yes | no |
| 10. | _____ | Saturn and Uranus have moons? | yes | no |

❑ **Exercise 49. Warm-up.** (Chart 3-10)
Match the questions with the correct answers.

1. Where is the lost-and-found? ___
2. Is the lost-and-found office in this building? ___
3. What is in this building? ___

a. The lost-and-found.
b. Yes, it is.
c. Down the hall.

---

### 3-10 Simple Present Tense: Asking Information Questions with *Where* and *What*

| *(WHERE/ WHAT)* | + *DO/ DOES* | + SUBJECT + | MAIN VERB | | SHORT ANSWER | |
|---|---|---|---|---|---|---|
| (a) | **Do** | they | *live* | in Miami? → | **Yes**, they do. **No**, they don't. | |
| (b) **Where** | **do** | they | *live?* | → | **In Miami.** | |
| (c) | **Does** | Gina | *live* | in Rome? → | **Yes**, she does. **No**, she doesn't. | |
| (d) **Where** | **does** | Gina | *live?* | → | **In Rome.** | |
| (e) | **Do** | they | *need* | help? → | **Yes**, they do. **No**, they don't. | |
| (f) **What** | **do** | they | *need?* | → | **Help.** | |
| (g) | **Does** | Lee | *need* | help? → | **Yes**, he does. **No**, he doesn't. | |
| (h) **What** | **does** | Lee | *need?* | → | **Help.** | |

(a) = a yes/no question
(b) = an information question

**Where** asks for information about a place.

The form of yes/no questions and information questions is the same:
**Do/Does** + *subject* + *main verb*

**What** asks for information about a thing.

---

❑ **Exercise 50. Looking at grammar.** (Chart 3-10)
Make questions.

1. A: _____*Does Hana eat lunch in the cafeteria every day?*_____
   B: Yes, she does. (Hana eats lunch in the cafeteria every day.)

2. A: _____*Where does Hana eat lunch every day?*_____
   B: In the cafeteria. (Hana eats lunch in the cafeteria every day.)

3. A: _____
   B: Rice. (She eats rice for lunch every day.)

4. A: _____
   B: At the post office. (Alfonso works at the post office.)

5. A: _____
   B: Yes, he does.  (Alfonso works at the post office.)

6. A: _____
   B: Yes, I do.  (I live in an apartment.)

7. A: _____
   B: In an apartment.  (I live in an apartment.)

8. A: _____
   B: Popcorn.  (Hector likes popcorn for a snack.)

9. A: _____
   B: At the University of Toronto.  (Ming goes to school at the University of Toronto.)

10. A: _____
    B: Biology.  (Her major is biology.)

11. A: _____
    B: To class.  (I go to class every morning.)

12. A: _____
    B: In class.  (The students are in class right now.)

❑ **Exercise 51. Let's talk: pairwork.** (Chart 3-10)
Work with a partner.  Ask and answer questions with *where*.

*Example:* live
   → Where do you live?

| PARTNER A | PARTNER B |
|---|---|
| 1. live | 1. buy your clothes |
| 2. eat lunch every day | 2. go on weekends |
| 3. go after class | 3. sit during class |
| 4. study at night | 4. eat dinner |
| 5. go to school | 5. do your homework |
| 6. buy school supplies | 6. go on vacation |

❑ **Exercise 52. Reading.** (Chart 3-10)
Read the story and answer the questions.

### Opposite Roommates

I have two roommates.  One of them, Fernando, is always neat and clean.  He washes his clothes once or twice a week.  My other roommate, Matt, is the opposite of Fernando.  For example, Matt doesn't change the sheets on his bed.  He keeps the same sheets week after week.  He never washes his clothes.  He wears the same dirty jeans every day.  He doesn't care if his clothes smell!  Fernando's side of the room is always neat.  He makes his bed, hangs up his clothes, and puts everything away.  Matt's side of the room is always a mess. He doesn't make his bed, hang up his clothes, or put things away. What habits do you think I prefer?

1. What are some of Fernando's habits?
2. What are some of Matt's habits?
3. Who is a good roommate for you? Why?

❏ **Exercise 53. Let's talk: class activity.** (Chart 3-10)
Ask your teacher questions to get more information about each person's life.* Decide who has the best life and why.

*Example:*
STUDENT A: Where does Antonio live?
  TEACHER: On a boat.
STUDENT B: What does Lena do?
  TEACHER: She teaches skiing.
STUDENT C: What pets does Lisa have?
  TEACHER: She has a snake.

Continue asking questions until your chart is complete.

| | **Where does she/he live?** | **What does he/she do?** | **Where does she/he work?** | **What pets does he/she have?** |
|---|---|---|---|---|
| ANTONIO | on a boat | | | |
| LENA | | teaches skiing | | |
| KANE | | | at a jewelry store | |
| LISA | | | | a snake |
| JACK | | | | |

❏ **Exercise 54. Warm-up.** (Chart 3-11)
Answer the questions.

1. What time does Alberto's alarm clock go off? _____

2. When does Alberto get out of bed? _____

8:00 A.M.             8:30 A.M.

*Teacher: See *Let's Talk: Answers*, p. 501.

## 3-11 Simple Present Tense: Asking Information Questions with *When* and *What Time*

| QUESTION* + *DO*/ + SUBJECT + MAIN | | | | | SHORT ANSWER | *When* and *what time* ask for information about time. |
|---|---|---|---|---|---|---|
| WORD | *DOES* | | VERB | | | |
| (a) **When** | do | you | go | to class? → | **At nine o'clock.** | |
| (b) **What time** | do | you | go | to class? → | **At nine o'clock.** | |
| (c) **When** | does | Anna | eat | dinner? → | **At six** P.M. | |
| (d) **What time** | does | Anna | eat | dinner? → | **At six** P.M. | |
| (e) **What time** do you **usually** go to class? | | | | | The frequency adverb usually comes immediately after the subject in a question: *Question word* + **does**/**do** + *subject* + **usually** + *main verb* | |

*\*Where, when, what, what time, who,* and *why* are examples of question words.*

❑ **Exercise 55. Looking at grammar.** (Chart 3-11)

Make questions.

1. A: _____*When/What time do you eat breakfast?*_____
   B: At 7:30. (I eat breakfast at 7:30 in the morning.)

2. A: _____*When/What time do you usually eat breakfast?*_____
   B: At 7:00. (I usually eat breakfast at 7:00.)

3. A: _____
   B: At 6:45. (I usually get up at 6:45.)

4. A: _____
   B: At 6:30. (Maria usually gets up at 6:30.)

5. A: _____
   B: At 8:15. (The movie starts at 8:15.)

6. A: _____
   B: Around 11:00. (I usually go to bed around 11:00.)

7. A: _____
   B: At 12:30. (I usually eat lunch at 12:30.)

8. A: _____
   B: At 5:30. (The restaurant opens at 5:30.)

9. A: _____

    B: At 9:05. (The train leaves at 9:05.)

10. A: _____

    B: Between 6:30 and 8:00. (I usually eat dinner between 6:30 and 8:00.)

11. A: _____

    B: At a quarter after eight. (Classes begin at a quarter after eight.)

12. A: _____

    B: At 10:00 P.M. (The library closes at 10:00 P.M. on Saturday.)

❑ **Exercise 56. Let's talk: interview.** (Chart 3-11)

Walk around the room. Ask a question beginning with **when** or **what time**. Write the answer and your classmate's name. Then ask another classmate a different question with **when** or **what time**. Share a few of your answers with the class.

*Example:* eat breakfast
STUDENT A: When/What time do you eat breakfast?
STUDENT B: I usually eat breakfast around seven o'clock.

| ACTIVITY | NAME | ANSWER |
|---|---|---|
| 1. wake up | | |
| 2. usually get up | | |
| 3. eat breakfast | | |
| 4. leave home in the morning | | |
| 5. usually get to class | | |
| 6. eat lunch | | |
| 7. get home from school | | |
| 8. have dinner | | |
| 9. usually study in the evening | | |
| 10. go to bed | | |

□ **Exercise 57. Looking at grammar.** (Chapter 3)
Use the information about Professor Vega to make questions and answers.

1. *be \ he \ a physics teacher*

   _____Is he a physics teacher?_____

   _____No, he isn't._____

2. *what \ teach \ he*

   _____What does he teach?_____

   _____He teaches Psychology 101 and_____

   _____Child Psychology 205._____

**Professor Vega**

*Office hours:*
Tuesday and Thursday
3:00 - 4:00

*Classes:*
Psychology 101, Room 213
9:00 - 10:00 daily

Child Psychology 205, Room 201
11:00 - 12:50
Tuesday and Thursday

3. *teach \ he \ Psychology 102*

   _____ ? _____

4. *where \ teach \ he \ Child Psychology 205*

   _____ ? _____

5. *be \ he \ in his office \ every day*

   _____ ? _____

6. *be \ he \ in his office \ at 9:00*

   _____ ? _____

7. *teach \ he \ at 7:00 A.M.*

   _____ ? _____

8. *what time \ leave \ he \ the office on Tuesdays and Thursdays*

   _____ ? _____

9. *be \ he \ a professor*

   _____ ? _____

□ **Exercise 58. Looking at grammar.** (Chapter 3)
Complete the questions in the conversations. Use *is, are, does,* or *do.*

CONVERSATION 1:

A: What time _____does_____ the movie start?
   ¹

B: Seven-fifteen. _____ you want to go with us?
                      ²

A: Yes. What time _____ it now?
                       3

B: Almost seven o'clock. _____ you ready to leave?
                                  4

A: Yes, let's go.


CONVERSATION 2:

A: Where _____ my keys to the car?
                 5

B: I don't know. Where _____ you usually keep them?
                               6

A: In my purse. But they're not there.

B: Are you sure?

A: Yes. _____ you see them?
               7

B: No. _____ they in one of your pockets?
              8

A: I don't think so.

B: _____ your husband have them?
           9

A: No. He has his own set of car keys.

B: Well, good luck!

A: Thanks.


CONVERSATION 3:

A: _____ you go to school?
          10

B: Yes.

A: _____ your brother go to school too?
          11

B: No, he works full-time.

A: Where _____ he work?
                 12

B: At a hotel.

A: _____ he happy?
          13

B: Yes, he loves his job.

❑ **Exercise 59. Check your knowledge.** (Chapter 3)
Correct the mistakes.

           *lives*
1. Niko ~~live~~ in Greece.

2. Lisa comes usually to class on time.

3. Diego use his cell phone often.

4. Amira carry a notebook computer to work every day.

5. She enjoy her job.

6. Miguel don't like milk.  He never drink it.

7. Tina doesn't speaks Chinese.  She speakes Spanish.

8. You a student?

9. Does your roommate sleeps with the window open?

10. Where your parents live?

11. What time is your English class begins?

12. Olga isn't need a car.  She have a bicycle.

13. I no speak English.

14. Omar speak English every day.

15. A:  Do you like strong coffee?

    B:  Yes, I like.


❑ **Exercise 60. Looking at grammar.** (Chapter 3)
Make questions.  Use your own words.

1. A: _____ ?
   B: No, I don't.

2. A: _____ ?
   B: Yes, I am.

3. A: _____ ?
   B: In an apartment.

4. A: _____ ?
   B: Six-thirty.

5. A: _____ ?

   B: Monday.

6. A: _____ ?

   B: No, he doesn't.

7. A: _____ ?

   B: No, she isn't.

8. A: _____ ?

   B: South of the United States.

9. A: _____ ?

   B: Yes, it is.

10. A: _____ ?

    B: Yes, they do.

11. A: _____ ?

    B: In Southeast Asia.

12. A: _____ ?

    B: Yes, I do.

❑ **Exercise 61. Speaking and writing: pairwork.** (Chapter 3)

*Part I*. Work with a partner. Take turns asking about things you have and don't have (for example, a car, a computer, a pet, children, a TV set, a briefcase, etc.). Take notes.

*Example:*
PARTNER A: Do you have a car?
PARTNER B: No.
PARTNER A: Do you have a computer?
PARTNER B: Yes, but it's not here. It's in my country.
Etc.

*Part II*. Take turns asking about things you like and don't like.

*Example:*
PARTNER B: Do you like pizza?
PARTNER A: Yes.
PARTNER B: Do you like the music of (name of a group or singer)?
PARTNER A: No, I don't.
Etc.

**Part III.** Write about your partner.
- Give a physical description.
- Write about things this person has and doesn't have.
- Write about things this person likes and doesn't like.

Here is some vocabulary to help you describe your partner.

| HAIR TYPE | HAIR COLOR | | EYE COLOR |
|---|---|---|---|
| straight | brown | blond | brown |
| curly | black | dark | blue |
| wavy | red | light | green |
| bald | | | gray |

| straight | curly | wavy | bald |

*Writing sample:*

   My partner is Jin. He is very tall. He has brown eyes and black hair, and he has a nice smile. He is very friendly.

   Jin has an apartment near school. He doesn't have a car, but he has a bike. He rides his bike to school. He has a laptop computer. His family doesn't live here. He talks to them by video a few times a week.

   He is often homesick. He likes to watch movies from his country in the evening. He enjoys comedy and drama. He likes many kinds of music. He listens to music on his cell phone. He doesn't really like the food here. He likes spicy food. The food here is not spicy. Unfortunately, he is not a good cook, so he doesn't cook much. He likes to eat with his friends. They are good cooks.

**Part IV.** Editing check: Work individually or change papers with a partner. Check (✓) for the following:

1. ____ capital letter at the beginning of each sentence

2. ____ capital letter at the beginning of a person's name

3. ____ period at the end of each sentence

4. ____ paragraph indents

5. ____ a verb in every sentence

6. ____ correct use of **doesn't** or **isn't** in negative sentences

7. ____ correct spelling (use a dictionary or spell-check)

# Chapter 4
## Using the Present Progressive

❑ **Exercise 1. Warm-up.** (Chart 4-1)
Complete the sentences with the given words.

David

Nancy

*happy/sad*

1. David is _____.

2. Nancy is _____.

*laughing/crying*

He is _____.

She is _____.

---

### 4-1 *Be* + *-ing:* the Present Progressive

| | | |
|---|---|---|
| **am** + **-ing** | (a) I *am sitting* in class right now. | In (a): When I say this sentence, I am in class. I am sitting. I am not standing. The action (sitting) is happening right now, and I am saying the sentence at the same time. |
| **is** + **-ing** | (b) Rita *is sitting* in class right now. | |
| **are** + **-ing** | (c) You *are sitting* in class right now. | |
| | | **am, is, are** = helping verbs <br> **sitting** = the main verb |
| | | **am, is, are** + **-ing** = the present progressive* |

* The present progressive is also called the "present continuous."

❏ **Exercise 2. Looking at grammar.** (Chart 4-1)
Complete the sentences with the correct form of *be* (*am*, *is*, or *are*).

*Right now . . .*

1. it _____*is*_____ raining outside.

2. we _____ sitting in the college library.

3. you _____ writing.

4. some students _____ studying.

5. I _____ looking out the window.

6. two women _____ waiting for a bus.

7. they _____ talking.

8. a bus _____ coming.

❏ **Exercise 3. Looking at grammar.** (Chart 4-1)
Complete each sentence with the present progressive of the verb in *italics*.

1. *stand*      She ____*is standing*_____.

2. *sleep*      You _____.

3. *read*       He _____.

4. *eat*        I _____.

5. *help*       We _____.

6. *play*       They _____.

7. *snow*       It _____.

❏ **Exercise 4. Let's talk: class activity.** (Chart 4-1)
Your teacher will act out some verbs. Answer questions about these actions. Close your book for this activity.

*Example:* read
TEACHER: (*acts out reading*) I am reading. What am I doing?
STUDENT: You are reading.

1. write                4. count
2. sit                  5. wave
3. stand                6. look at the ceiling

**Exercise 5. Let's talk: pairwork.** (Chart 4-1)
Work with a partner. Take turns describing the pictures. Use the present progressive form
of the verbs from the box.

*Example:*
PARTNER A: The woman is driving a car.
PARTNER B: (*points to the picture*)
PARTNER A: Your turn.

| | | | | |
|---|---|---|---|---|
| fish | get on (a bus) | laugh | sing | swim |
| fix (a computer) | kick (a soccer ball) | read | sleep | walk |

❑ **Exercise 6. Let's talk: class activity.** (Chart 4-1)

Act out the directions your teacher gives you. Describe the actions using the present progressive. Continue the action during the description. Close your book for this activity.

*Example:*

TEACHER TO STUDENT A: Please smile. What are you doing?
STUDENT A: I'm smiling.
TEACHER TO STUDENTS A + B: Please smile. (*Student A*), what are you and (*Student B*) doing?
STUDENT A: We're smiling.
TEACHER TO STUDENT B: What are you and (*Student A*) doing?
STUDENT B: We're smiling.
TEACHER TO STUDENT C: What are (*Student A* and *Student B*) doing?
STUDENT C: They're smiling.
TEACHER TO STUDENT B: What is (*Student A*) doing?
STUDENT B: He/She is smiling.

1. Stand up.
2. Sit down.
3. Sit in the middle of the room.
4. Stand in the back of the room.
5. Stand between ( ___ ) and ( ___ ).
6. Touch your desk.
7. Look at the ceiling.
8. Hold up your right hand.
9. Hold up your left hand.
10. Clap your hands.

❑ **Exercise 7. Listening.** (Chart 4-1)

Read the story. Then listen to each sentence and look at the picture of Tony. Circle the correct answer. Compare your answers with your classmates' answers.

Tony is not a serious student. He is lazy. He doesn't go to class much. He likes to sit in the cafeteria. Sometimes he sits alone, and sometimes he visits with friends from his country. He is in the cafeteria right now. What is he doing?

*Example:* Tony is talking on his cell phone. (yes) no

1. yes no
2. yes no
3. yes no
4. yes no
5. yes no
6. yes no
7. yes no
8. yes no
9. yes no
10. yes no

❑ **Exercise 8. Warm-up.** (Chart 4-2)
Answer the questions.

| count | ride | sleep | stop |
|-------|------|-------|------|

1. Which verb ends in a consonant + **-e**? _____
2. Which verb ends in two consonants? _____
3. Which verb ends in two vowels + one consonant? _____
4. Which verb ends in one vowel + one consonant? _____

## 4-2 Spelling of *-ing*

| | END OF VERB | → | *-ING* FORM |
|------|-------------|---|-------------|
| RULE 1 | A CONSONANT* + **-e** | → | DROP THE **-e** AND ADD **-ing** |
| | smil*e* | → | smil*ing* |
| | wri*te* | → | wri*ting* |
| RULE 2 | ONE VOWEL* + ONE CONSONANT | → | DOUBLE THE CONSONANT AND ADD **-ing**** |
| | si*t* | → | si*tting* |
| | ru*n* | → | ru*nning* |
| RULE 3 | TWO VOWELS + ONE CONSONANT | → | ADD **-ing**; DO NOT DOUBLE THE CONSONANT |
| | rea*d* | → | rea*ding* |
| | rai*n* | → | rai*ning* |
| RULE 4 | TWO CONSONANTS | → | ADD **-ing**; DO NOT DOUBLE THE CONSONANT |
| | sta*nd* | → | sta*nding* |
| | pu*sh* | → | pu*shing* |

*Vowels = *a, e, i, o, u*. Consonants = *b, c, d, f, g, h, j, k, l, m, n, p, q, r, s, t, v, w, x, y, z.*
**Exception to Rule 2: Do not double *w, x,* and *y. snow → snowing; fix → fixing; say → saying*

❑ **Exercise 9. Looking at spelling.** (Chart 4-2)
Write the *-ing* form of the given verbs.

1. take _____*taking*_____
2. come _____
3. dream _____
4. bite _____
5. hit _____
6. rain _____

7. hurt _____
8. plan _____
9. bake _____
10. snow _____
11. study _____
12. stop _____

## Exercise 10. Looking at spelling. (Chart 4-2)

Your teacher will act out a sentence. On a separate piece of paper, write the word that ends in **-ing**. Close your book for this activity.

*Example:* wave
TEACHER: (*waves*) I'm waving.
STUDENT: (*writes*) ____waving____

1. smile
2. read
3. drink
4. sit
5. eat
6. clap
7. write
8. fly
9. sleep
10. sneeze
11. cut a piece of paper
12. cry

## Exercise 11. Looking at grammar. (Chart 4-2)

Complete the sentences. Use the present progressive form of the verbs from the box.

| call | charge | eat | search | send | wait |

**At work**

1. People are standing in the lobby. They ____are waiting____ for the elevator.

2. A secretary _____ an email to the staff.

3. A customer is using an office phone. He _____ his office.

4. Several people are in the lunchroom. They _____ lunch.

5. A manager has his cell phone on his desk. He _____ his battery.

6. An employee needs information. She _____ the Internet.

## Exercise 12. Warm-up. (Chart 4-3)

Choose the correct completion.

1. The birds   are / aren't   flying.
2. They   are / aren't   sitting on a telephone wire.
3. A car   is / isn't   driving by.

## 4-3 Present Progressive: Negatives

| | |
|---|---|
| (a) I **am not** *sleeping.* I am awake. <br> (b) Ben **isn't** *listening.* He's daydreaming. <br> (c) Mr. and Mrs. Silva **aren't** *watching* TV. They're reading. | Present progressive negative: <br> **am** <br> **is** } + **not** + **-ing** <br> **are** |

Ben

Mr. and Mrs. Silva

❏ **Exercise 13. Looking at grammar.** (Chart 4-3)
Make two sentences about each situation, one negative and one affirmative. Use the present progressive.

*Example:* Sandra: standing up / sitting down

Sandra _____*isn't standing up.*_____

She __*'s sitting down.*_____

SITUATION 1:
Otto: watching TV / talking on the phone

Otto _____

He _____

SITUATION 2:
Anita:  listening to music / playing soccer

Anita _____

She _____

SITUATION 3:
Sofia and Bruno:  reading / eating lunch

Sofia and Bruno _____

They _____

SITUATION 4:
Ted:  making photocopies / fixing the photocopy machine

Ted _____

He _____

❑ **Exercise 14. Looking at grammar.** (Chart 4-3)

***Part I.*** Read the paragraph.

    Jamal is a car mechanic.  He owns a car repair business.  He is very serious and works very hard.


Right now Jamal is at work.  What is he doing?  Check (✓) the phrases that make sense.

1.  ✓  talk to customers
2. _____ play soccer in a park
3. _____ change the oil in a car
4. _____ watch a movie in a theater
5. _____ put on a new tire

6. _____ answer the office phone
7. _____ give a customer a bill
8. _____ repair an engine
9. _____ eat at a restaurant
10. _____ replace a windshield wiper

windshield wipers


***Part II.*** Make true sentences about Jamal.

1. _____*He is talking to customers.*_____

2. _____*He isn't playing soccer in a park.*_____

3. _____

4. _____

5. _____

6. _____

7. _____

8. _____

9. _____

10. _____

❏ **Exercise 15. Let's talk.** (Chart 4-3)

Work in small groups. Take turns making sentences about the people in the list. Say what they are doing right now and what they are not doing right now.

*Example:* a neighbor
→ Mrs. Martinez is working in her office right now.
→ She is not working in her garden.

1. someone in your family
2. your favorite actor, writer, or sports star
3. a friend from childhood

4. a classmate
5. the leader of your country

❏ **Exercise 16. Warm-up.** (Chart 4-4)

Choose the correct answer.

1. Are you lying on a bed?
   a. Yes, I am.                    b. No, I'm not.

2. Is your teacher dancing?
   a. Yes, he/she is.               b. No, he/she isn't.

3. Are the students in your class singing?
   a. Yes, they are.                b. No they aren't.

## 4-4 Present Progressive: Questions

| QUESTION | SHORT ANSWER (LONG ANSWER) |
|---|---|
| | |

|  | BE + SUBJECT + -ING | | | SHORT ANSWER (LONG ANSWER) |
|---|---|---|---|---|
| (a) | *Is* | Marta | *sleeping?* | → Yes, *she is*. (She's sleeping.) |
| | | | | → No, *she's not*. (She's not sleeping.) |
| | | | | → No, *she isn't*. (She isn't sleeping.) |
| (b) | *Are* | you | *watching* TV? | → Yes, *I am*. (I'm watching TV.) |
| | | | | → No, *I'm not*. (I'm not watching TV.) |

| | QUESTION WORD + BE + SUBJECT + -ING | | | | |
|---|---|---|---|---|---|
| (c) | *Where* | is | Marta | *sleeping?* | → *In bed*. (She's sleeping in bed.) |
| (d) | *What* | is | Ted | *watching?* | → *A movie*. (Ted is watching a movie). |
| (e) | *Why* | are | you | *watching* TV? | → *Because I like this program*. (I'm watching TV because I like this program.) |

❑ **Exercise 17. Looking at grammar.** (Chart 4-4)
Make questions.

1. A: _____*Is the teacher helping*_____ students?

   B: Yes, she is. (The teacher is helping students.)

2. A: _____?

   B: Yes, he is. (Ivan is talking on his phone.)

3. A: _____?

   B: No, I'm not. (I'm not sleeping.)

4. A: _____ TV?

   B: No, they aren't. (The students aren't watching TV.)

5. A: _____ outside?

   B: No, it isn't. (It isn't raining outside.)

6. A: _____?

   B: Yes, he is. (John is riding a bike.)

❑ **Exercise 18. Vocabulary and speaking: pairwork.** (Chart 4-4)
**Part I.** Work with a partner. Check (✓) the expressions you know. Your teacher will explain the ones you don't know.

| *do* | *make* | *take* |
|---|---|---|
| ____ do the dishes | ____ make breakfast | ____ take a nap |
| ____ do the laundry | ____ make a bed | ____ take a shower |
| ____ do homework | ____ make a phone call | ____ take a bath |
| ____ do the ironing | ____ make a mess | ____ take a test |
| | | ____ take a break |
| | | ____ take medicine |

**Part II.** With your partner, take turns asking and answering questions about the pictures. Find the differences. You can look at your book before you speak. When you speak, look at your partner. Partner A: Use the pictures on p. 107. Partner B: Use the pictures in Let's Talk: Answers, p. 501.

*Example:*

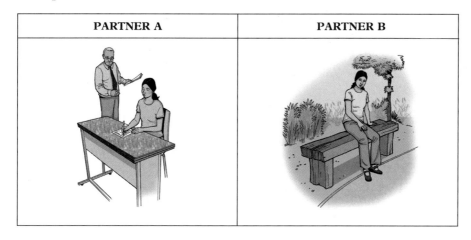

| PARTNER A | PARTNER B |
|-----------|-----------|

PARTNER A:  Is the girl in your picture taking a test?
PARTNER B:  No, she isn't.
PARTNER A:  What is she doing?
PARTNER B:  She's taking a break.

**PARTNER A**

1
2
3
4
5
6

**Exercise 19. Looking at grammar.** (Chart 4-4)
Make questions with *where*, *why*, and *what*.

1. A: _____*What are you reading?*_____

   B: My grammar book.  (I'm reading my grammar book.)

2. A: _____

   B: Because we're doing an exercise.  (I'm reading my grammar book because we're
   doing an exercise.)

3. A: _____

   B: A sentence.  (I'm writing a sentence.)

4. A: _____

   B: In the back of the room.  (Yoshi is sitting in the back of the room.)

5. A: _____

   B: In a hotel.  (I'm staying in a hotel.)

6. A: _____

   B: Jeans and a sweatshirt.  (Jonas is wearing jeans and a sweatshirt today.)

7. A: _____

   B: Because I'm happy.  (I'm smiling because I'm happy.)


❑ **Exercise 20. Looking at grammar.** (Chart 4-4)
Make questions.  Give short answers to yes/no questions.

1. A: What _____*are you writing?*_____

   B: A thank-you note.  (I'm writing a thank-you note.)

2. A: _____*Is Ali reading a book?*_____

   B: No, _____*he isn't / he's not.*_____ (Ali isn't reading a book.)

3. A: _____

   B: Yes, _____ (Magda is eating lunch.)

4. A: Where _____

   B: At the Sunrise Café.  (She's eating lunch at the Sunrise Café.)

5. A: _____

   B: No, _____ (Sam isn't drinking a cup of coffee.)

6. A: What _____

   B: A glass of lemonade.  (He's drinking a glass of lemonade.)

7. A: _____

   B: No, _____ (The girls aren't playing in the street.)

8. A: Where _____

   B: In the park.  (They're playing in the park.)

9. A: Why _____

   B: Because they don't have school today.  (They're playing in the park because they don't have school today.)

10. A: _____

    B: Yes.  (The girls are playing together.)

11. A: _____?

    B: No.  (A parent isn't watching them.)

❑ **Exercise 21. Warm-up.** (Chart 4-5)

Answer the questions with *yes* or *no*.

1. Do you eat breakfast every day?
2. Do you talk on the phone every day?
3. Do you study English every day?
4. Are you eating breakfast right now?
5. Are you talking on the phone right now?
6. Are you studying English right now?

## 4-5 Simple Present Tense vs. the Present Progressive

| | SIMPLE PRESENT | PRESENT PROGRESSIVE |
|---|---|---|
| | The simple present expresses habits or usual activities. Common time words are **every day**, **every year**, **every month**, **often**, **sometimes**, and **never**. The simple present uses **do** and **does** in negatives and questions. | The present progressive expresses actions that are happening right now, while the speaker is speaking. Common time words are **now**, **right now**, and **today**. The present progressive uses **am**, **is**, and **are** in negatives and questions. |

| STATEMENT | | | |
|---|---|---|---|
| | I | *talk* | |
| | You | *talk* | |
| | He, She, It | *talks* | *every day.* |
| | We | *talk* | |
| | They | *talk* | |

| | | | | |
|---|---|---|---|---|
| | I | *am* | *talking* | |
| | You | *are* | *talking* | |
| | He, She, It | *is* | *talking* | *now.* |
| | We | *are* | *talking* | |
| | They | *are* | *talking* | |

| NEGATIVE | | | |
|---|---|---|---|
| | I | *don't* | *talk.* |
| | You | *don't* | *talk.* |
| | He, She, It | *doesn't* | *talk.* |
| | We | *don't* | *talk.* |
| | They | *don't* | *talk.* |

| | | | | |
|---|---|---|---|---|
| | I | *am* | *not* | *talking.* |
| | You | *are* | *not* | *talking.* |
| | He, She, It | *is* | *not* | *talking.* |
| | We | *are* | *not* | *talking.* |
| | They | *are* | *not* | *talking.* |

| QUESTION | | | |
|---|---|---|---|
| | *Do* | I | *talk?* |
| | *Do* | you | *talk?* |
| | *Does* | he, she, it | *talk?* |
| | *Do* | we | *talk?* |
| | *Do* | they | *talk?* |

| | | | |
|---|---|---|---|
| | *Am* | I | *talking?* |
| | *Are* | you | *talking?* |
| | *Is* | he, she it | *talking?* |
| | *Are* | we | *talking?* |
| | *Are* | they | *talking?* |

☐ **Exercise 22. Looking at grammar.** (Chart 4-5)
Choose the correct completion.

1. Mari is working ⟨now.⟩ every day.
2. Mari works at a pharmacy now. every day.
3. I am working today. every day.
4. It's snowing now. every day.
5. You are making breakfast today. every day.
6. You make breakfast right now. every day.
7. We eat vegetables right now. every day.
8. We are eating outside right now. every day.

❏ **Exercise 23. Looking at grammar.** (Chart 4-5)
Complete the sentences with the correct form of the words in parentheses.

1. Ahmed (*talk*) _____*talks*_____ to his classmates every day in class.

   Right now he (*talk*) _____*is talking*_____ to Yoko. He (*talk, not*)

   _____ to his friend Omar right now.

2. It (*rain*) _____ a lot in this city, but it (*rain, not*) _____

   right now. The sun (*shine*) _____. (*it, rain*) _____

   a lot in your hometown?

3. Hans and Anna (*sit*) _____ next to each other in class every day, so they often

   (*help*) _____ each other with their grammar exercises. Right now Anna (*help*)

   _____ Hans with an exercise on verbs.

4. Roberto (*cook*) _____ his own dinner every evening. Right now he

   is in his kitchen. He (*cook*) _____ rice and beans.

   (*he, cook*) _____ meat for his dinner tonight too? No,

   he is a vegetarian. He (*eat, never*) _____ meat. (*you, eat*)

   _____ meat? (*you, be*) _____ a vegetarian?

❏ **Exercise 24. Listening.** (Chart 4-5)
Listen to each sentence. Choose the correct completion.

*Examples:* You will hear:     Pedro is sleeping late . . .
           You will choose: (now)     every day

1. now     every day
2. now     every day
3. now     every day
4. now     every day
5. now     every day
6. now     every day
7. now     every day
8. now     every day

Work with a partner. Take turns asking and answering questions about Isabel's activities.
Use the present progressive and the simple present.

*Example:* check her phone for messages
PARTNER A: Is Isabel checking her phone for messages?
PARTNER B: Yes, she is.
PARTNER A: Does she check her phone for messages every day?
PARTNER B: Yes, she does.
PARTNER A: Your turn now.

| | | |
|---|---|---|
| drink tea | ride her bike | take a walk |
| listen to music | say "hi" to her neighbor | talk on her phone |
| play her guitar | write a report | text |
| play tennis | swim | watch TV |

❑ **Exercise 26. Looking at grammar.** (Chart 4-5)

Complete each question with <u>all</u> the correct answers.

> a teacher    at school    early    sick    study    studying    work

1. a. Are you _____ *a teacher / early / studying / at school / sick* _____ ?

   b. Do you _____ *work / study* _____ ?

> angry    a dancer    cook    dance    driving    ready    understand

2. a. Do you _____ ?

   b. Are you _____ ?

> a problem    help    here    new    raining    ready    true    work

3. a. Is it _____ ?

   b. Does it _____ ?

❑ **Exercise 27. Looking at grammar.** (Chart 4-5)

Complete the sentences with **Do, Does, Is,** or **Are.**

**On the subway**

1. _____ *Do* _____ you have your ticket?

2. _____ *Is* _____ your ticket in your wallet?

3. _____ the train usually leave on time?

4. _____ the train on time?

5. _____ the tickets cheap?

6. _____ you looking at a map?

7. _____ you have enough money?

8. _____ the train here?

9. _____ we have extra time?

10. _____ the train leaving?

11. _____ the conductor check for tickets?

❏ **Exercise 28. Listening.** (Chart 4-5)

Listen to the conversation. Complete the sentences with the words you hear.

*Example:* You will hear: Are you doing an exercise?

You will write: ___Are you doing___ an exercise?

A: What are you doing? _____ on your English paper?

   <sub>1</sub>

B: No. _____. _____ an email to my sister.

   <sub>2</sub>                    <sub>3</sub>

A: _____ to her often?

   <sub>4</sub>

B: Yes, but I _____ a lot of emails to anyone else.

   <sub>5</sub>

A: _____ to you often?

   <sub>6</sub>

B: No, but she _____ me a lot.

   <sub>7</sub>

❏ **Exercise 29. Looking at grammar.** (Chart 4-5)

Complete the sentences with the correct form of the words in parentheses.

1. A: Tom is on the phone.

   B: (*he, talk*) ___Is he talking___ to his wife?

   A: Yes.

   B: (*he, talk*) ___Does he talk___ to her often?

   A: Yes, he (*talk*) ___talks___ to her every day during his lunch break.

2. A: I (*walk*) _____ to school every day. I (*take, not*) _____

   _____ the bus. (*you, take*) _____ the bus?

   B: No, I don't.

3. A: Selena is in the hallway.

   B: (*she, talk*) _____ to her friends?

   A: No, she isn't. She (*run*) _____ to her next class.

4. A: I (*read*) _____ the newspaper every day.

   B: (*you, read*) _____ it online?

   A: No, I don't. I (*read, not*) _____ it online.

5. A: What (*you, read*) _____ right now?

   B: I (*read*) _____ my grammar book.

6. A: (*you, want*) _____ your coat?

   B: Yes.

   A: (*be, this*) _____ your coat?

   B: No, my coat (*hang*) _____ in the closet right now.

**Part I.** Read the paragraph. Look at new vocabulary with your teacher first.

### Reni's Job

Reni is a server at a restaurant. She works long hours, and the restaurant pay is minimum wage. She earns extra money from tips. Reni is an excellent server. She is friendly and fast. Customers leave her good tips. Fifteen percent is average, but often she gets twenty percent. Today Reni is working an extra shift. A co-worker is sick, so Reni is taking her hours. Reni is feeling tired at the moment, but she is also happy because the tips are good. She is earning a lot of extra money today.

*Do you know these words?*

server
minimum wage
tips
average
shift
co-worker

**Part II.** Complete the sentences with **Is, Do,** or **Does.**

1. _____Is_____ Reni a good server?

2. _____ the restaurant pay Reni a lot of money?

3. _____ customers leave her good tips?

4. _____ Reni work extra hours every day?

5. _____ Reni working extra hours today?

6. _____ she happy today?

7. _____ she earning extra money?

8. _____ she usually get good tips?

9. _____ servers earn a lot of money from tips?

**Part III.** Discuss possible answers to these questions.

1. In your opinion, what are some important qualities for a restaurant server? Check (✓) the items.

   _____ fast            _____ formal

   _____ friendly        _____ speaks other languages

   _____ talkative       _____ smiles a lot

   _____ polite          _____ has a good memory

2. Do customers leave tips at restaurants in your country? If yes, what percentage is an average tip? Do you like to leave tips?

3. What is more important for you at a restaurant: the food or the service?

4. In some countries, a usual workday is eight hours, and a usual workweek is 40 hours. What is the usual workday and workweek in your country?

❏ **Exercise 31. Warm-up.** (Chart 4-6)
Read the sentences. What do you notice about the verbs in red?

Right now, I am waiting at a bus stop. I see an ambulance. I hear a siren. A car and a motorcycle are stopping. The ambulance is going fast.

## 4-6 Non-Action Verbs Not Used in the Present Progressive

| | Some verbs are NOT used in the present progressive. They are called "non-action verbs." |
|---|---|
| (a) I'm hungry *right now*. I *want* an apple.<br>    INCORRECT: *I am wanting an apple.* | In (a): **Want** is a non-action verb. *Want* expresses a physical or emotional need, not an action. |
| (b) I *hear* a siren. *Do* you *hear* it too?<br>    INCORRECT: *I'm hearing a siren.*<br>                  *Are you hearing it too?* | In (b): **Hear** is a non-action verb. *Hear* expresses a sensory experience, not an action. |

NON-ACTION VERBS

| | | |
|---|---|---|
| dislike | hear | believe |
| hate | see | know |
| like | smell | think (*meaning* believe)* |
| love | taste | understand |
| need | | |
| want | | |

*Sometimes *think* is used in progressive verbs. See Chart 4-8 for a discussion of *think about* and *think that*.

❏ **Exercise 32. Looking at grammar.** (Chart 4-6)
Complete the sentences. Use the simple present or the present progressive form of the verbs in parentheses.

1. Alicia is in her room right now. She (*listen*) _____*is listening*_____ to a podcast.

   She (*like*) _____*likes*_____ the podcast.

2. It (*snow*) _____ right now. It's beautiful! I (*like*)

   _____ this weather.

3. I (*know*) _____ Jessica Santos. She's in my class.

4. The teacher (*talk*) _____ to us right now. I (*understand*)

   _____ everything she's saying.

5. Emilio is at a restaurant right now. He (*eat*) _____ dinner. He

   (*like*) _____ the food. It (*taste*) _____ good.

6. Sniff-sniff. I (*smell*) _____ gas. (*you, smell*) _____ it?

7. Taro (*tell*) _____ us a story right now.  I (*believe*)

_____ his story.

8. Ugh!  Someone (*smoke*) _____ a cigar.  It (*smell*)

_____ terrible!  I (*hate*) _____ cigars.

9. Look at Mr. Gomez.  He (*hold*) _____

a kitten in his hand.  He (*love*) _____ the kitten.

Mr. Gomez (*smile*) _____ .

(Chart 4-6)

❑ **Exercise 33.  Let's talk: interview.**  (Chart 4-6)

Ask two students each question.  Write their answers in the chart.  Share some of their answers with the class.

| QUESTION | STUDENT A | STUDENT B |
|---|---|---|
| 1.  What \ you \ like? | | |
| 2.  What \ babies \ around the world \ like? | | |
| 3.  What \ you \ want? | | |
| 4.  What \ children around the world \ want? | | |
| 5.  What \ you \ love? | | |
| 6.  What \ teenagers around the world \ love? | | |
| 7.  What \ you \ dislike or hate? | | |
| 8.  What \ people around the world \ dislike or hate? | | |
| 9.  What \ you \ need? | | |
| 10.  What \ elderly people around the world \ need? | | |

❑ **Exercise 34. Warm-up.** (Chart 4-7)
Complete the sentences with the given phrases.

1. *am looking at / am watching*

    a. I _____ my cell phone. It is 10:00 P.M.

    b. I _____ a movie. It is very funny.

2. *hear / am listening to*

    a. I _____ the teacher carefully. She is explaining

    grammar to me.

    b. Shh! I _____ a noise. Maybe someone is downstairs!

---

### 4-7 *See, Look At, Watch, Hear,* and *Listen To*

| | |
|---|---|
| *SEE, LOOK AT,* and *WATCH*<br><br>(a) I *see* many things in this room. | In (a): **see** = a non-action verb. Seeing happens because my eyes are open. Seeing is a physical reaction, not a planned action. |
| (b) I'*m looking at* the clock. I want to know the time. | In (b): **look at** = an action verb. Looking is a planned or purposeful action. Looking happens for a reason. |
| (c) Bob *is watching* TV. | In (c): **watch** = an action verb. I *watch* something for a long time, but I *look at* something for a short time. |
| *HEAR* and *LISTEN TO*<br><br>(d) I'm in my apartment. I'm trying to study. I *hear* music from the next apartment. The music is loud. | In (d): **hear** = a non-action verb. Hearing is an unplanned act. It expresses a physical reaction. |
| (e) I'm in my apartment. I'm studying. I have an iPod. I'*m listening to* music. I like to listen to music when I study. | In (e): **listen (to)** = an action verb. Listening happens for a purpose. |

---

❑ **Exercise 35. Let's talk: class activity.** (Chart 4-7)
Your teacher will ask you questions. Close your book for this activity.

*Example:*
TEACHER: Look at the floor. What do you see?
STUDENT: I see shoes/dirt/etc.

1. What do you see in this room? Now look at something. What are you looking at?
2. Turn to p. 107 of this book. What do you see? Now look at one thing on that page. What are you looking at?
3. Look at the board. What do you see?
4. What programs do you like to watch on TV?
5. What sports do you like to watch?

6. What animals do you like to watch when you go to the zoo?
7. What do you hear at night in the place where you live?
8. What do you listen to when you go to a concert?
9. What do you listen to when you are at home?

❑ **Exercise 36. Looking at grammar.** (Chart 4-7)
Complete the sentences. Use the simple present or the present progressive form of the verbs in parentheses.

SITUATION 1:

I (*sit*) _____*am sitting*_____ in class right now. I (*sit, always*)

_____*always sit*_____ in the same seat every day. Rashid is my partner

today. We (*do*) _____ a pairwork exercise. Right now we (*speak*)

_____ English. We both (*know*) _____

French, so sometimes we (*speak*) _____ French to each other. Of

course, our teacher (*want*) _____ us to speak English.

Sandro is in the corner of the room. He (*work, not*) _____.

He (*look*) _____ around the room. Kim (*check*)

_____ the answer key in his grammar book. Francisco

(*stare*) _____ at the clock. Abdullah (*smile*)

_____. Lidia (*tap*) _____ her foot. Hans

(*chew*) _____ gum.

SITUATION 2:

The person on the bench in the picture on page 120 is Caroline. She's an accountant.

She (*work*) _____ for the government. She (*have*) _____ an

hour for lunch every day. She (*eat, often*) _____ lunch in the

park. She (*bring, usually*) _____ a sandwich and some fruit

with her to the park. She (*sit, usually*) _____ on a bench, but

sometimes she (*sit*) _____ on the grass and (*watch*) _____

people and animals. She (*sees, often*) _____ joggers and squirrels. She

(*relax*) _____ when she eats at the park.

Right now I (*look*) _____ at the picture of Caroline. She (*be, not*)

_____ at home in the picture. She (*be*) _____ at the park. She
      11                                              12

(*sit*) _____ on a bench. She (*eat*) _____ her
         13                                                    14

lunch. A jogger (*run*) _____ on a path through the park. A squirrel
                        15

(*sit*) _____ on the ground in front of Caroline. The squirrel
         16

(*eat*) _____ a nut. Caroline (*watch*) _____
         17                                                18

the squirrel. She (*watch, always*) _____ squirrels
                                          19

when she eats lunch in the park. Some ducks (*swim*) _____
                                                            20

in the pond in the picture, and some birds (*fly*) _____ in
                                                         21

the sky. A police officer (*ride*) _____ a horse. He (*ride*)
                                   22

_____ a horse through the park every day. Near Caroline, a family
      23

(*have*) _____ a picnic. They (*go*) _____ on a picnic
            24                                        25

every week.

❏ **Exercise 37. Warm-up.** (Chart 4-8)
Do you agree or disagree with each sentence? Circle *yes* or *no*.

1. I think about my parents every day.                    yes    no

2. I am thinking about my parents right now.              yes    no

3. I think that it is difficult to be a good parent.      yes    no

## 4-8 Think About and Think That

| | | | | | | In (a): Ideas about my family are in my mind every day. |
|---|---|---|---|---|---|---|
| | | *THINK* | + | *ABOUT* + | A NOUN | |
| (a) | I | **think** | | **about** | **my family** every day. | In (b): My mind is busy now. Ideas about grammar are in my mind right now. |
| (b) | I | **am thinking** | | **about** | **grammar** right now. | |

| | | | | | | In (c): In my opinion, Emma is lazy. I believe that Emma is lazy. People use **think that** when they want to say (to state) their beliefs. The present progressive is often used with **think about**. The present progressive is almost never used with **think that**. |
|---|---|---|---|---|---|---|
| | | *THINK* | + | *THAT* + | A STATEMENT | |
| (c) | I | **think** | | **that** | **Emma is lazy.** | |
| (d) | Ed | **thinks** | | **that** | **I am lazy.** | |
| (e) | I | **think** | | **that** | **the weather is nice.** | *INCORRECT:* I am thinking that Emma is lazy. |

| (f) I **think that** Marco is a nice person. | Examples (f) and (g) have the same meaning. People often omit **that** after **think**, especially in speaking. |
|---|---|
| (g) I **think** Marco is a nice person. | |

❑ **Exercise 38. Grammar and speaking.** (Chart 4-8)
Use *I think that* to give your opinion. Share a few of your opinions with the class.

1. English grammar is easy / hard / fun / interesting.

   _____*I think that English grammar is interesting.*_____

2. People in this city are friendly / unfriendly / kind / cold.

   _____

3. The food at (*name of a place*) is delicious / terrible / good / excellent / awful.

   _____

4. Baseball / football / soccer / golf is interesting / boring / confusing / etc.

   _____

❑ **Exercise 39. Writing and speaking.** (Chart 4-8)
Complete the sentences with your own words. Share a few of your completions with the class.

1. I think that the weather today is _____

2. I think my classmates are _____

3. Right now I'm thinking about _____

4. In my opinion, English grammar is _____

5. In my opinion, soccer is _____

6. I think that my parents are _____

7. I think this school is _____

8. I think about _____ often.

9. I think that _____

10. In my opinion, _____

❏ **Exercise 40. Let's talk: game.** (Charts 4-5 → 4-8)
Work in small groups. One person will think about an animal or a food. The other students will ask questions and try to guess the answer.

*Example:* animal
STUDENT A: I'm thinking about an animal
STUDENT B: Is it big?
STUDENT A: No.
STUDENT C: Does it have wings?
STUDENT A: Yes.
STUDENT D: Is it a mosquito?
STUDENT A: Yes!

Another student chooses an animal or food.

❏ **Exercise 41. Reading.** (Chart 4-5 → 4-8)
Read the paragraph and the statements. Circle "T" for true and "F" for false.

**Sleep: How Much Do People Need?**

Adults need about eight hours of sleep a night. Some need more and some need less, but this is an average amount. Newborn babies need the most sleep, about 14 to 16 hours every 24 hours. They sleep for about four hours. Then they wake up, eat, and then sleep again. As babies grow, they need a little less sleep, about 10 to 14 hours. Here is an interesting fact. Teenagers also need about 10 to 14 hours of sleep a night. Some people think teenagers sleep a lot because they are lazy. Actually, their bodies are changing, so they need a lot of rest. How much sleep do you get every night? Is it enough?

1. Everyone needs eight hours of sleep a night.                  T  F

2. Newborn babies sleep 14 to 16 hours and then wake up.         T  F

3. Teenagers need a lot of sleep.                                T  F

4. Teenagers and adults need the same amount of sleep.           T  F

**Exercise 42. Looking at grammar.** (Chapter 4)
Choose the correct completion.

1. Lola and Pablo _____ TV right now.
   a. watch b. watching (c.) are watching

2. A: _____ you writing to your parents?

   B: No. I'm studying.
   a. Are b. Do c. Don't

3. I _____ like to write letters.
   a. no b. don't c. am not

4. A: Jack has six telephones in his apartment.

   B: I _____ you. No one needs six telephones in one apartment.
   a. am believe b. am not believing c. don't believe

5. When I want to know the time, I _____ a clock.
   a. see b. look at c. watch

6. A: Do you know Fatima?

   B: Yes, I do. I _____ she is a very nice person.
   a. am thinking b. thinking c. think

7. Where _____ Boris? Upstairs or downstairs?
   a. does b. is c. lives

8. Oh, no! Paul _____. He is allergic to cats.
   a. is sneezing b. doesn't sneeze c. sneezes

9. A: You look sad.

   B: Yes, I _____ about my family back in my country. I miss them.
   a. think b. am thinking c. thinking

❑ **Exercise 43. Check your knowledge.** (Chapter 4)
Correct the mistakes.

       *raining*         *don't*
1. It's ~~rainning~~ today. I ~~no~~ like the rain.

2. I like New York City. I am thinking that it is a wonderful city.

3. Does Abdul be sleeping right now?

4. Why you are going downtown today?

5. I am liking flowers. They are smelling good.

6. Bill at a restaurant right now. He usually eat at home, but today he eatting dinner at a restaurant.

7. Alex is siting at his desk. He writting a letter.

8. Where do they are sitting today?

❑ **Exercise 44. Reading and writing.** (Chapter 4)

*Part I.* Read the paragraph. Look at new vocabulary with your teacher first.

### A Sleepless Night

    Mila is in bed. It is 3:00 A.M. She is very tired, but she isn't sleeping. She is thinking about medical school. She is worrying about her final exams tomorrow. She needs to pass because she wants to be a doctor. She is tossing and turning in bed. She wants a few more days to study. She is thinking about possible test questions. She is wide-awake. She isn't going back to sleep tonight.

*Do you know these words?*

medical school
final exams
pass
toss and turn
wide-awake

*Part II.* Imagine it is 3:00 A.M. You are in bed, and you are wide-awake. You are having a sleepless night. What are you thinking about? Write a paragraph. Use both simple present and present progressive verbs.

*Part III.* Editing check: Work individually or change papers with a partner. Check (✓) for the following:

1. _____ paragraph indent

2. _____ capital letter at the beginning of each sentence

3. _____ period at the end of each sentence

4. _____ a verb in every sentence

5. _____ use of present progressive for activities right now

6. _____ correct spelling (use a dictionary or spell-check)

# Chapter 5

# Talking About the Present

□ **Exercise 1. Warm-up.** (Chart 5-1)

Match the questions to the pictures.

| Picture A | Picture B | Picture C |
|---|---|---|
|  |  |  |
| It's 11:00. | It's Saturday. | It's July. |
| 1. What month is it? | 2. What time is it? | 3. What day is it? |

## 5-1 Using *It* to Talk About Time

| QUESTION | | ANSWER | |
|---|---|---|---|
| (a) What day is it? | → | *It's* Monday. | In English, people use *it* to express (to talk about) time. |
| (b) What month is it? | → | *It's* September. | |
| (c) What year is it? | → | *It's* (2014). | |
| (d) What's the date today? | → | *It's* September 15th. | |
| | → | *It's* the 15th of September. | |
| (e) What time is it? | → | *It's* 9:00.* | |
| | → | *It's* nine. | |
| | → | *It's* nine o'clock. | |
| | → | *It's* 9:00 A.M. | |

*American English uses a colon (two dots) between the hour and the minutes: 9:00 A.M. British English uses one dot: 9.00 A.M.

❑ **Exercise 2. Looking at grammar.** (Chart 5-1)
Make questions. Begin each question with **What**.

1. A: _____*What day is it?*_____
   B: It's Tuesday.

2. A: _____
   B: It's March 14th.

3. A: _____
   B: (It's) ten-thirty.

4. A: _____
   B: (It's) March.

5. A: _____
   B: (It's) six-fifteen.

6. A: _____
   B: (It's) Wednesday.

7. A: _____
   B: (It's) the 1st of April.

8. A: _____
   B: (It's) 2014.

9. A: _____
   B: It's 7:00 A.M.

| Sun | Mon | Tues | Wed | Thurs | Fri | Sat |
|-----|-----|------|-----|-------|-----|-----|
|     |     |      |     | 1     | 2   | 3   |
| 4   | 5   | 6    | 7   | 8     | 9   | 10  |
| 11  | 12  | 13   | 14  | 15    | 16  | 17  |
| 18  | 19  | 20   | 21  | 22    | 23  | 24  |
| 25  | 26  | 27   | 28  | 29    | 30  | 31  |

a calendar page

❏ **Exercise 3. Warm-up. (Chart 5-2)**
Which answers are true for you?  Complete item 3 with the time your English class meets.

1. I go to school

____ on Monday.

____ on Tuesday.

____ on Wednesday.

____ on Thursday.

____ on Friday.

____ on Saturday.

____ on Sunday.

2. I have class

____ in the morning.

____ in the evening.

____ at night.

3. I have class from _____ to _____.
            (time)        (time)

## 5-2  Prepositions of Time

| | | |
|---|---|---|
| *AT* | (a)  We have class *at* one o'clock. <br> (b)  I have an appointment with the doctor *at* 3:00. <br> (c)  We sleep *at* night. | *at* + a specific time on the clock <br><br> *at* + *night* |
| *IN* | (d)  My birthday is *in* October. <br> (e)  I was born *in* 1989. <br> (f)  We have class *in* the morning. <br> (g)  Bob has class *in* the afternoon. <br> (h)  I study *in* the evening. | *in* + a specific month <br> *in* + a specific year <br> *in* + *the morning* <br> *in* + *the afternoon* <br> *in* + *the evening* |
| *ON* | (i)  I have class *on* Monday(s). <br> (j)  I was born *on* October 31. <br> (k)  I was born *on* October 31, 1991. | *on* + a specific day of the week <br> *on* + a specific date |
| *FROM . . . TO* | (l)  We have class *from* 1:00 *to* 2:00. | *from* (a specific time) *to* (a specific time) |

❏ **Exercise 4. Looking at grammar. (Chart 5-2)**
Complete the sentences with prepositions of time.

1. *We have class . . .*

a.  ___*at*___ ten o'clock.

b.  _____ ten _____ eleven.

c.  _____ the morning and _____ the afternoon.

2. *I study* . . .

    a. _____ the evening.

    b. _____ night.

3. *I was born* . . .

    a. _____ May.

    b. _____ 1990.

    c. _____ May 21.

    d. _____ May 21, 1990.

4. a. The post office isn't open _____ Sundays.

    b. It's open _____ 8:00 A.M. _____ 5:00 P.M., Monday through Saturday.

    c. The post office closes _____ 5:00 P.M.

❏ **Exercise 5. Let's talk: pairwork.** (Chart 5-2)
Complete the sentences with information about your partner. Share some of your partner's answers with the class.

1. When do you eat breakfast?

    a. I eat breakfast in _____*the morning*_____.

    b. I eat breakfast at _____.

    c. I eat breakfast from _____ to _____.

2. When do you study?

    a. I study at _____.

    b. I study in _____.

    c. I study on _____.

    d. I study from _____ to _____.

3. Tell about the time of your birth.

    a. I was born in _____.

    b. I was born on _____.

    c. I was born at _____.

❑ **Exercise 6. Listening and grammar.** (Chart 5-2)

*Part I.* Listen to each description. Write the name of the person.

*Example:* You will hear:  I was born in June.  I go to class in the morning.
My name is . . .

You will write:  ___Lisa___

| June 2, 1992 7:00 A.M. | June 24, 1985 1:00 P.M. | July 7, 1997 7:00 P.M. | July 24, 1990 11:00 A.M. |
| Lisa | Marta | Shen | Ron |

1. _____      3. _____

2. _____      4. _____

*Part II.* Use the information in the pictures to complete the sentences.

1. I was born _____ July.  I was born _____ July 7.  My name is

   _____.

2. I was born _____ 1985.  I was born _____ June 24, 1985.  My name

   is _____.

3. I go to class _____ the morning.  I go to class _____ 7:00.  My name

   is _____.

4. Hi, my name is _____.  I was born _____ July.  I was born

   _____ July 24.  I go to class _____ the morning.

❑ **Exercise 7. Warm-up.** (Chart 5-3)
Which answers are true for you?

   A: In your hometown, how's the weather in the summer?

   B: It's sunny / cloudy / rainy / cold / hot / windy.

   A: What's the weather like in the winter?

   B: It's sunny / cloudy / rainy / cold / hot / windy.

## 5-3 Using *It* and *What* to Talk About the Weather

| | |
|---|---|
| (a) *It's* sunny today. <br> (b) *It's* hot and humid today. <br> (c) *It's* a nice day today. | In English, people usually use *it* when they talk about the weather. |
| (d) *What's the weather like* in Istanbul in January? <br> (e) *How's the weather* in Moscow in the summer? <br> (f) *What's the temperature* in Bangkok today? | People commonly ask about the weather by saying *What's the weather like?* OR *How's the weather?* <br> *What* is also used to ask about the temperature. |

❏ **Exercise 8. Let's talk: pairwork.** (Chart 5-3)

How's the weather today? Choose *yes* or *no*. Share your answers with a partner. Do you and your partner agree? Report some of your answers to the class.

| | | | | | | | |
|---|---|---|---|---|---|---|---|
| 1. hot | yes | no | | 8. sunny | yes | no |
| 2. warm | yes | no | | 9. nice | yes | no |
| 3. cool | yes | no | | 10. clear | yes | no |
| 4. chilly | yes | no | | 11. partly cloudy | yes | no |
| 5. cold | yes | no | | 12. humid★ | yes | no |
| 6. freezing | yes | no | | 13. windy | yes | no |
| 7. below freezing | yes | no | | 14. stormy | yes | no |

❏ **Exercise 9. Let's talk: small groups.** (Chart 5-3)

Change the Fahrenheit (F) temperatures to Celsius★★ (C) by choosing temperatures from the box. Then describe the temperature in words.

| 38°C | 24°C | ✓10°C | 0°C | −18°C |
|---|---|---|---|---|

| | FAHRENHEIT | CELSIUS | DESCRIPTION |
|---|---|---|---|
| 1. | 50°F | _10°C_ | _cool, chilly_ |
| 2. | 32°F | _____ | _____ |
| 3. | 100°F | _____ | _____ |
| 4. | 75°F | _____ | _____ |
| 5. | 0°F | _____ | _____ |

★*humid* = hot and wet
★★*Celsius* is also called "Centigrade."

❏ **Exercise 10. Let's talk: small groups.** (Chart 5-3)
Read the chart and follow the instructions.

---

"Approximate" means "close but not exact." Here is a fast way to get an **approximate** number when you convert from one temperature system to another.[*]

---

- To change **Celsius to Fahrenheit**: DOUBLE THE CELSIUS NUMBER AND ADD 30.

  *Examples:* 12°C × 2 = 24 + 30 =  54°F  (Exact numbers: 12°C = 53.6°F)
  20°C × 2 = 40 + 30 =  70°F  (Exact numbers: 20°C = 68°F)
  35°C × 2 = 70 + 30 = 100°F  (Exact numbers: 35°C = 95°F)

- To change **Fahrenheit to Celsius**: SUBTRACT 30 FROM THE FAHRENHEIT NUMBER AND THEN DIVIDE BY 2.

  *Examples:* 60°F − 30 = 30 ÷ 2 = 15°C.  (Exact numbers: 60°F = 15.6°C.)
  80°F − 30 = 50 ÷ 2 = 25°C.  (Exact numbers: 80°F = 26.7°C.)
  90°F − 30 = 60 ÷ 2 = 30°C.  (Exact numbers: 90°F = 32.2°C.)

---

[*]To get exact numbers, use these formulas: $C = 5/9 \ (°F − 32)$ OR $F = 9/5 \ (°C) + 32$.

Change the temperatures from Celsius to Fahrenheit and from Fahrenheit to Celsius.
Calculate the approximate numbers.

1.  22°C   *22°C = approximately 74°F (22°C × 2 = 44 + 30 = 74°F)*

2.  2°C   _____

3.  30°C   _____

4.  16°C   _____

5.  25°F   _____

6.  70°F   _____

7.  100°F   _____

❑ **Exercise 11. Let's talk: interview.** (Chart 5-3)

Interview your classmates about their hometowns. Ask questions about the name of the hometown, its location, its population, its weather, and its average temperature in a particular month (of your choice). Share some of their answers with the class.

*Example:*
STUDENT A: What's your hometown?
STUDENT B: Athens.
STUDENT A: Where is it?
STUDENT B: In southeastern Greece near the Aegean Sea.
STUDENT A: What's the population of Athens?
STUDENT B: Almost four million.
STUDENT A: What's the weather like in Athens in May?
STUDENT B: It's mild. Sometimes it's a little rainy.
STUDENT A: What's the average temperature in May?
STUDENT B: The average temperature is around 21° Celsius.

Write down the information you get here.

| NAME | Spyros | | | |
|------|--------|--|--|--|
| HOMETOWN | Athens | | | |
| LOCATION | SE Greece | | | |
| POPULATION | almost 4 million | | | |
| WEATHER | mild in May, around 21°C, in the mid-seventies Fahrenheit | | | |

❑ **Exercise 12. Warm-up.** (Chart 5-4)
Complete the sentences.

1. There   is / isn't   a whiteboard in this room.

2. There   are / aren't   computers in this room.

3. There are _____ students in this room.
<br>    (number)

---

## 5-4  *There + Be*

| | THERE + BE + | | SUBJECT + | PLACE | **There + be** is used to say that something exists in a particular place. |
|---|---|---|---|---|---|
| (a) | **There** | **is** | **a bird** | in the tree. | |
| (b) | **There** | **are** | **four birds** | in the tree. | |

*There + be* is used to say that something exists in a particular place.

Notice: The subject follows *be*:

   *there + is + singular noun*
   *there + are + plural noun*

(c) **There's** a bird in the tree.
(d) **There're** four birds in the tree.

CONTRACTIONS:
   *there + is = there's*
   *there + are = there're*

---

❑ **Exercise 13. Looking at grammar.** (Chart 5-4)
Complete the sentences with *is* or *are*. Then choose *yes* or *no*. Compare your answers with your classmates' answers.

1. There _____*is*_____ a grammar book on my desk.                    yes     no

2. There _____*are*_____ many grammar books in this room.            yes     no

3. There _____ comfortable chairs in this classroom.          yes     no

4. There _____ a nice view from the classroom window.         yes     no

5. There _____ interesting places to visit in this area.      yes     no

6. There _____ a good place to eat near school.               yes     no

7. There _____ fun activities to do on weekends in this area. yes     no

8. There _____ difficult words in this exercise.              yes     no

❑ **Exercise 14. Let's talk: pairwork.** (Chart 5-4)
Work with a partner. Complete each sentence with words from the box or your own words.
You can look at your book before you speak. When you speak, look at your partner.

| | | |
|---|---|---|
| a book | a map | a notebook |
| books | papers | notebooks |
| tall buildings | a park | restaurants |
| a bulletin board | a pen | a sink |
| a calendar | a pencil | stores |
| chairs | a pencil sharpener | students |
| a chalkboard | people | a teacher |
| a clock | a picture | a whiteboard |
| a coffee shop | pictures | a window |
| desks | a post office | windows |
| light switches | | |

1. PARTNER A: There is . . . on this desk.
   PARTNER B: There are . . . on that desk.

2. PARTNER A: There are . . . on that wall.
   PARTNER B: There is . . . on this wall.

3. PARTNER A: There are . . . in this room.
   PARTNER B: There is also . . . in this room.

4. PARTNER A: There is . . . near our school.
   PARTNER B: There are also . . . near our school.

❑ **Exercise 15. Let's talk: small groups.** (Chart 5-4)
First, everyone in your group puts two or three objects (e.g., a coin, some keys, a pen, a dictionary) on a table in the classroom. Then take turns describing the items on the table. Begin with *There is* and *There are*.

*Example:*
STUDENT A: There are three dictionaries on the table.
STUDENT B: There are some keys on the table.
STUDENT C: There is a pencil sharpener on the table.

❑ **Exercise 16. Listening.** (Chart 5-4)
Listen to each sentence. Choose the word you hear. *Note:* You will hear contractions for *There is* and *There are*.

*Example:* You will hear:    There're several windows in this room.
           You will choose: There's    (There're)

| | | | | | |
|---|---|---|---|---|---|
| 1. There's | There're | | 5. There's | There're |
| 2. There's | There're | | 6. There's | There're |
| 3. There's | There're | | 7. There's | There're |
| 4. There's | There're | | 8. There's | There're |

**Exercise 17. Warm-up.** (Chart 5-5)

Answer the questions.

| | | | |
|---|---|---|---|
| 1. Is there an elevator in this building? | | yes | no |
| 2. Are there stairs in this building? | | yes | no |

---

## 5-5 *There + Be:* Yes/No Questions

| QUESTION | | | | | | SHORT ANSWER |
|---|---|---|---|---|---|---|
| | *BE* | + | *THERE* | + | *SUBJECT* | |
| (a) | *Is* | | *there* | | *an apple* | in the refrigerator? → Yes, *there is.* |
| | | | | | | → No, *there isn't.* |
| (b) | *Are* | | *there* | | *eggs* | in the refrigerator? → Yes, *there are.* |
| | | | | | | → No, *there aren't.* |

---

❏ **Exercise 18. Let's talk: pairwork.** (Chart 5-5)

Work with a partner. Ask questions about the refrigerator in the picture. Use the nouns in the list. Begin with **Is there** or **Are there**.

*Example:* a piece of cheese
PARTNER A: Is there a piece of cheese in the refrigerator?
PARTNER B: Yes, there is.
PARTNER A: Your turn now.

*Example:* onions
PARTNER B: Are there onions in the refrigerator?
PARTNER A: No, there aren't.
PARTNER B: Your turn now.

| PARTNER A | PARTNER B |
|---|---|
| 1. a carton of eggs | 1. strawberries |
| 2. a loaf of bread | 2. oranges |
| 3. apples | 3. a bottle of orange juice |
| 4. a cube of butter | 4. a bowl of rice |
| 5. potatoes | 5. a bag of flour |
| 6. vegetables | 6. pickles |

**Exercise 19. Let's talk: small groups.** (Chart 5-5)
Take turns asking and answering questions about this city. Begin with *Is there* or *Are
there*. If the answer is "I don't know," ask someone else.

*Example:* a zoo
STUDENT A: Is there a zoo in (*name of this city*)?
STUDENT B: Yes, there is. / No, there isn't.
STUDENT B: (*to Student C*) Is there an airport near (*name of this city*)?
STUDENT C: I don't know.
STUDENT B: (*to Student D*) Is there an airport near (*name of this city*)?
STUDENT D: Yes, there is. / No, there isn't.
Etc.

1. a zoo
2. an airport
3. lakes
4. good restaurants
5. a good Chinese restaurant
6. an art museum

7. an aquarium
8. interesting bookstores
9. a subway system
10. public swimming pools
11. a good public transportation system
12. a movie theater

❏ **Exercise 20. Let's talk: class activity.** (Chart 5-5)
Solve the puzzle. *Teacher's Note:* See *Let's Talk: Answers,* p. 502, to answer your students'
questions.

The Romero family needs to decide where to stay for their summer vacation. They
want a hotel with everything in the list below. Your teacher has information about several
hotels. Ask her/him questions using the list. Then write *yes* or *no* in the correct column of
the chart. Which hotel has everything that the Romeros want?

*List:*

| a swimming pool | hiking trails | ocean-view rooms |
| a beach | horses to ride | |

*Example:*
STUDENT A: Is there a swimming pool at Hotel 1?
   TEACHER: Yes, there is.
STUDENT B: Are there hiking trails at Hotel 3?
   TEACHER: Yes, there are.

| | A SWIMMING POOL | A BEACH | HIKING TRAILS | HORSES | OCEAN-VIEW ROOMS |
|---|---|---|---|---|---|
| HOTEL 1 | *yes* | | | | |
| HOTEL 2 | | *yes* | | | |
| HOTEL 3 | | | *yes* | | |
| HOTEL 4 | | | | *yes* | |
| HOTEL 5 | | | | | *yes* |

**Exercise 21. Warm-up.** (Chart 5-6)
Answer the questions.

1. How many students are there at this school?
2. How many people are there in your country?
3. How many people are there on the earth?

## 5-6  *There + Be:* Asking Questions with *How Many*

| QUESTION | | | | | SHORT ANSWER |
|---|---|---|---|---|---|
| *HOW MANY* + SUBJECT + *ARE* + *THERE* + PLACE | | | | | |
| (a) *How many* chapters are there in this book? → | | | | | Fifteen. (There are 15 chapters in this book.) |
| (b) *How many* provinces are there in Canada? → | | | | | Ten. (There are ten provinces in Canada.) |

| | |
|---|---|
| (c) How many *words* do you see?  INCORRECT: *How many word do you see?* | Notice: The noun that follows *how many* is plural. |

❏ **Exercise 22. Let's talk: class activity.** (Chart 5-6)
Ask and answer questions about this classroom. Use *How many* and the given words.

*Example:* desks
STUDENT A: How many desks are there in this room?
STUDENT B: Thirty-two. OR There are thirty-two desks in this room.
STUDENT A: That's right. OR No, I count thirty-three desks.

1. windows       3. students       5. women       7. grammar books
2. laptops        4. teachers       6. men          8. dictionaries

❏ **Exercise 23. Let's talk: pairwork.** (Chart 5-6)
Work with a partner. Ask questions. Begin with *How many*.

*Example:* days in a week
PARTNER A: How many days are there in a week?
PARTNER B: Seven. OR There are seven days in a week.
PARTNER A: Right. There are seven days in a week. Your turn now.

| PARTNER A | PARTNER B |
|---|---|
| 1. chapters in this book | 1. pages in this book |
| 2. doors in this room | 2. people in this room |
| 3. floors in this building | 3. letters in the English alphabet (26) |
| 4. states in the United States (50) | 4. provinces in Canada (10) |
| 5. countries in North America (3) | 5. continents in the world (7) |

Guess the person.  Notice the prepositions in red.

*Who am I?*

1. I live in London.
2. I live on Downing Street.
3. I live at 10 Downing Street.

---

## 5-7 Prepositions of Place

| | |
|---|---|
| (a)  My book is **on** my desk. | In (a):  *on* = a preposition<br>*my desk* = object of the preposition<br>*on my desk* = a prepositional phrase |
| (b)  Ned lives **in** Miami.<br>           **in** Florida.<br>           **in** the United States.<br>           **in** North America. | A person lives **in** a city, a state, a country, a continent. |
| (c)  Meg lives **on** Hill Street. | **on** a street, avenue, road, etc. |
| (d)  She lives **at** 4472 Hill Street. | **at** a street address |
| (e)  My father is **in** the kitchen. | In (e):  *in* is used with rooms:  **in** *the kitchen,* **in** *the classroom,* **in** *the hall,* **in** *my bedroom, etc.* |
| (f)  Ivan is **at** work.<br><br>(g)  Yoko is **at** school.<br><br>(h)  Olga is **at** home. | **At** + *work, school, home* expresses activity:<br><br>In (f):  Ivan is working at his office (or other place of work).<br><br>In (g):  Yoko is a student.  She is studying.  (Or, if she is a teacher, she is teaching.)<br><br>In (h):  Olga is doing things at her home. |
| (i)  Siri is **in** bed.<br><br>(j)  Tim is **in** class.<br><br>(k)  Mr. Lee is **in** the hospital.<br><br>(l)  Paul is **in** jail/prison. | **In** + *bed, class, hospital, jail* has these special meanings:<br><br>In (i):  Siri is resting or sleeping *under* the covers.<br><br>In (j):  Tim is studying (or teaching).<br><br>In (k):  Mr. Lee is sick.  He is a patient.<br><br>In (l):  Paul is a prisoner.  He is not free to leave.<br><br>NOTE:  American English = *in the hospital*<br>            British English = *in hospital* |

❑ **Exercise 25. Looking at grammar.** (Chart 5-7)
Complete the sentences with *in*, *on*, or *at*.

Write about Alonso.

1. Alonso lives _____ Canada.

2. He lives _____ Toronto.

3. He lives _____ Lake Street.

4. He lives _____ 5541 Lake Street _____ Toronto, Canada.

Alonso Sales
5541 Lake Street
Toronto, Canada

Write about Dr. Eng.

5. Dr. Eng lives on _____.

6. He lives in _____.

7. He lives at _____.

Dr. John Eng
342 First Street
Miami, Florida

Write about yourself.

8. I live _____.
    (name of country)

9. I live _____.
    (name of city)

10. I live _____.
    (name of street)

11. I live _____.
    (street address)

**Exercise 26. Game.** (Chart 5-7)
Work in teams. Complete the sentences with *in, on,* or *at.* Then guess the person, building, or company. Use words from the box. The team with the most correct answers wins.

| | | |
|---|---|---|
| Alexandria Pyramids | Facebook | Nike |
| Apple | Giza Pyramids | president of the U.S. |
| Boeing | Louvre Museum | prime minister of Canada |
| Eiffel Tower | Microsoft | vice president of the U.S. |

1. I am a building.

   a. I am _____ Paris.

   b. I am _____ Anatole Avenue.

   c. I am _____ 5 Anatole Avenue.

   ANSWER: _____

2. I am a person.

   a. I live _____ Ottawa.

   b. I live _____ 24 Sussex Drive.

   c. I live _____ Sussex Drive.

   ANSWER: _____

3. I am a building.

   a. I am _____ Pyramid Street.

   b. I am _____ 124 Pyramid Street.

   c. I am _____ Egypt.

   ANSWER: _____

4. I am a company.

   a. I am _____ Oregon.

   b. I am _____ Bowerman Drive.

   c. I am _____ One Bowerman Drive.

   ANSWER: _____

5. I am a person.

   a. I live _____ Pennsylvania Avenue.

   b. I live _____ 600 Pennsylvania Avenue N.W.

   c. I live _____ the United States.

   ANSWER: _____

6. I am a company.

   a. I am _____ Illinois.

   b. I am _____ 100 North Riverside Plaza.

   c. I am _____ Chicago.

   ANSWER: _____

❑ **Exercise 27. Looking at grammar.** (Chart 5-7)
Complete the sentence with *at* or *in.*

*Rachel isn't . . .*

1. _____ her bedroom.

2. _____ bed.

3. _____ work.

4. _____ prison.

5. _____ home.

6. _____ jail.

7. _____ class.

8. _____ Africa.

9. _____ the hall.

10. _____ the hospital.  She's well now.

**Exercise 28. Looking at grammar.** (Chart 5-7)
Complete the sentences with *at* or *in*.

1. When I was _____ work yesterday, I had an interesting phone call.

2. Poor Anita. She's _____ the hospital again for more surgery.

3. Mr. Gow is a teacher, but he isn't _____ school today. He's sick, so he is

   _____ home.

4. Last year at this time, Eric was _____ Vietnam. This year he's _____ Spain.

5. There's a fire extinguisher _____ the hall.

6. There are thirty-seven desks _____ our classroom.

7. Rob is _____ jail. He's going to be _____ prison for a long time.

8. Our hotel rooms are on the same floor. I'm _____ 501 and you're _____ 505.

9. Singapore is _____ Asia.

10. The kids are _____ the kitchen. They're making dinner for us!

11. A: Is Jennifer _____ home?

    B: No, she's still _____ class.

12. A: Where's Jack?

    B: He's _____ his room.

    A: What's he doing?

    B: He's _____ bed. He has a headache.


❏ **Exercise 29. Warm-up.** (Chart 5-8)
Answer the questions.

*Right now . . .*

1. who is in front of you?

2. who is behind you?

3. who is beside you?

4. who is far away from the teacher?

5. who is in the middle of the room?

6. who is near the door?

## 5-8 More Prepositions of Place: A List

| | | | | |
|---|---|---|---|---|
| above | beside | in back of | in the middle of | on |
| around | between | in the back of | inside | on top of |
| at | far (away) from | in front of | near | outside |
| behind | in | in the front of | next to | under |
| below | | | | |

(a) The book is *beside* the cup.
(b) The book is *next to* the cup.
(c) The book is *near* the cup.

(d) The book is *between* two cups.

(e) The book is *far away from* the cup.

(f) The cup is *on* the book.
(g) The cup is *on top of* the book.

(h) The cup is *under* the book.

(i) The cup is *above* the book.

(j) The hand is *around* the cup.

(k) The man is *in back of* the bus.
(l) The man is *behind* the bus.

(m) The man is *in the back of* the bus.

(n) The man is *in front of* the bus.
   In (k), (l), and (n): the man is *outside* the bus.

(o) The man is *in the front of* the bus.

(p) The man is *in the middle of* the bus.
   In (m), (o), and (p): the man is *inside* the bus.

❏ **Exercise 30. Looking at grammar.** (Chart 5-8)
Describe the pictures by completing the sentences with prepositional expressions of place.

1. The apple is ___*on / on top of*___ the plate.

2. The apple is _____ the plate.

3. The apple is _____ the plate.

4. The apple is _____ the glass.

5. The apple isn't near the glass. It is _____ the glass.

6. The apple is _____ the glass.

7. The apple is _____ two glasses.

8. The hand is _____ the glass.

9. The dog isn't inside the car. The dog is _____ the car.

10. The dog is in _____ of the car.

11. The dog is in _____ of the car.

12. The dog is in _____ of the car.

13. The dog is in _____ of the car.

**Exercise 31. Let's talk: pairwork.** (Charts 5-4 → 5-8)
Work with a partner. Ask and answer questions about the picture. Use the questions below and the words from the box to help you.

Questions: *Where is the . . . ?* OR *Where are the . . . ?* OR *How many . . . are there?*

*Examples:*
PARTNER A: Where is the bird?
PARTNER B: The bird is on the table.
PARTNER A: Your turn to ask.

PARTNER B: How many birds are there?
PARTNER A: There is one bird.
PARTNER B: Your turn to ask.

| | | | |
|---|---|---|---|
| bikes | butterflies | guitar | river |
| bird | clouds | mountains | train |
| boat | fish | knife | trees |
| boots | fishing pole | picnic bench | |
| bridge | flowers | picnic table | |

□ **Exercise 32. Listening.** (Chart 5-8)

Listen to the statements about the picture on p. 144. Choose "T" for true and "F" for false.

*Example:* You will hear:     A bike is in the water.

You will choose:  T     (F)

| | | | | | | |
|---|---|---|---|---|---|---|
| 1. T   F | | 6. T   F | | 11. T   F | | |
| 2. T   F | | 7. T   F | | 12. T   F | | |
| 3. T   F | | 8. T   F | | 13. T   F | | |
| 4. T   F | | 9. T   F | | 14. T   F | | |
| 5. T   F | | 10. T   F | | 15. T   F | | |

□ **Exercise 33. Let's talk: pairwork.** (Chart 5-8)

Work with a partner. Choose a small object (a pen, pencil, coin, etc.). Give and follow directions. You can look at your book before you speak. When you speak, look at your partner.

*Example:* (*a small object such as a coin*)
PARTNER A (*book open*):    Put it on top of the desk.
PARTNER B (*book closed*):   (*Partner B puts the coin on top of the desk.*)

1. Put it on your head.
2. Put it above your head.
3. Put it between your fingers.
4. Put it near me.
5. Put it far away from me.
6. Put it under your book.
7. Put it below your knee.
8. Put it in the middle of your grammar book.

*Change roles.*
9. Put it inside your grammar book.
10. Put it next to your grammar book.
11. Put it on top of your grammar book.
12. Put it in front of me.
13. Put it behind me.
14. Put it in back of your back.
15. Put it in the back of your grammar book.
16. Put your hand around it.

**Exercise 34. Vocabulary and grammar.** (Chapters 4 and 5)

*Part I.* Work in pairs or as a class. Answer the questions. (Alternate questions if working in pairs.) Use the vocabulary from the box to help you.

| | | |
|---|---|---|
| burn | a bowl / a bowl of salad | meat / a piece of meat |
| eat dinner | a candle | a plate |
| have a steak for dinner | a cup / a cup of coffee | a restaurant |
| hold a knife and a fork | a fork | a saucer |
| | a glass / a glass of water | a spoon |
| | a knife | a steak |
| | a vase of flowers | a table |
| | | a server |

1. What is Jill doing?
2. What do you see on the table?
3. What is Jill holding in her right hand? in her left hand?
4. What is in the bowl?
5. What is on the plate?

6. What is in the cup?
7. What is burning?
8. Is Jill eating breakfast?
9. Is Jill at home? Where is she?
10. What is she cutting?

*Part II.* Complete the sentences.

1. Jill is sitting _____ a table.

2. There is a candle _____ the table.

3. There is coffee _____ the cup.

4. Jill _____ holding a knife _____ her right hand.

5. She's eating _____ a restaurant.

6. She _____ eating at home.

7. She _____ eating breakfast.

❑ **Exercise 35. Vocabulary and grammar.** (Chapters 4 and 5)

*Part I.* Work in pairs or as a class. Answer the questions. (Alternate questions if working in pairs.) Use the vocabulary from the box to help you.

> read a book         the circulation desk
> study at the library    a librarian
> take notes           a shelf (singular)
>                        shelves (plural)★

1. What is Jon doing?
2. What do you see in the picture?
3. Is Jon at home? Where is he?
4. Is Jon reading a newspaper?
5. Where is the librarian standing?
6. Is Jon right-handed or left-handed?

*Part II.* Complete the sentences.

1. Jon is studying _____ the library.

2. He is sitting _____ a table.

3. He is sitting _____ a chair.

4. His legs are _____ the table.

5. There are books _____ the shelves.

6. Jon is writing _____ a piece of paper.

7. He's taking notes _____ a piece of paper.

8. He _____ reading a newspaper.

9. The librarian _____ standing _____ the circulation desk.

10. Another student is sitting _____ Jon.

---

★See Chart 6-6, p. 174, for information about nouns with irregular plural forms.

❑ **Exercise 36. Vocabulary and grammar.** (Chapters 4 and 5)

*Part I.* Work in pairs or as a class. Answer the questions. (Alternate questions if working in pairs.) Use the vocabulary from the box to help you.

| | | |
|---|---|---|
| cash a check | a bank teller | a man (singular) |
| stand in line | a counter | men (plural)★ |
| | a line | people (plural)★ |
| | | a woman (singular) |
| | | women (plural)★ |

1. What is Megan doing?
2. Is Megan at a store? Where is she?
3. What do you see in the picture?
4. Who is standing behind Megan, a man or a woman?
5. Who is standing at the end of the line, a man or a woman?

6. How many men are there in the picture?
7. How many women are there in the picture?
8. How many people are there in the picture?
9. How many people are standing in line?

*Part II.* Complete the sentences.

1. Megan is _____ a bank.

2. Four people _____ standing in line.

3. Megan is standing _____ the counter.

4. The bank teller is standing _____ the counter.

5. A woman _____ standing _____ Megan.

6. Megan _____ standing _____ the end _____ the line.

7. A man _____ standing _____ the end _____ the line.

8. A businessman _____ standing _____ the woman in the skirt and the man with the beard.

*See Chart 6-6, p. 174, for information about nouns with irregular plural forms.

**148** CHAPTER 5

These sentences have the same meaning. Which speaker sounds more polite to you?

| 5-9 *Would Like* | |
|---|---|
| (a) I'm thirsty. I **want** a glass of water.<br>(b) I'm thirsty. I **would like** a glass of water. | Examples (a) and (b) have the same meaning, but **would like** is usually more polite than **want**. *I would like* is a nice way of saying *I want*. |
| (c) **I would like**<br>   **You would like**<br>   **She would like**<br>   **He would like**   } a glass of water.<br>   **We would like**<br>   **They would like** | Notice in (c):<br>   There is no final **-s** on **would**.<br>   There is no final **-s** on **like**. |
| (d) CONTRACTIONS<br>   **I'd** = **I would**<br>   **you'd** = **you would**<br>   **she'd** = **she would**<br>   **he'd** = **he would**<br>   **we'd** = **we would**<br>   **they'd** = **they would** | **Would** is often contracted with pronouns in both speaking and writing.<br>In speaking, **would** is usually contracted with nouns too.<br>WRITTEN: Ray would like to come.<br>SPOKEN: "Ray'd like to come." |
| *WOULD LIKE* + INFINITIVE<br>(e) I **would like**   **to eat**   a sandwich. | Notice in (e): **would like** can be followed by an infinitive. |
| *WOULD* + SUBJECT + *LIKE*<br>(f) **Would**   you   **like**   some tea? | In a question, **would** comes before the subject. |
| (g) Yes, I **would**. (I would like some tea.) | **Would** is used alone in short answers to questions with **would like**. It is not contracted in short answers. |

❏ **Exercise 38. Grammar.** (Chart 5-9)
Change the sentences to *would like*.

1. **Dan wants** a cup of coffee.

→ _____Dan would like_____ a cup of coffee.

2. **He wants** some sugar in his coffee.

→ _____He would like_____ some sugar in his coffee.

3. **Hassan and Eva want** some coffee too.

→ _____ some coffee too.

4. **They want** some sugar in their coffee too.

→ _____ some sugar in their coffee too.

5. **I want to thank** you for your help.

→ _____ you for your help.

6. **My friend wants to thank** you too.

→ _____ you too.

7. **My friends want to thank** you too.

→ _____ you too.


❏ **Exercise 39. Let's talk: class activity.** (Chart 5-9)
Your teacher will ask you questions. Answer the questions. Close your book for this activity.

1. Who's hungry right now? ( _____ ), are you hungry? What would you like?
2. Who's thirsty? ( _____ ), are you thirsty? What would you like?
3. Who's sleepy? What would you like to do?
4. What would you like to do this weekend?
5. What would you like to do after class today?
6. What would you like to have for dinner tonight?
7. What countries would you like to visit?
8. What cities would you like to visit in (*the United States, Canada, etc.*)?
9. What languages would you like to learn?
10. Pretend that you are a host at a party at your home and your classmates are your guests. Ask them what they would like to eat or drink.
11. Think of something fun to do tonight or this weekend. Use *would you like* and invite a classmate to join you.

❑ **Exercise 40. Warm-up.** (Chart 5-10)
What is the difference in meaning between these sentences?

I like chocolate.

I would like some chocolate.

| 5-10 | *Would Like* vs. *Like* |
| --- | --- |
| (a)  I *would like to go* to the zoo. | In (a): *I would like to go to the zoo* means *I want to go to the zoo.* ***Would like*** indicates that I want to do something now or in the future. |
| (b)  I *like to go* to the zoo. | In (b): *I like to go to the zoo* means *I enjoy the zoo.* ***Like*** indicates that I always, usually, or often enjoy something. |

❑ **Exercise 41. Listening.** (Chart 5-10)
Listen to the sentences and choose the verbs you hear.  Some sentences have contractions.

*Example:* You will hear:     I'd like some tea.

    You will choose:  like     ('d like)

| | | | | | |
| --- | --- | --- | --- | --- | --- |
| 1. | like | 'd like | 6. | likes | 'd like |
| 2. | like | 'd like | 7. | like | 'd like |
| 3. | like | 'd like | 8. | like | 'd like |
| 4. | likes | 'd like | 9. | like | 'd like |
| 5. | like | 'd like | 10. | like | 'd like |

❑ **Exercise 42. Let's talk: class activity.** (Charts 3-7, 5-9, and 5-10)
Discuss possible completions for the sentences. Use your own words.

1. I need to _____ every day.

2. I want to _____ today.

3. I like to _____ every day.

4. I would like to _____ today.

5. I don't like to _____ every day.

6. I don't want to _____ today.

7. Do you like to _____?

8. Would you like to _____?

9. I need to _____ and _____ today.

10. _____ would you like to _____ this evening?

❑ **Exercise 43. Let's talk: pairwork.** (Charts 5-9 and 5-10)
Work in pairs. Ask and answer questions. You can look at your book before you speak. When you speak, look at your partner.

*Example:*
PARTNER A: Do you like apples?
PARTNER B: Yes, I do. OR No, I don't.
PARTNER A: Would you like an apple right now?
PARTNER B: Yes, I would. OR Yes, thank you. OR No, but thank you for asking.
PARTNER A: Your turn now.

| PARTNER A | PARTNER B |
|---|---|
| 1. Do you like coffee?<br>Would you like a cup of coffee? | 1. Do you like chocolate?<br>Would you like some chocolate right now? |
| 2. Do you like to watch movies?<br>Would you like to go to a movie with me later today? | 2. Do you like to go shopping?<br>Would you like to go shopping with me later today? |
| 3. What do you like to do on weekends?<br>What would you like to do this weekend? | 3. What do you like to do in your free time?<br>What would you like to do in your free time tomorrow? |
| 4. What do you need to do this evening?<br>What would you like to do this evening? | 4. Do you like to travel?<br>What countries would you like to visit? |

❏ **Exercise 44. Vocabulary and grammar.** (Chapters 4 and 5)

*Part I.* Work in pairs or as a class. Answer the questions. (Alternate questions if working in pairs.) Use the vocabulary from the box to help you.

| | | |
|---|---|---|
| the date | a bank | first name/given name |
| sign a check★ | cash | middle initial |
| sign her name | a check | last name/family name/surname |
| write a check | | name and address |

1. What is Mary doing?
2. What is Mary's address?
3. What is Mary's full name?
4. What is Mary's middle initial?
5. What is Mary's last name?

6. How much money does Mary want?
7. What is in the upper-left corner of the check?
8. What is in the lower-left corner of the check?
9. What is the name of the bank?

*Part II.* Complete the sentences.

1. Mary is writing a _____.

2. She is signing _____ name.

3. The date on the check is _____.

4. Mary lives _____ 3471 Tree Street.

5. Mary lives _____ Chicago, Illinois.

6. Mary is writing a check for _____.

---

★*Check* (American English) is spelled *cheque* in British and Canadian English. The pronunciation of *check* and *cheque* is the same.

❏ **Exercise 45. Vocabulary and grammar.** (Chapters 4 and 5)

*Part I.* Work in pairs or as a class. Answer the questions. (Alternate questions if working in pairs.) Use the vocabulary from the box to help you.

| cook | (in the) kitchen | bread |
|------|------------------|-------|
| cook dinner | a list/a grocery list | butter |
| make dinner | a pepper shaker | coffee |
| taste (food) | a pot | an egg |
| | a refrigerator | pepper |
| | a salt shaker | salt |
| | | a stove |
| | | a clock |

1. What is Dave doing?
2. What do you see in the picture?
3. Where is Dave?
4. Is Dave tasting his dinner?
5. Is Dave a good cook?

6. Where is the refrigerator?
7. What is on the refrigerator?
8. Is the food on the stove hot or cold?
9. Is the food in the refrigerator hot or cold?

*Part II.* Complete the sentences.

1. Dave is making dinner. He's _____ the kitchen.

2. There is a pot _____ the stove.

3. The stove is _____ the refrigerator.

4. There is a grocery list _____ the refrigerator door.

5. Dave needs _____ to the grocery store.

6. A salt shaker and a pepper shaker are _____ the stove.

7. There is hot food _____ top _____ the stove.

8. There is cold food _____ the refrigerator.

**154** CHAPTER 5

❏ **Exercise 46. Vocabulary and grammar. (Chapters 4 and 5)**

*Part I.* Work in pairs or as a class. Answer the questions. (Alternate questions if working in pairs.) Use the vocabulary from the box to help you.

| | | |
|---|---|---|
| sing | a cat | a living room |
| sit on a sofa/a couch | a dog | a rug |
| sleep | a fish | a singer |
| swim | a fishbowl | a TV set/a television set |
| watch TV/television | a floor | |
| | a lamp | |

1. What are Nate and Lisa doing?
2. What do you see in the picture?
3. Are Nate and Lisa in the kitchen? Where are they?
4. Where is the lamp?
5. Where is the rug?
6. Where is the dog?
7. Where is the cat?

8. Is the cat walking? What is the cat doing?
9. What is the dog doing?
10. What is on top of the TV set?
11. Is the fish watching TV?
12. What is on the TV screen? What are Nate and Lisa watching?

*Part II.* Complete the sentences.

1. Nate and Lisa _____ watching TV. They like _____ watch TV.

2. They _____ sitting _____ a sofa.

3. They _____ sleeping.

4. There is a rug _____ the floor.

5. A dog _____ sleeping _____ the rug.

6. A cat _____ sleeping _____ the sofa.

❑ **Exercise 47. Let's talk: game.** (Chapters 4 and 5)

Work in teams. Make sentences about the picture. Every sentence needs to have a preposition. Use the vocabulary from the box to help you. One team member writes the sentences on paper. Your teacher will give you a time limit. The team with the most grammatically correct sentences wins.

| | | |
|---|---|---|
| draw a picture | a clock | a piece of paper |
| talk on the phone | a calendar | a telephone book |
| talk to (someone) | a heart | a wall |
| talk to each other | a phone/a telephone | |
| | a picture | |
| | a picture of a mountain | |

Nick          Kate

❑ **Exercise 48. Looking at grammar.** (Chapters 4 and 5)

Choose the correct completion.

1. Jack lives _____ China.
   (a.) in           b. at           c. on

2. I need _____ a new notebook.
   a. buy           b. to buy           c. buying

3. _____ a cup of tea?
   a. Would you like           b. Do you like           c. Are you like

4. There _____ twenty-two desks in this room.
   a. be           b. is           c. are

5. Pilots sit _____ an airplane.
   a. in front of           b. in the front of           c. front of

6. I live _____ 6601 Fourth Avenue.
   a. in           b. on           c. at

7. The students _____ do their homework.
   a. don't want      b. aren't wanting      c. don't want to

8. _____ a TV in Marisa's bedroom?
   a. Are there      b. There      c. Is there

❏ **Exercise 49. Check your knowledge.** (Chapter 5)
Correct the mistakes.

1. Do you want ⌃*to* go downtown with me?

2. There's many problems in big cities today.

3. I'd like see a movie tonight.

4. We are needing to find a new apartment soon.

5. Mr. Rice woulds likes to have a cup of tea.

6. How many students there are in your class?

7. What day it is today?

8. I am like to leave right now.

9. How the weather in Kenya?

10. The teacher would like to checking our homework now.

❏ **Exercise 50. Looking at grammar.** (Chapters 4 and 5)
Complete the sentences with your own words. Use your own paper.

1. I need ____ because ____.

2. I want ____ because ____.

3. I would like ____.

4. Would you like ____?

5. Do you like ____?

6. There is ____.

7. There are ____.

8. I'm listening to ____,
   but I also hear ____.

9. I'm looking at ____,
   but I also see ____.

10. I'm thinking about ____.

11. I think that ____.

12. In my opinion, ____.

13. How many ____ are
    there ____?

14. Is there ____?

15. Are there ____?

❑ **Exercise 51. Reading and writing.** **(Chapters 4 and 5)**

*Part I.* Read the sample paragraph. <u>Underline</u> the verbs.

**A Happy Dream**

    I am walking alone in a big field of flowers. There are thousands of colorful flowers around me. The air smells very sweet. The sun is shining, and the sky is bright blue. There are some tall trees, and the wind is gently blowing. Birds are singing in the trees. I am feeling very calm. I have no worries. My life is very peaceful. I would like to stay here forever. I don't want to wake up.

*Part II.* Write about a dream that you remember that describes a place. It can be a happy or a sad dream. If you can't remember a dream, imagine one. Use present verbs.

Include this information:

1. Where are you?
2. What are you doing?
3. Describe the place. What is there around you?
4. How are you feeling?

*Part III.* Editing check: Work individually or change papers with a partner. Check (✓) for the following:

1. ____ paragraph indent

2. ____ capital letter at the beginning of each sentence

3. ____ period at the end of each sentence

4. ____ a verb in every sentence

5. ____ correct use of prepositions of place

6. ____ use of present progressive for activities right now

7. ____ *there is* + singular noun

8. ____ *there are* + plural noun

9. ____ correct spelling (use a dictionary or spell-check)

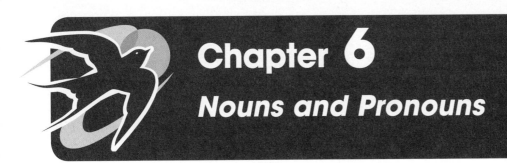

# Chapter 6
## Nouns and Pronouns

❑ **Exercise 1. Warm-up.** (Chart 6-1)

Work in small groups. Make lists of things that belong to each category. Compare your lists with other groups' lists. All of the words you use in this exercise are called "nouns."

1. Name clothing you see in this room. (*shirt,* etc.)

2. Name kinds of fruit. (*apple,* etc.)

3. Name things you drink. (*coffee,* etc.)

4. Name parts of the body. (*head,* etc.)

5. Name kinds of animals. (*horse,* etc.)

6. Name famous cities in the world⋆ (*Paris, Tokyo,* etc.)

7. Name languages.⋆ (*English,* etc.)

8. Name school subjects. (*history,* etc.)

---

### 6-1 Nouns: Subjects and Objects

| | |
|---|---|
| NOUN<br>(a) \| **Birds** \| fly. \|<br>    subject   verb | A NOUN is used as the SUBJECT of a sentence.<br>A NOUN is used as the OBJECT of a verb.⋆<br><br>In (a): **Birds** is a NOUN. It is used as the subject of the sentence. |
| NOUN         NOUN<br>(b) \| **Karl** \| is holding \| a **pen**. \|<br>    subject   verb   object | In (b): **pen** is a NOUN. It has the article **a** in front of it; **a pen** is used as the object of the verb **is holding**.<br>Objects are NOUNS, and they come after a verb. |

⋆Some verbs can be followed by an object. These verbs are called transitive verbs (*v.t.* in a dictionary). Some verbs cannot be followed by an object. These verbs are called intransitive verbs (*v.i.* in a dictionary).

---

⋆The names of cities and languages begin with capital letters.

## Exercise 2. Looking at grammar. (Chart 6-1)
Check (✓) the words that are nouns.

1. ____ eat
2. _✓_ dog
3. ____ nice
4. ____ math
5. ____ write
6. ____ have

7. ____ flowers
8. ____ juice
9. ____ ears
10. ____ Paris
11. ____ great
12. ____ English

## Exercise 3. Looking at grammar. (Chart 6-1)
For each sentence, write the object or write "no object."

NOUN

1. Cats catch mice.  What do cats catch?　　　　　object = ____*mice*____

2. Cats purr.  What do cats do?　　　　　　　　　object = ____*no object*____

3. Mice like cheese.  What do mice like?　　　　　object = _____

4. Mice don't like people.  Who don't mice like?　object = _____

5. Cats and mice have whiskers.  What do cats and
   mice have?　　　　　　　　　　　　　　　　object = _____

6. Cats sleep a lot.  What do cats do?　　　　　　object = _____

7. Cats scratch furniture.  What do cats scratch?　object = _____

## Exercise 4. Looking at grammar. (Chart 6-1)
Check (✓) the sentences that have objects.  <u>Underline</u> the objects.

1. a.  _✓_ I am writing an <u>email</u>.
   b.  _✓_ I am writing an <u>email</u> right now.
   c.  ____ I am writing right now.

2. a.  ____ Students memorize vocabulary.
   b.  ____ Some students memorize every day.
   c.  ____ Some students memorize vocabulary every day.

3. a.  ____ The printer needs paper.
   b.  ____ The printer needs ink and paper.
   c.  ____ The printer has problems.

4. a. _____ The company is hiring.

   b. _____ The company is hiring workers.

   c. _____ The company is hiring today.

5. a. _____ Babies cry.

   b. _____ Babies cry frequently.

   c. _____ Babies cry loudly.

❏ **Exercise 5. Warm-up.** (Chart 6-2)
Complete each sentence with a preposition that describes the picture. Are the words in the box nouns, verbs, or adjectives?

| above | across | in | on | under |
|-------|--------|----|----|-------|

1. The man is _____ the ground.

2. The man is _____ the plane.

3. The plane is _____ the sky.

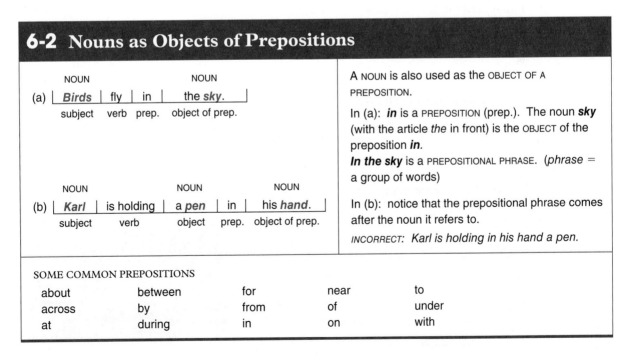

## 6-2 Nouns as Objects of Prepositions

| | NOUN | | | NOUN | |
|---|------|---|---|------|---|
| (a) | *Birds* | fly | in | the *sky*. | |
| | subject | verb | prep. | object of prep. | |

A NOUN is also used as the OBJECT OF A PREPOSITION.

In (a): *in* is a PREPOSITION (prep.). The noun *sky* (with the article *the* in front) is the OBJECT of the preposition *in*.
*In the sky* is a PREPOSITIONAL PHRASE. (*phrase* = a group of words)

| | NOUN | | NOUN | | NOUN |
|---|------|---|------|---|------|
| (b) | *Karl* | is holding | a *pen* | in | his *hand*. |
| | subject | verb | object | prep. | object of prep. |

In (b): notice that the prepositional phrase comes after the noun it refers to.
INCORRECT: *Karl is holding in his hand a pen.*

SOME COMMON PREPOSITIONS

| about | between | for | near | to |
|-------|---------|------|------|-------|
| across | by | from | of | under |
| at | during | in | on | with |

□ **Exercise 6. Looking at grammar.** (Chart 6-2)

Check (✓) the phrases that have prepositions. <u>Underline</u> the noun that is the object of each preposition.

1. ____ right now

2. ____ at noon

3. ____ on the counter

4. ____ in my closet

5. ____ some salt and pepper

6. ____ two days a week

7. ____ under the chair

8. ____ with a broom

a broom

□ **Exercise 7. Looking at grammar.** (Chart 6-2)

<u>Underline</u> the prepositions. Circle the object of each preposition.

1. a. A tutor helps Sari <u>with</u> her (homework.)

   b. A tutor helps Sari on Tuesday afternoons.

   c. A tutor helps Sari in the library.

2. a. The teacher erases the board.

   b. The teacher erases the board after class.

   c. The teacher erases the board with an eraser.

3. a. Elin cleans windows.

   b. Elin cleans in the afternoons.

   c. Elin cleans five days a week.

4. a. I do my homework in the library.

   b. I do my homework every weekend.

   c. I do my homework with my friends.

5. a. Birds fly during the day.

   b. Birds live in nests.

   c. Birds sit on eggs.

❑ **Exercise 8. Looking at grammar.** (Charts 6-1 and 6-2)
Write the noun(s) for each sentence. Describe the grammatical structure of the sentences as shown in the examples.

*Examples:* Alicia studies chemistry.  Noun(s): ___Alicia, chemistry___

| Alicia | studies | chemistry. | (none) | (none) |
|--------|---------|------------|--------|--------|
| subject | verb | object of verb | preposition | object of prep. |

The kids are playing in the park.  Noun(s): ____kids, park____

| The kids | are playing | (none) | in | the park. |
|----------|-------------|--------|-----|-----------|
| subject | verb | object of verb | preposition | object of prep. |

1. Kids like candy.  Noun(s): _____

| | | | | |
|--|--|--|--|--|
| subject | verb | object of verb | preposition | object of prep. |

2. Dayo lives in Africa.  Noun(s): _____

| | | | | |
|--|--|--|--|--|
| subject | verb | object of verb | preposition | object of prep. |

3. The sun is shining.  Noun(s): _____

| | | | | |
|--|--|--|--|--|
| subject | verb | object of verb | preposition | object of prep. |

4. Lev is reading books about movies and filmmaking.  Noun(s): _____

| | | | | |
|--|--|--|--|--|
| subject | verb | object of verb | preposition | object of prep. |

5. Dara doesn't eat chicken or beef.  Noun(s): _____

| | | | | |
|--|--|--|--|--|
| subject | verb | object of verb | preposition | object of prep. |

6. Monkeys and birds eat fruit and insects.  Noun(s): _____

| | | | | |
|--|--|--|--|--|
| subject | verb | object of verb | preposition | object of prep. |

Do you agree or disagree with each sentence?  Circle *yes* or *no*.

1. I cook delicious meals.                    yes       no

2. I like raw vegetables.                     yes       no

3. Fresh fruit is expensive.                   yes       no

---

## 6-3 Adjectives with Nouns

| | |
|---|---|
| (a) I don't like **cold weather**.<br>       adj. + noun<br>(b) Alex is a **happy child**.<br>       adj. + noun<br>(c) The **hungry boy** has a **fresh apple**.<br>   adj. + noun    adj. + noun | An ADJECTIVE (adj.) describes a noun.  In grammar, we say that adjectives modify nouns.  The word *modify* means "change a little."  Adjectives give a little different meaning to a noun: *cold weather, hot weather, nice weather, bad weather.*<br>Adjectives come in front of nouns. |
| (d) The *weather*   *is*   **cold**.<br>    noun  + *be* + adj. | Reminder:  An adjective can also follow **be**; the adjective describes the subject of the sentence. (See Chart 1-7, p. 16.) |

COMMON ADJECTIVES

| | | | |
|---|---|---|---|
| beautiful - ugly | good - bad | angry | hungry |
| big - little | happy - sad | bright | important |
| big - small | large - small | busy | intelligent |
| boring - interesting | long - short | delicious | interesting |
| cheap - expensive | noisy - quiet | exciting | kind |
| clean - dirty | old - new | famous | lazy |
| cold - hot | old - young | favorite | nervous |
| dangerous - safe | poor - rich | free | nice |
| dry - wet | sour - sweet | fresh | ripe |
| easy - hard | strong - weak | healthy | serious |
| easy - difficult | | honest | wonderful |

---

❑ **Exercise 10. Looking at grammar.** (Chart 6-3)

Circle the nouns.  <u>Underline</u> the adjectives.  Draw an arrow from each adjective to the noun it describes.

1. Jake has an <u>expensive</u> (bike.)

2. My sister has a beautiful house.

3. We often eat at an Italian restaurant.

4. Valentina sings her favorite songs in the shower.

5. Olga likes American hamburgers.

6. You like sour apples, but I like sweet fruit.

❑ **Exercise 11. Let's talk: small groups.** (Chart 6-3)

Work in small groups. Take turns adding adjectives to the sentences. Use any adjectives that make sense. Think of at least three possible adjectives to complete each sentence.

1. I don't like ___cold / hot / wet / rainy / bad / etc.___ weather.

2. Do you like _____ food?

3. I admire _____ people.

4. _____ people make me angry.

5. Pollution is a/an _____ big problem.

6. I had a/an _____ experience yesterday.

7. I don't like _____ cities.

8. I had a/an _____ dinner last night.

❑ **Exercise 12. Let's talk: small groups.** (Chart 6-3)

***Part I.*** Complete each sentence with the name of a country and the adjective that goes with it.

1. Food from ___China___ is ___Chinese___ food.

2. Food from ___Mexico___ is _____ food.

3. Food from _____ is _____ food

4. Food from _____ is _____ food.

5. Food from _____ is _____ food.

6. Food from _____ is _____ food.

7. Food from _____ is _____ food.

8. Food from _____ is _____ food.

***Part II.*** What is the favorite ethnic food in your group? Give an example of this kind of food. Then find out the most popular ethnic food in other groups.

*Example:* Favorite ethnic food?
GROUP A: Italian
*Example:* An example of Italian food?
GROUP A: spaghetti

Favorite ethnic food in our group: _____

An example of this kind of food: _____

***Part III.*** Working as a class, make a list of adjectives of nationality.

**Exercise 13. Warm-up.** (Chart 6-4)

Choose <u>all</u> the correct completions for each sentence.

| he | him | it |
|----|-----|-----|
| she | her | |

1. I understand _____.

2. You don't understand _____.

3. _____ understands us.

## 6-4 Subject Pronouns and Object Pronouns

| SUBJECT PRONOUNS | OBJECT PRONOUNS | SUBJECT — OBJECT |
|---|---|---|
| (a) *I* speak English. | Bob knows *me*. | I — me |
| (b) *You* speak English. | Bob knows *you*. | you — you |
| (c) *She* speaks English. | Bob knows *her*. | she — her |
| (d) *He* speaks English. | Bob knows *him*. | he — him |
| (e) *It* starts at 8:00. | Bob knows *it*. | it — it |
| (f) *We* speak English. | Bob talks to *us*. | we — us |
| (g) *You* speak English. | Bob talks to *you*. | you — you |
| (h) *They* speak English. | Bob talks to *them*. | they — them |
| (i) I know <u>*Tony*</u>. <u>*He*</u> is a friendly person. | A pronoun has the same meaning as a noun. In (i): *He* has the same meaning as *Tony*. | |
| (j) I like <u>*Tony*</u>. I know <u>*him*</u> well. | In (j): *Him* has the same meaning as *Tony*. In grammar, we say that a pronoun "refers to" a noun. The pronouns *he* and *him* refer to the noun *Tony*. | |
| (k) I have <u>*a red book*</u>. <u>*It*</u> is on my desk. | Sometimes a pronoun refers to a *noun phrase*. In (k): *It* refers to the whole phrase *a red book*. | |

❏ **Exercise 14. Looking at grammar.** (Chart 6-4)

Complete the sentences with the correct subject and object pronouns.

1. Jack loves Janey. _____*He*_____ loves _____*her*_____ very much.

2. Janey loves Jack. _____ loves _____ very much.

3. Janey and Jack love their daughter, Mia. _____ love _____ very much.

4. Janey and Jack love their son, Todd. _____ love _____ very much.

5. Todd loves his little sister, Mia. _____ loves _____ very much.

6. Janey loves her children. _____ loves _____ very much.

7. Jack loves his children. _____ loves _____ very much.

8. Janey and Jack love Todd and Mia. _____ love _____ very much.

❏ **Exercise 15. Looking at grammar.** (Chart 6-4)
Choose the correct answers.

1. Rita has a book. (She) / It bought her /(it) last week.

2. I know the new students, but Franco doesn't know him / them yet.

3. Where are my keys? Are they / them in your purse?

4. Ary is in Canada. She / Her is studying at a university.

5. Bert lives in my dorm. I eat breakfast with he / him every morning.

6. Sandra is my neighbor. I talk to she / her every day. She / Her and I / me have interesting conversations.

7. I have two pictures on my bedroom wall. I like it / them. It / They are beautiful.

8. Zola and I have a dinner invitation. Mr. and Mrs. Soto want we / us to come to dinner at their house.

9. Min has a new car. He / It is a convertible.

10. My husband and I have a new car. We / Us got it / him last month.

❏ **Exercise 16. Let's talk: interview.** (Chart 6-4)
Interview your classmates. Find someone who can answer *yes* to a question. Then ask the follow-up question using the appropriate object pronoun.

*Example:*
STUDENT A: Do you send emails?
STUDENT B: No, I don't.
STUDENT A: (*Ask another student.*) Do you send emails?
STUDENT C: Yes, I do.

*Follow-up question:*
STUDENT A: When do you send **them**?
STUDENT C: I send **them** all day.

1. Do you do your homework?
   When do you . . . ?

2. Do you visit friends?
   When do you . . . ?

3. Do you read newspapers or magazines?
   When do you . . . ?

4. Do you talk to (*name of classmate*)?
   When do you . . . ?

5. Do you watch TV?
   When do you . . . ?

6. Do you buy groceries?
   When do you . . . ?

7. Do you wear boots?
   When do you . . . ?

8. Do you use a laptop computer?
   When do you . . . ?

❑ **Exercise 17. Looking at grammar.** (Chart 6-4)
Complete the sentences with the correct pronouns.

1. A: Do you know Zuri and Obi?

   B: Yes, _____*I*_____ do. I live near _____*them*_____.

2. A: Is the chemical formula for water $H_3O$?

   B: No, _____ isn't. _____ is $H_2O$.

3. A: Do Julia and you want to come to the movie with us?

   B: Yes, _____ would. Julia and _____ would like to go to the movie

      with _____ .

4. A: Do Mr. and Mrs. Kelly live in the city?

   B: No, _____ don't. _____ live in the suburbs. I visited

      _____ last month.

5. A: Do you know how to spell "Mississippi"?

   B: Sure! I can spell _____ . _____ is easy to spell.

6. A: Is Paul Peterson in your class?

   B: Yes, _____ is. I sit next to _____ .

❑ **Exercise 18. Listening.** (Chart 6-4)
Listen to the sentences. Notice that the "h" in *her* and *him* is often dropped in spoken
English. The "th" in *them* can also be dropped. *Him* and *them* may sound the same.

1. Renata knows Oscar. She knows him very well.
2. Where does Shelley live? Do you have her address?
3. There's Vince. Let's go talk to him.
4. There are Dave and Lois. Let's go talk to them.

5. I'm looking online for JoAnne's phone number. What's her last name again?

6. I need to see our airline tickets. Do you have them?

❑ **Exercise 19. Listening.** (Charts 1-5 and 6-4)

Listen to each conversation and write the words you hear.

*Example:* You will hear: How is Mr. Park doing?

You will write: How _____*is*_____ Mr. Park doing?

You will hear: Great! I see him every week at the office.

You will write: Great! I see _____*him*_____ every week at the office.

1. A: Mika and _____ downtown this afternoon. Do you want to

come _____?

B: I don't think so, but thanks anyway. Chris and _____ to

the library. _____ study for our test.

2. A: Hi, Abby. How do you like your new apartment?

B: _____ great. I have a new roommate too. She's very nice.

A: What's _____ name?

B: Rita Lopez. Do you _____?

A: No, but I know _____ brother. He's in my math class.

3. A: Do you see Mike and George very much?

B: Yes, I see _____ often. We play video games at my house.

A: Who usually wins?

B: Mike. We never beat _____!

❏ **Exercise 20. Warm-up.** (Chart 6-5)

How many? Choose the correct number.

| | | | |
|---|---|---|---|
| 1. cup | | one | two or more |
| 2. class | | one | two or more |
| 3. countries | | one | two or more |
| 4. knives | | one | two or more |
| 5. radio | | one | two or more |

## 6-5 Nouns: Singular and Plural Forms

| SINGULAR | PLURAL | |
|---|---|---|
| (a) one pen<br>one apple<br>one cup<br>one elephant | two pens<br>three apples<br>four cups<br>five elephants | To make the plural form of most nouns, add **-s**. |
| (b) baby<br>city | babies<br>cities | End of noun: *consonant* + **-y**<br>Plural form: change **y** to **i**, add **-es** |
| (c) boy<br>key | boys<br>keys | End of noun: *vowel* + **-y**<br>Plural form: add **-s** |
| (d) wife<br>thief | wives<br>thieves | End of noun: **-fe** or **-f**<br>Plural form: change **f** to **v**, add **-s** or **-es** |
| (e) dish<br>match<br>class<br>box | dishes<br>matches<br>classes<br>boxes | End of noun: **-sh, -ch, -ss, -x**<br>Plural form: add **-es**<br>Pronunciation: /əz/ |
| (f) tomato<br>potato | tomatoes<br>potatoes | End of noun: *consonant* + **-o**<br>Plural form: add **-es** |
| zoo<br>radio | zoos<br>radios | End of noun: *vowel* + **-o**<br>Plural form: add **-s** |

❏ **Exercise 21. Looking at grammar.** (Chart 6-5)

Complete the sentences. Use the plural form of the words in the boxes. Use each word only once.

*Part I.*

| baby | city | cowboy | key | party |
|---|---|---|---|---|
| ✓ boy | country | dictionary | lady | tray |

1. Mr. and Mrs. Novak have one daughter and two sons. They have one girl and two
_____ boys _____.

2. The students in my class come from many _____.

3. Women give birth to _____.

4. My money and my _____ are in my pocket.

5. I know the names of many _____ in the United States and Canada.

6. I like to go to _____ because I like to meet and talk to people.

7. People carry their food on _____ in a cafeteria.

8. We always check our _____ when we write compositions.

9. Good evening, _____ and gentlemen.

10. _____ ride horses.

**Part II.**

| knife | leaf | life | thief | wife |

11. It is fall. The _____ are falling from the trees.

12. Sue and Ann are married. They have husbands. They are

_____.

13. We all have some problems in our _____.

14. Police officers catch _____.

15. Please put the _____, forks, and spoons on
the table.

**Part III.**

| | | | |
|---|---|---|---|
| bush | glass | sandwich | tomato |
| class | match | sex | zoo |
| dish | potato | tax | |

16. Steve drinks eight _____ of water every day.

17. There are two _____: male and female.

18. Please put the _____ and the silverware on the table.

19. All citizens pay money to the government every year. They pay their _____.

20. I can see trees and _____ outside the window.

21. I want to light the candles. I need some _____.

22. When I make a salad, I use lettuce and _____.

23. Sometimes Pam has a hamburger and French-fried _____
    for dinner.

24. Some animals live all of their lives in _____.

25. Mehmet is a student. He likes his _____.

26. We often eat _____ for lunch.

 ❏ **Exercise 22. Listening.** (Chart 6-5)
Choose the word you hear.

1. toy     (toys)            6. box       boxes
2. table   tables           7. package   packages
3. face    faces            8. chair     chairs
4. hat     hats             9. edge      edges
5. office  offices         10. top       tops

□ **Exercise 23. Listening.** (Chart 6-5)

Listen to each sentence. Circle the word you hear.

1. desk        (desks)
2. place       places
3. sandwich    sandwiches
4. sentence    sentences
5. apple       apples

6. exercise    exercises
7. piece       pieces
8. rose        roses
9. bush        bushes
10. college    colleges

a rose

a rose bush

□ **Exercise 24. Grammar and speaking.** (Chart 6-5)

Write the correct ending. Write **Ø** if no ending is necessary. Then decide if you agree
or disagree with the sentence. Share some of your answers with a partner or the class.
Remember: **a = one**.

1. I like banana _s_ , strawberry _ies_ , and peach _es_ .          yes    no

2. I eat a banana____ every day.                                    yes    no

3. My favorite animals are elephant____.                            yes    no

4. A baby elephant____ is cute.                                     yes    no

5. Baby____ are cute.                                               yes    no

6. The grammar exercise____ in this book are easy.                  yes    no

7. A ride on a motorcycle____ is fun.                               yes    no

8. A ride on an airplane____ is comfortable.                        yes    no

9. This exercise____ is easy.                                       yes    no

10. Cockroach____ are ugly, and they scare me.                      yes    no

a cockroach

Write ***a*** before the singular nouns.

1. a. _____ child

   b. _____ children

2. a. _____ teeth

   b. _____ tooth

3. a. _____ foot

   b. _____ feet

## 6-6 Nouns: Irregular Plural Forms

| SINGULAR | PLURAL | EXAMPLES |
|---|---|---|
| (a) *child* | **children** | Mr. Smith has one *child*.  Mr. Cook has two **children**. |
| (b) *foot* | **feet** | I have a right *foot* and a left *foot*.  I have two **feet**. |
| (c) *man* | **men** | I see a *man* on the street.  I see two **men** on the street. |
| (d) *mouse* | **mice** | My cat sees a *mouse*.  Cats like to catch **mice**. |
| (e) *tooth* | **teeth** | My *tooth* hurts.  My **teeth** are white. |
| (f) *woman* | **women** | There's one *woman* in our class.  There are ten **women** in your class. |
| (g) *sheep* | **sheep** | Annie drew a picture of one *sheep*.  Tommy drew a picture of two **sheep**. |
| (h) *fish* | **fish** | Bob has an aquarium.  He has one *fish*.  Sue has an aquarium.  She has seven **fish**. |
| (i) *(none)** | **people** | There are fifteen **people** in this room. (Notice: *People* does not have a final **-s**.) |

\* ***People*** is always plural.  It has no singular form.

❏ **Exercise 26. Looking at grammar.** (Chart 6-6)
Complete the sentences with the correct form of the noun in each picture.

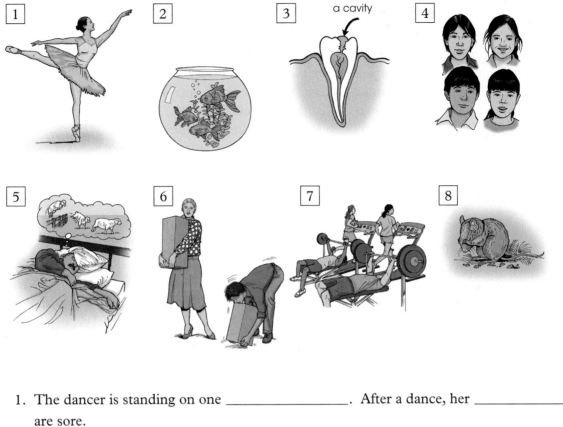

1. The dancer is standing on one _____. After a dance, her _____
   are sore.

2. There are three _____ in the bowl. One _____ is blowing
   bubbles.

3. The dentist is checking my _____. One _____
   has a cavity.

4. Janine has four _____. I have one _____.

5. Sometimes, I have trouble sleeping, so I count _____. One
   _____, two _____, . . . one hundred _____.
   Oh, no, I'm still awake!

6. This _____ is strong. This _____ is weak.

7. Are _____ stronger than _____, or are
   _____ stronger than _____?

8. There is a _____ in my bedroom wall. There are _____ under my
   house.

□ **Exercise 27. Reading and grammar.** (Charts 6-5 and 6-6)

*Part I.* Read the story. Look at new vocabulary with your teacher first.

### An Online Shopper

Tara likes to buy clothes online. She lives far away from stores and shopping malls. She knows many good online sites. She frequently checks for sales. She finds shirts, pants, and jackets for her husband and children. She buys skirts, dresses, warm coats, and hats for herself. But she doesn't get shoes online. She has big feet and often shoes don't fit. Sometimes she returns her purchases. For Tara, the best websites have free shipping for returns.

*Do you know these words?*

malls
sales
purchases
free shipping

*Part II.* Add plural endings to the nouns. Write Ø for "no ending."

1. Tara shops at online site____.

2. She lives far away from mall____.

3. She checks website____ for sale____.

4. She like to buy clothes for her husband____ and child____.

5. She buys jacket____, skirt____, shirt____, dress____, and coat____.

6. She doesn't buy shoe____ online because she has big f____.

7. Tara likes website____ with free shipping for return____.

□ **Exercise 28. Looking at grammar.** (Charts 6-1 → 6-6 )

A *complete sentence* is a group of words that has a subject and a verb. An *incomplete sentence* is a group of words that does not have a subject and a verb.

If the words are a complete sentence, change the first letter to a capital letter and add final punctuation (a period or a question mark). If the words are an incomplete sentence, write "NC" to mean "not complete."

1. M̸onkeys like bananas.

2. in my garden → *NC*

3. D̸o you like sour apples?

4. this class ends at two o'clock

5. teaches English

6. my mother works

7. in an office

8. my mother works in an office

9. does your brother have a job

10. does not work

11. my sister lives in an apartment

12. has a roommate

13. the apartment has two bedrooms

14. a small kitchen and a big living room

15. on the third floor

❏ **Exercise 29. Looking at grammar.** (Charts 6-1 → 6-6)
Choose the correct completion.

1. My sister and I live together. Our parents often call or visit _____.
   a. us    b. them    c. we    d. they

2. Dan has a broken leg. I visit _____ every day.
   a. he    b. him    c. them    d. it

3. Maya and I are good friends. _____ spend a lot of time together.
   a. They    b. You    c. We    d. She

4. Our kids enjoy the zoo. We often take _____ to the zoo.
   a. it    b. they    c. them    d. him

5. Cristina drives an old car. She takes good care of _____.
   a. her    b. them    c. it    d. him

6. Mark and _____ don't know Mr. Sung.
   a. I    b. me    c. us    d. them

7. Ms. Vargas is a lawyer in Chicago. Do you know _____?
   a. them    b. it    c. him    d. her

8. Ahmed lives near Yoko and _____.
   a. I    b. me    c. he    d. she

9. My sister and a friend are visiting me. _____ are visiting here for two days.
   a. She    b. They    c. We    d. Them

10. Do _____ have the correct time?
    a. you    b. them    c. him    d. her

❑ **Exercise 30. Warm-up.** (Chart 6-7)
Complete the sentences.

*Who does this book belong to?*

1. STUDENT A:  It's his book     OR     It's his.
2. STUDENT B:  It's her book.     OR     It's hers.
3. STUDENT C:  It's your book.     OR     It's yours.
4. STUDENT D:  It's our book.     OR     It's _____.
5. STUDENT E:  It's their book.     OR     It's _____.

*Do you know this exception?*

6. It's my book.     OR     It's _____.

---

### 6-7 Possessive Pronouns: *Mine, Yours, His, Hers, Ours, Theirs*

| | POSSESSIVE ADJECTIVE | POSSESSIVE PRONOUN | |
|---|---|---|---|
| (a) This book belongs to me. <br> It is *my* book. <br> It is *mine*. | my <br> your <br> her <br> his <br> our <br> their | mine <br> yours <br> hers <br> his <br> ours <br> theirs | A POSSESSIVE ADJECTIVE is used in front of a noun: *my* book. |
| (b) That book belongs to you. <br> It is *your* book. <br> It is *yours*. | | | |
| (c) That book is *mine*. <br> INCORRECT: *That is mine book.* | | | A POSSESSIVE PRONOUN is used alone, without a noun following it, as in (c). |

---

❑ **Exercise 31. Looking at grammar.** (Chart 6-7)
Write or say the correct possessive pronoun.

1. It's your money.  It's _____.

2. It's our money.  It's _____.

3. It's her money.  It's _____.

4. It's their money.  It's _____.

5. It's his money.  It's _____.

6. It's my money.  It's _____.

7. The money belongs to Matt.  It's _____.

8. The money belongs to Elena.  It's _____.

9. The money belongs to Matt and Elena.  It's _____.

10. The money belongs to Stuart and me.  It's _____.

□ **Exercise 32. Looking at grammar.** (Charts 2-5, 6-2, 6-4, and 6-7)
Complete the sentences. Use object pronouns, possessive adjectives, and possessive pronouns.

1. *I* own this book.

   a. This book belongs to _____*me*_____.

   b. This is _____*my*_____ book.

   c. This book is _____*mine*_____.

2. *They* own these books.

   a. These books belong to _____.

   b. These are _____ books.

   c. These books are _____.

3. *You* own that book.

   a. That book belongs to _____.

   b. That is _____ book.

   c. That book is _____.

4. *She* owns this pen.

   a. This pen belongs to _____.

   b. This is _____ pen.

   c. This pen is _____.

5. *He* owns that pen.

   a. That pen belongs to _____.

   b. That is _____ pen.

   c. That pen is _____.

6. *We* own those books.

   a. Those books belong to _____.

   b. Those are _____ books.

   c. Those books are _____.

❏ **Exercise 33. Looking at grammar.** (Charts 2-5 and 6-7)
Write the correct completion.

1. Is this _____*your*_____ pen?
   <u>your / yours</u>

2. Please give this dictionary to Oksana. It's _____.
   <u>her / hers</u>

3. A: Don't forget _____ hat. Here.
      <u>your / yours</u>

   B: No, that's not _____ hat. _____ is green.
      <u>my / mine</u>      <u>My / Mine</u>

4. A: Please take this bouquet of flowers as a gift from me. Here. They're

      _____.
      <u>your / yours</u>

   B: Thank you. You're very thoughtful.

5. A: That car belongs to Mr. and Mrs. Townsend.

   B: No, that's not _____. _____ car is new.
      <u>their / theirs</u>   <u>Their / Theirs</u>

6. A: Malik and I really like _____ new apartment. It has lots of space.
      <u>our / ours</u>

      How do you like _____?
      <u>your / yours</u>

   B: _____ is small, but it's comfortable.
      <u>Our / Ours</u>

7. A: Excuse me. Is this _____ umbrella?
      <u>your / yours</u>

   B: I don't have an umbrella. Ask Jay. Maybe it's _____.
      <u>he / his</u>

8. A: This isn't _____ phone.
      <u>my / mine</u>

   B: Are you sure?

   A: Yes, I have a flip phone. This one belongs to Carla. _____ is a
      <u>Her / Hers</u>
      smartphone.

❏ **Exercise 34. Warm-up.** (Chart 6-8)
Choose all the grammatically correct sentences.

1. His bedroom is messy.
2. The boy his bedroom is messy.
3. The boy bedroom is messy.
4. The boy's bedroom is messy.

## 6-8 Possessive Nouns

| | | SINGULAR NOUN | POSSESSIVE FORM | To show that a person possesses something, add an apostrophe (') and **-s** to a singular noun. |
|---|---|---|---|---|
| (a) | My *friend* has a car. My ***friend's*** car is blue. | **friend** | **friend's** | POSSESSIVE NOUN, SINGULAR: *noun + apostrophe (') +* **-s** |
| (b) | The *student* has a book. The ***student's*** book is red. | **student** | **student's** | |

| | | PLURAL NOUN | POSSESSIVE FORM | Add an apostrophe (') at the end of a plural noun (after the **-s**). |
|---|---|---|---|---|
| (c) | The *students* have books. The ***students'*** books are red. | **students** | **students'** | POSSESSIVE NOUN, PLURAL: *noun +* **-s** *+ apostrophe (')* |
| (d) | My *friends* have a car. My ***friends'*** car is blue. | **friends** | **friends'** | |

❏ **Exercise 35. Looking at grammar.** (Chart 6-8)
Complete the sentences with the correct nouns.

1. Rebecca's dress is very colorful.

   The _____*dress*_____ belongs to _____*Rebecca*_____.

2. Dave's car was expensive.

   The _____ belongs to _____.

3. Where is Samir's room?

   The _____ belongs to _____.

4. Is the doctor's office crowded?

   The _____ belongs to _____.

❏ **Exercise 36. Looking at grammar.** (Chart 6-8)
Choose the correct answer for each boldfaced noun.

1. My **teacher's** office is large.               one teacher     more than one
2. My **teachers'** office is large.               one teacher     more than one
3. The **nurses'** uniform is green.               one nurse       more than one
4. The **nurse's** uniform is green.               one nurse       more than one
5. My **friends'** work is interesting.            one friend      more than one
6. The **dentist's** schedule is busy.             one dentist     more than one

❑ **Exercise 37. Looking at grammar.** (Chart 6-8)

Complete the sentences with your classmates' names.

1. _____ hair is short and straight.

2. _____ grammar book is on her desk.

3. _____ last name is _____.

4. I don't know _____ address.

5. _____ eyes are brown.

6. _____ shirt is blue.

7. _____ backpack is on the floor.

8. I need to borrow _____ pen.


❑ **Exercise 38. Game.** (Chart 6-8)

Work in teams. Complete the sentences with words from the box. You may use a word more than one time. The team with the most correct answers wins.

| | | |
|---|---|---|
| brother | father | son |
| children | mother | wife |
| daughter | sister | |

**Family relationships**

1. My uncle is my father's _____.

2. My grandmother is my mother's _____.

3. My brother-in-law is my husband's _____.

4. My sister's _____ are my nieces and nephews.

5. My niece is my brother's _____.

6. My nephew is my sister's _____.

7. My aunt's _____ is my mother.

8. My wife's _____ is my mother-in-law.

9. My brother's _____ is my sister-in-law.

10. My father's _____ and _____ are my grandparents.

❏ **Exercise 39. Looking at grammar.** (Charts 2-5, 6-7, and 6-8)
Complete the sentences. Use the correct possessive form of the given words.

1. I     a. This bookbag is _____mine_____.

  Ava     b. That bookbag is _____Ava's_____.

  I     c. _____My_____ bookbag is red.

  she     d. _____Hers_____ is green.

2. we     a. These books are _____.

  they     b. Those books are _____.

  we     c. _____ books are on the table.

  they     d. _____ are on the desk.

3. Don     a. This raincoat is _____.

  Kate     b. That raincoat is _____.

  he     c. _____ is light brown.

  she     d. _____ is light blue.

4. I     a. This notebook is _____.

  you     b. That one is _____.

  I     c. _____ has _____ name on it.

  you     d. _____ has _____ name on it.

5. Ray     a. _____ apartment is on Pine Street.

  we     b. _____ is on Main Street.

  he     c. _____ apartment has three rooms.

  we     d. _____ has four rooms.

6. I     a. This is _____ pen.

  you     b. That one is _____.

  I     c. _____ is in _____ pocket.

  you     d. _____ is on _____ desk.

7. we    a. _____ car is a Chevrolet.

   they    b. _____ is a Volkswagen.

   we    c. _____ gets 17 miles to the gallon.

   they    d. _____ car gets 30 miles to the gallon.

8. Gabi    a. These books are _____.

   Evan    b. Those are _____.

   she    c. _____ are on _____ desk.

   he    d. _____ are on _____ desk.

❑ **Exercise 40. Listening.** (Chart 6-8)

 Listen to each sentence and choose the word you hear.

*Example:* You will hear:   Your dad's job sounds interesting.

        You will choose:  dad   (dad's)

| | | | |
|---|---|---|---|
| 1. Mack | Mack's | 5. friend | friend's |
| 2. Mack | Mack's | 6. friend | friend's |
| 3. teacher | teacher's | 7. manager | manager's |
| 4. teacher | teacher's | 8. cousin | cousin's |

❑ **Exercise 41. Looking at grammar.** (Chart 6-8)

Add apostrophes where necessary.

    *Brian's*
1. ~~Brians~~ last name is Wolf.

2. Stefan likes to work late at night. → (*no change*)

3. My teachers give a lot of homework.

4. My teachers names are Ms. Cordova and Mr. Durisova.

5. My teachers first name is Ellen.

6. The teacher collected all the students test papers at the end of the class.

7. Nicole is a girls name.

8. Erica and Natalie are girls names.

9. Do you know Monicas brother?

10. Ryans friends visited him last night.

**Exercise 42. Warm-up.** (Chart 6-9)
Choose the correct answer.

1. Who is that?
   a. It's Tom.
   b. It's Tom's.

2. Whose is that?
   a. It's Tom.
   b. It's Tom's.

## 6-9 Questions with *Whose*

| | | |
|---|---|---|
| (a) *Whose book* is this? | → *Mine.*<br>→ It's *mine.*<br>→ It's *my* book. | *Whose* asks about possession.<br>*Whose* is often used with a noun (e.g., *whose book*), as in (a) and (b). |
| (b) *Whose books* are these? | → *Rita's.*<br>→ They're *Rita's.*<br>→ They're *Rita's* books. | |
| (c) *Whose* is this? (*The speaker is pointing to one book.*)<br>(d) *Whose* are these? (*The speaker is pointing to some books.*) | | *Whose* can be used without a noun if the meaning is clear, as in (c) and (d). |
| (e) *Who's* your teacher? | | In (e): *Who's* = *who is*<br>*Whose* and *who's* have the same pronunciation. |

Whose is this? There's no name on it. Who's the artist?

❑ **Exercise 43. Looking at grammar.** (Chart 6-9)
Choose the correct answer.

1. Whose birthday is today?
   a. Audrey's.
   b. Audrey.

2. Who is on the phone?
   a. Audrey's.
   b. Audrey.

3. Who is working at the bakery?
   a. Allen.
   b. Allen's.

4. Whose bakery is the best?
   a. Allen.
   b. Allen's.

5. Who's going to join us for lunch?
   a. Toshi's.
   b. Toshi.

6. Whose dirty socks are on the floor?
   a. Julian's.
   b. Julian.

❏ **Exercise 44. Looking at grammar.** (Chart 6-9)
Complete the sentences with **Whose** or **Who's**.

1. _____ your roommate this year?

2. _____ pen is this?

3. _____ on the phone?

4. _____ that?

5. _____ is that?

6. _____ making so much noise?

❏ **Exercise 45. Listening.** (Chart 6-9)
Listen to each sentence. Choose **Whose** or **Who's**.

1. Whose     Who's          6. Whose     Who's

2. Whose     Who's          7. Whose     Who's

3. Whose     Who's          8. Whose     Who's

4. Whose     Who's          9. Whose     Who's

5. Whose     Who's         10. Whose     Who's

❏ **Exercise 46. Looking at grammar.** (Charts 2-6, 2-7, and 6-9)
Write the correct completion.

1. Whose watch ____*is*____ ____*this*____?
                 is / are      this / these

2. Whose glasses _____ _____?
                   is / are        that / those

3. Whose hat _____ _____?
               is / are        that / those

4. Whose shoe _____ _____?
                is / are        this / these

5. Whose keys _____ _____?
                is / are        this / these

❏ **Exercise 47. Let's talk: pairwork.** (Chart 6-9)
Work with a partner. Touch or point to something in the classroom that belongs to someone and ask a question with **Whose**.

*Example:*
PARTNER A: (*points to a book*) Whose book is this?
PARTNER B: It's mine. / Mine. / It's my book.
PARTNER A: Your turn.

❑ **Exercise 48. Warm-up.** (Chart 6-10)
Choose the answer that describes the picture. Only one answer is correct.

a. Woman's Restroom
b. Women's Restroom

---

### 6-10 Possessive: Irregular Plural Nouns

| | |
|---|---|
| (a) The **children's** toys are on the floor. | Irregular plural nouns (*children, men, women, people*) have an irregular plural possessive form. The apostrophe (') comes <u>before</u> the final -*s*. |
| (b) That store sells **men's** clothing. | REGULAR PLURAL POSSESSIVE NOUN: |
| (c) That store sells **women's** clothing. | *the students' books* |
| (d) I like to know about other **people's** lives. | IRREGULAR PLURAL POSSESSIVE NOUN: *the women's books* |

---

❑ **Exercise 49. Looking at grammar.** (Charts 6-8 and 6-10)
Complete each sentence with the possessive form of the given noun.

*These books belong to . . .*

1. Maggie.        They're _____Maggie's_____ books.

2. my friend.     They're _____ books.

3. my friends.    They're _____ books.

4. the child.     They're _____ books.

5. the children.  They're _____ books.

6. the woman.     They're _____ books.

7. the women.     They're _____ books.

❑ **Exercise 50. Looking at grammar.** (Charts 6-8 and 6-10)
Complete each sentence with the possessive form of the given noun.

1. children That store sells _____*children's*_____ books.

2. women Vanessa and Angelina are _____ names.

3. person A biography is the story of a _____ life.

4. people Biographies are the stories of _____ lives.

5. students _____ lives are busy.

6. brother Do you know my _____ wife?

7. wife Vanya fixed his _____ old

   sewing machine.

8. dog My _____ name is Fido.

9. dogs My _____ names are Fido and Rover.

10. men Are Jim and Tom _____ names?

11. man, woman Chris can be a _____ nickname or a

   _____ nickname.

12. children Our _____ school is near our house.


❑ **Exercise 51. Looking at grammar.** (Charts 6-8 and 6-10)
Choose the correct completion.

1. The ____ work hard.
   a. students    b. student's    c. students'

2. My ____ name is Honey.
   a. cats    b. cat's    c. cats'

3. My ____ are traveling in Spain.
   a. cousins    b. cousin's    c. cousins'

4. My ____ is meeting them in two weeks.
   a. uncle    b. uncle's    c. uncles'

5. The three ____ coats are in the closet.
   a. boys    b. boy's    c. boys'

6. The _____ is riding his bike.
   a. boys          b. boy          c. boys'

7. We have three _____ and one girl in my family.
   a. boys          b. boy's          c. boys'

8. Two of my _____ live near me.
   a. friends          b. friend's          c. friends'

9. My _____ names are Frank and Martin.
   a. friend          b. friend's          c. friends'

10. My best _____ name is Andy.
    a. friends          b. friend's          c. friends'

❑ **Exercise 52. Check your knowledge.** (Chapter 6)
Correct the mistakes.

1. Jamil a car has. → *Jamil has a car.*

2. Babys cry.

3. Kurt helps Justin and I.

4. Our teacher gives tests difficult.

5. Charlie is cutting with a lawnmower the grass.

6. Do you know Yuko roommate?

7. My roommate desk is always a mess.

8. There are nineteen peoples in my class.

9. Veronica and Victor have three childrens.

10. Excuse me. Where is the men room?

11. There is twenty classroom in this building.

12. Mr. Torro is our teacher. Me like he very much.

13. Does that store sell children toys?

14. Whose is book on the chair?

15. It is mine book.

a lawnmower

❏ **Exercise 53. Grammar and writing.** (Chapter 6)

***Part I.*** Read the paragraph. Look at the boldface words. Write "S" if the word is singular and "P" if it is plural.

                          S

My favorite **store** is City Market. It is a grocery store. I like this store because it has many kinds of **groceries**. I can buy interesting **ingredients** there. I often cook **dishes** from my **country**. City Market has a big **selection** of rice and fresh **vegetables**. I like to buy fresh, not frozen, vegetables and meat, but the meat at City Market is expensive, so I don't buy much. The store is near my **house**, and I can walk to it. The **people** are friendly and helpful.

***Part II.*** Where do you like to shop? It can be a grocery store, clothes store, online store, etc. Complete the sentences. Combine the sentences into a paragraph. Add a few extra details to make your writing more interesting. Begin with ***My favorite store is . . . .***

1. My favorite store is _____ .

2. I like this store because it _____ .

3. I often/sometimes buy _____ .

4. I don't like to buy _____ .

5. The store is _____ .

***Part III.*** Work individually or change papers with a partner. Check (✓) for the following:

1. ____ indented paragraph
2. ____ capital letter at the beginning of each sentence
3. ____ period at the end of each sentence
4. ____ a verb in every sentence
5. ____ correct use of **-s/-es/-ies** endings for plural nouns
6. ____ correct use of irregular plural forms
7. ____ correct spelling (use a dictionary or spell-check)

# Chapter **7**
## Count and Noncount Nouns

❑ **Exercise 1. Warm-up.** (Chart 7-1)
Which of the following can you count? There is only one possibility.

1. _____ sugar bowl

2. _____ sugar

---

## 7-1 Nouns: Count and Noncount

|  | SINGULAR | PLURAL |  |
|---|---|---|---|
| COUNT NOUN | *a book*<br>*one book* | *books*<br>*two books*<br>*some books*<br>*a lot of books* | **A COUNT NOUN**<br><br>SINGULAR: *a* + noun / *one* + noun     PLURAL: noun + *-s* |
| NONCOUNT NOUN | *mail*<br>*some mail*<br>*a lot of mail* | (no plural form) | **A NONCOUNT NOUN**<br><br>SINGULAR: Do not use *a*. Do not use *one*.     PLURAL: A noncount noun does not have a plural form. |

COMMON NONCOUNT NOUNS

| | | | |
|---|---|---|---|
| advice | mail | bread | pepper |
| furniture | money | cheese | rice |
| help | music | coffee | salt |
| homework | traffic | food | soup |
| information | vocabulary | fruit | sugar |
| jewelry | weather | meat | tea |
| luck | work | milk | water |

**Exercise 2. Looking at grammar.** (Chart 7-1)

Look at the *italicized* words. <u>Underline</u> the noun. Is it count or noncount?

| | | | |
|---|---|---|---|
| 1. He is sitting on *a <u>chair</u>*. | (count) | noncount |
| 2. He is sitting on *old <u>furniture</u>*. | count | (noncount) |
| 3. She has *a coin*. | count | noncount |
| 4. She has *some money*. | count | noncount |
| 5. The street is full of *heavy traffic*. | count | noncount |
| 6. There are *a lot of cars* in the street. | count | noncount |
| 7. I know *a fact* about bees. | count | noncount |
| 8. I have *some information* about bees. | count | noncount |
| 9. The teacher gives us *a lot of homework*. | count | noncount |
| 10. We have *an easy assignment*. | count | noncount |
| 11. I like *classical music*. | count | noncount |
| 12. Would you like *some coffee?* | count | noncount |
| 13. Our school has *a big library*. | count | noncount |
| 14. We are learning *new vocabulary* every day. | count | noncount |
| 15. I need *some advice*. | count | noncount |
| 16. Peter has *a good job*. | count | noncount |
| 17. He likes *his work*. | count | noncount |
| 18. Margo wears *a lot of bracelets*. | count | noncount |

❏ **Exercise 3. Vocabulary and grammar.** (Chart 7-1)

Describe the pictures. Add **-s** to the ends of the words if necessary or write Ø (no ending).

| PICTURE | DESCRIPTION |
|---|---|
| | 1. one ring *Ø* |
| | 2. two ring *s* |

| PICTURE | DESCRIPTION |
|---|---|
| | 3. three ring _s_ |
| | 4. some jewelry _Ø_ |
| | 5. two letter____ |
| | 6. one postcard____ |
| | 7. some mail____ |
| | 8. one couch____ |
| | 9. two table____ |
| | 10. some chair____ |
| | 11. some furniture____ |
| | 12. a. a lot of car____<br>b. a lot of traffic____ |
| | 13. a. a lot of money____<br>b. a lot of coin____ |

**Exercise 4. Looking at grammar: small groups.** (Chart 7-1)
Work in small groups. List the noncount nouns. Find the count nouns that are close in meaning. Use **a/an** with the count nouns.

| | | | |
|---|---|---|---|
| advice | desk | jewelry | music |
| assignment | fact | job | song |
| bracelet | furniture | ✓ letter | suggestion |
| cloud | homework | ✓ mail | weather |
| coin | information | money | work |

|  | NONCOUNT | COUNT |
|---|---|---|
| 1. | _mail_ | _a letter_ |
| 2. | _____ | _____ |
| 3. | _____ | _____ |
| 4. | _____ | _____ |
| 5. | _____ | _____ |
| 6. | _____ | _____ |
| 7. | _____ | _____ |
| 8. | _____ | _____ |
| 9. | _____ | _____ |
| 10. | _____ | _____ |

❑ **Exercise 5. Looking at grammar.** (Chart 7-1)
Complete the nouns with **-s** or **Ø** (no article).

1. a house____, one house____, two house____, a lot of house____, some house____

2. a car____, one car____, four car____, a lot of car____

3. water____, some water____, a lot of water____

4. a computer____, three computer____, some computer____, a lot of computer____

❑ **Exercise 6. Game.** (Chart 7-1)
Work in teams. Complete the sentences with as many nouns as possible. Write the names of things you see in the classroom. The team with the most grammatically correct nouns wins.

*I see . . .*

1. a
2. two
3. five
4. some
5. a lot of
6. many

Work in groups or individually. The object of the game is to fill in each list with nouns that belong to the category of that list. If possible, write one noun that begins with each letter of the alphabet. When you finish your lists, count the nouns you have. That is your score. Who has the highest score?

|   | **LIST 1**<br>Things in nature | **LIST 2**<br>Things you eat<br>and drink | **LIST 3**<br>Animals and<br>insects | **LIST 4**<br>Things for sale<br>at (*name of a local<br>store*) |
|---|---|---|---|---|
| A | air | | | |
| B | bushes | | | |
| C | | | | |
| D | | | | |
| E | earth | | | |
| F | fish | | | |
| G | grass | | | |
| H | | | | |
| I | ice | | | |
| J | | | | |
| K | | | | |
| L | leaves | | | |
| M | | | | |
| N | | | | |
| O | ocean | | | |
| P | plants | | | |
| Q | | | | |
| R | rain | | | |
| S | stars | | | |
| T | trees | | | |
| U | | | | |
| V | | | | |
| W | water | | | |
| X | | | | |
| Y | | | | |
| Z | | | | |
| | Score: ___13___ | Score: _____ | Score: _____ | Score: _____ |

❑ **Exercise 8. Warm-up** (Chart 7-2)

Are the words in red correct or incorrect?

1. I work in an office.
2. It is in a hotel.
3. I take an elevator to the top floor.
4. I have an amazing view.

## 7-2 Using *A* vs. *An*

| | |
|---|---|
| (a) *A dog* is *an animal.* | *A* and *an* are used in front of singular count nouns. <br><br> In (a): *dog* and *animal* are singular count nouns. |
| (b) I work in *an office.* <br><br> (c) Mr. Tang is *an old man.* | Use *an* in front of words that begin with the vowels *a, e, i,* and *o*: *an apartment, an elephant, an idea, an ocean.* <br><br> In (c): Notice that *an* is used because the adjective (*old*) begins with a vowel and comes in front of a singular count noun (*man*). |
| (d) I have *an uncle.* <br><br> COMPARE <br> (e) He works at *a university.* | Use *an* if a word that begins with "u" has a vowel sound: *an uncle, an ugly picture.* <br><br> Use *a* if a word that begins with "u" has a /yu/ sound: *a university, a usual event.* |
| (f) I need *an hour* to finish my work. <br><br> COMPARE <br> (g) I live in *a house.* He lives in *a hotel.* | In some words that begin with "h," the "h" is not pronounced. Instead, the word begins with a vowel sound and *an* is used: *an hour, an honor.* <br><br> In most words that begin with "h," the "h" is pronounced. Use *a* if the "h" is pronounced. |

❑ **Exercise 9. Looking at grammar.** (Chart 7-2)

Complete the sentences with *a* or *an*.

1. Lars is eating _____ apple.

2. Tia is eating _____ banana.

3. Alice works in _____ office.

4. I have _____ idea.

5. I have _____ good idea.

6. Ada is taking _____ easy class.

7. Cuba is _____ island near the United States.

8. _____ hour has sixty minutes.

9. _____ healthy person gets regular exercise.

10. Elsa is _____ honest worker.

11. Markus needs _____ math tutor.

12. Bashir has _____ exciting job. He is _____ pilot. He flies helicopters.

❏ **Exercise 10. Listening.** (Chart 7-2)
Listen to each sentence. Choose the word you hear.

*Example:* You will hear:     I come from a small town.
You will choose: (a)     an

1. a     an                    6. a     an
2. a     an                    7. a     an
3. a     an                    8. a     an
4. a     an                    9. a     an
5. a     an                    10. a     an

❏ **Exercise 11. Warm-up** (Chart 7-3)
Answer the questions about the nouns in the box.

| a bike | some cars | some motorcycles |
| some pollution | some traffic | a truck |

1. Which nouns are count? _____

2. Which nouns are noncount? _____

3. Which nouns are singular count? _____

4. Which nouns are plural count? _____

Can you make a rule about when to use **some?**

## 7-3 Using *A/An* vs. *Some*

| | |
|---|---|
| (a) I have *a pen*. | ***A/An*** is used in front of SINGULAR COUNT nouns.<br>In (a): The word ***pen*** is a singular count noun. |
| (b) I have ***some** pens*. | ***Some*** is used in front of PLURAL COUNT nouns.<br>In (b): The word ***pens*** is a plural count noun. |
| (c) I have ***some** rice*. | ***Some*** is used in front of NONCOUNT nouns.*<br>In (c): The word ***rice*** is a noncount noun. |

* Reminder: Noncount nouns do not have a plural form. Noncount nouns are grammatically singular.

❏ **Exercise 12. Looking at grammar.** (Chart 7-3)

Look at each noun and circle the correct word: *a, an,* or *some*. Then decide if the noun is singular count, plural count, or noncount.

| | | | | | SINGULAR COUNT | PLURAL COUNT | NONCOUNT |
|---|---|---|---|---|---|---|---|
| 1. | a | an | (some) | letters | | ✓ | |
| 2. | a | an | (some) | mail | | | ✓ |
| 3. | (a) | an | some | letter | ✓ | | |
| 4. | a | an | some | table | | | |
| 5. | a | an | some | tables | | | |
| 6. | a | an | some | furniture | | | |
| 7. | a | an | some | car | | | |
| 8. | a | an | some | automobiles | | | |
| 9. | a | an | some | buses | | | |
| 10. | a | an | some | traffic | | | |
| 11. | a | an | some | advice | | | |
| 12. | a | an | some | egg | | | |
| 13. | a | an | some | eggs | | | |
| 14. | a | an | some | hour | | | |
| 15. | a | an | some | minutes | | | |

❑ **Exercise 13. Looking at grammar.** (Chart 7-3)
Write each word from the box in the correct column.

| ✓ answer | computer | evening | ideas | uncle | word |
| ✓ boy | day | idea | mail | vocabulary | words |

| *a* | *an* | *some* |
|---|---|---|
| ___boy___ | ___answer___ | _____ |
| _____ | _____ | _____ |
| _____ | _____ | _____ |
| _____ | _____ | _____ |
| _____ | _____ | _____ |

❑ **Exercise 14. Looking at grammar.** (Chart 7-3)
Complete each sentence with *a, an,* or *some.* Is each noun singular count or noncount?

*I have . . .*

1. ___some___ fruit.      singular count    (noncount)

2. _____ apple.      singular count    noncount

3. _____ money.      singular count    noncount

4. _____ euro.      singular count    noncount

5. _____ sandwich.      singular count    noncount

6. _____ flour.      singular count    noncount

7. _____ soup.      singular count    noncount

8. _____ letter.      singular count    noncount

9. _____ information.      singular count    noncount

10. _____ water.      singular count    noncount

11. _____ word.      singular count    noncount

12. _____ homework.      singular count    noncount

13. _____ problem.      singular count    noncount

14. _____ answer.      singular count    noncount

**Exercise 15. Let's talk: small groups.** (Chart 7-3)
Work in small groups. Complete the lists with nouns. You may use adjectives with the nouns. Share some of your answers with the class.

1. things you usually see in an apartment

   a. a _____

   b. an _____

   c. some _____ (*plural noun*)

   d. some _____ (*noncount noun*)

2. things you usually see in a classroom

   a. a _____

   b. an _____

   c. some _____ (*plural noun*)

   d. some _____ (*noncount noun*)

3. things you usually see outdoors

   a. a _____

   b. an _____

   c. some _____ (*plural noun*)

   d. some _____ (*noncount noun*)

❏ **Exercise 16. Looking at grammar.** (Chart 7-3)
Complete the sentences with *a/an* or *some*.

1. Marisol is wearing ____*some*____ silver jewelry. She's wearing

   ____*a*____ necklace and ____*some*____ earrings.

2. Amir and I are busy. I have _____ homework to do.

   He has _____ work to do.

3. Asha has _____ job. She is _____ teacher.

4. We have _____ table, _____ couch, and _____ chairs
   in our living room.

5. We have _____ furniture in our living room.

6. Natalie is listening to _____ music.

7. I'm hungry. I would like _____ orange.

8. The kids are hungry. They would like _____ fruit. They would also like

   _____ cheese.

9. I need _____ information about the bus schedule.

10. I have a problem. I need _____ advice.

❑ **Exercise 17. Let's talk: pairwork.** (Chart 7-3)
Work with a partner. Use *a, an,* or *some* with the given word. Partner A: Your book is open to this page. Partner B: Your book is open to *Let's Talk: Answers,* p. 502.

*Example:* desks
PARTNER A: a desks
PARTNER B: Again?
PARTNER A: some desks
PARTNER B: Right.

   1. apple            6. word
   2. apples           7. music
   3. children         8. rice
   4. old man          9. hour
   5. men             10. island

*Change roles.*
Partner B: Your book is open to this page. Partner A: Your book is open to p. 502.

   11. animal          16. university
   12. animals         17. uncle
   13. people          18. bananas
   14. fruit           19. bread
   15. egg             20. vocabulary

❑ **Exercise 18. Looking at grammar.** (Chart 7-3)
Use the given word to complete the sentence. Add *-s* to a count noun (or give the irregular plural form). Do not add *-s* to a noncount noun.

   1. money      I need some _____ *money* _____.

   2. key        I see some _____ *keys* _____ on the table.

   3. man        Some _____ *men* _____ are standing in the street.

   4. flour      I need to buy some _____.

   5. flower     Andy wants to buy some _____ for his mom.

6. information     I need some _____.

7. jewelry     Fred is looking for some _____ for his wife.

8. child     Some _____ are playing in the park.

9. homework     I can't go to the movie because I have some _____ to do.

10. advice     Could you please give me some _____?

11. suggestion     I have some _____ for you.

12. help     I need some _____ with my homework.

13. sandwich     We're hungry. We want to make some _____.

14. animal     I see some _____ in the picture.

15. banana     The monkeys are hungry. They would like some _____.

16. water     I'm thirsty. I would like some _____.

17. weather     We're having some hot _____ right now.

18. picture     I have some _____ of my family in my wallet.

19. rice, bean     I usually have some _____ and _____ for dinner.

*Part I.* Read the story. Look at new vocabulary with your teacher first.

a coupon

some ice cream

*Do you know these words?*

on sale
brand
20% off

### A Coupon Shopper

Beth likes to shop with coupons. Coupons help her save **some** money. She usually gets coupons from newspapers, online, or in **some** stores. Today she is shopping for paper products like toilet paper and tissue. She has **a** coupon for free toilet paper. It says "Buy one package—get one free." She also wants **some** rice and butter. She doesn't have **a** coupon for rice, but her favorite rice is on sale. She has **a** coupon for butter, but it is still expensive with the coupon. She is looking for a cheaper brand. She also has **some** "20% off" coupons for frozen food. Ice cream sounds good. She loves ice cream, and she thinks **a** 20% coupon is good. Beth is happy because she is saving **some** money today.

*Part II.* Write the noun in the story that follows each word in **bold**. Can you say why *a* or *some* is used for each noun?

1. some ____money____

2. some _____

3. a _____

4. some _____

5. a _____

6. a _____

7. some _____

8. a _____

9. some _____

*Part III.* Answer the questions.

1. What do people generally buy with coupons?

2. Do people buy things they don't need when they shop with coupons?

3. Do you use coupons? Why or why not?

❑ **Exercise 20. Warm-up.** (Chart 7-4)
Answer the questions. Answers may vary.

1. What do you drink every day?

    a. _____ coffee

    b. _____ milk

    c. _____ tea

    d. _____ water

    e. _____ juice

2. What do you put your drink(s) in?

    a. _____ a cup

    b. _____ a glass

3. Which phrases sound OK to you?

    a. _____ a cup of coffee

    b. _____ a glass of water

    c. _____ a glass of coffee

    d. _____ a glass of tea

    e. _____ a cup of water

    f. _____ a cup of juice

## 7-4 Measurements with Noncount Nouns

| | |
|---|---|
| (a) I'd like **some** water. | Units of measure are used with noncount nouns to express a specific quantity. Examples: *a glass of, a cup of, a piece of.* |
| (b) I'd like **a glass of** water. | In (a): **some water** = an unspecific quantity |
| (c) I'd like **a cup of** coffee. | In (b): **a glass of water** = a specific quantity |
| (d) I'd like **a piece of** fruit. | |

COMMON EXPRESSIONS OF MEASURE

| | | |
|---|---|---|
| a bag of rice | a bunch of bananas | a jar of pickles |
| a bar of soap | a can of corn* | a loaf of bread |
| a bottle of olive oil | a carton of milk | a piece of cheese |
| a bowl of cereal | a glass of water | a sheet of paper |
| a box of candy | a head of lettuce | a tube of toothpaste |

bag      bar      bottle      box

can      carton      jar      tube      bunch

\* In British English: *a tin of corn*

❏ **Exercise 21. Vocabulary and grammar.** (Chart 7-4)

Complete the sentences. Use *a piece of, a cup of, a glass of, a bowl of*.

*I'm hungry and thirsty. I'd like . . .*

1. _____*a cup of*_____ coffee.          6. _____ soup.

2. _____ bread.          7. _____ meat.

3. _____ water.          8. _____ wine.

4. _____ tea.          9. _____ fruit.

5. _____ cheese.          10. _____ rice.


❏ **Exercise 22. Let's talk: pairwork.** (Chart 7-4)

Work with a partner. Look at the list of food and drinks. Check (✓) what you eat and drink every day. Add your own words to the list. Then tell your partner the usual <u>quantity</u> you have every day. Use *a piece of, two pieces of, a cup of, three cups of, a glass of, a bowl of*, or *one, two, a, some*, etc., in your answers. Share a few of your partner's answers with the class.

*Example:*

__✓__ egg                    __✓__ fruit

_____ banana              ____*ice cream*____

_____ coffee              ____*orange juice*____

PARTNER A:  I have one egg every day.
                I usually eat two pieces of fruit.
                I like a bowl of ice cream at night.
                I drink a glass of orange juice every morning.

List of food and drinks:

_____ egg              _____ rice

_____ soup            _____ ice cream

_____ fruit            _____ water

_____ bread          _____ chicken

_____ banana        _____ cheese

_____ apples        _____ tea

_____     _____

_____     _____

_____     _____

❑ **Exercise 23. Looking at grammar.** (Chart 7-4)
Complete the sentences with nouns.

1. I'm going to the store. I need to buy a carton of _____ *orange juice / milk / etc.* _____

2. I also need a tube of _____ and two bars of _____.

3. I need to find a can of _____ and a jar of _____.

4. I need to get a loaf of _____ and a box of _____.

5. I would like a head of _____ if it looks fresh.

6. Finally, I would like a couple of bottles of _____ and a jar of _____.

❑ **Exercise 24. Game.** (Chart 7-4)
Work in teams. Make a list of everything in the picture by completing the sentence
*I see* . . . . Try to use numbers (e.g., *three* spoons) or other units of measure (e.g., *a box of* candy). Use *a* for singular count nouns (e.g., *a fly*). Your teacher will give you a time limit. The team with the most correct answers wins.

*Example:* I see three spoons, a box of candy, a fly, etc.

❑ **Exercise 25. Let's talk: pairwork.** (Chart 7-4)
Work with a partner. Pretend that you are moving into a new apartment together. What do you need? First, make a list. Then write the things you need and indicate quantity (*two, some, a lot of*, etc.). List twenty to thirty things. Begin with *We need*.

*Example:*
PARTNER A: a couch and two beds
PARTNER B: a can opener
PARTNER A: pots and pans
PARTNER B: bookcases
PARTNER A: paint
          Etc.

*Possible answer:* We need one couch and two beds, one can opener, some pots and pans, a
            lot of bookcases, one can of paint, etc.

❏ **Exercise 26. Let's talk: pairwork.** (Chart 7-4)

Work with a partner. Complete the sentences with *a, an,* or *some* and the nouns.
Partner A:  Your book is open to this page. Partner B: Your book is open to
*Let's Talk: Answers,* p. 502. Help your partner with the correct responses if necessary.

1. *I'm hungry. I'd like* . . .
   a. food.
   b. apple.
   c. sandwich.
   d. bowl of soup.

2. *I'm thirsty. I'd like* . . .
   a. glass of milk.
   b. water.
   c. cup of tea.

3. *I'm sick. I need* . . .
   a. medicine.
   b. ambulance.

4. *I'm cold. I need* . . .
   a. coat.
   b. hat.
   c. warm clothes.★
   d. heat.

5. *I'm tired. I need* . . .
   a. sleep.
   b. break.
   c. relaxing vacation.

*Change roles.*
Partner B:  Your book is open to this page.  Partner A:  Your book is open to p. 502.

6. *I'm hungry. I'd like* . . .
   a. snack.
   b. fruit.
   c. orange.
   d. piece of chicken.

7. *I'm thirsty. I'd like* . . .
   a. juice.
   b. bottle of water.
   c. glass of iced tea.

8. *I'm sick. I need* . . .
   a. doctor.
   b. help.

9. *I'm cold. I need* . . .
   a. boots.
   b. blanket.
   c. hot bath.
   d. gloves.

10. *I'm tired. I need* . . .
    a. strong coffee.
    b. break.
    c. vacation.
    d. nap.

❏ **Exercise 27. Warm-up.** (Chart 7-5)

Which answers are true for you?

1. **Do you eat much fruit?**
   a. Yes, I eat a lot.   b. I eat a little.   c. No, I don't like fruit.

2. **Do you eat many bananas?**
   a. Yes, I eat a lot.   b. I eat a few.   c. No, I don't like bananas.

bananas

---

★*Clothes* is always plural. The word *clothes* does not have a singular form.

## 7-5 Using *Many, Much, A Few, A Little*

| | |
|---|---|
| (a) I don't get *many* letters. | *Many* is used with PLURAL COUNT nouns. |
| (b) I don't get *much* mail. | *Much* is used with NONCOUNT nouns. |
| (c) Jan gets *a few* letters. | *A few* is used with PLURAL COUNT nouns. |
| (d) Ken gets *a little* mail. | *A little* is used with NONCOUNT nouns. |

❑ **Exercise 28. Looking at grammar.** (Chart 7-5)

Complete the questions with *many* or *much*. Then give true answers. (If the answer is "zero," use "any" in the response.)

*Example:* How _____*much*_____ tea do you drink in a day?

*Possible answers:* I drink three cups.  I drink one cup.  I don't drink any tea.  Etc.

1. How _____*much*_____ money do you have in your wallet?

2. How _____*many*_____ roommates do you have?

3. How _____ languages do you speak?

4. How _____ homework does your teacher usually assign?

5. How _____ tea do you drink in a day?

6. How _____ coffee do you drink in a day?

7. How _____ sentences are there in this exercise?

8. How _____ moons does the Earth have?

❑ **Exercise 29. Grammar and speaking: pairwork.** (Chart 7-5)

Complete the sentences with *many* or *much*.  Then work with a partner.  Ask about each item.  Circle the answer your partner gives.  Who has more items in their kitchen?

*In your kitchen, do you have . . .*

1. _____*much*_____ sugar?                          Yes, I do.     No, I don't.

2. _____ paper bags?                        Yes, I do.     No, I don't.

3. _____ flour?                             Yes, I do.     No, I don't.

4. _____ salt?                              Yes, I do.     No, I don't.

5. _____ spices?                            Yes, I do.     No, I don't.

6. _____ olive oil?                         Yes, I do.     No, I don't.

7. _____ butter?                            Yes, I do.     No, I don't.

8. _____ dishwashing liquid?                Yes, I do.     No, I don't.

9. _____ cans of soup?     Yes, I do.    No, I don't.

10. _____ rolls of paper towels?    Yes, I do.    No, I don't.

❏ **Exercise 30. Looking at grammar.** (Chart 7-5)
Read the paragraph. Write *a little* or *a few* before each noun.

     Andrew is having a party, but he has a problem. He doesn't like to cook. His cabinets and refrigerator are almost empty. His friends are very surprised. When they get to his house, they find out he has only . . . .

1. _____ eggs.
2. _____ juice.
3. _____ potatoes.
4. _____ fruit.
5. _____ meat.

6. _____ vegetables.
7. _____ butter.
8. _____ ketchup.
9. _____ pieces of chicken.
10. _____ cans of soup.

❏ **Exercise 31. Looking at grammar.** (Chart 7-5)
*Part I.* Change *a lot of* to *many* or *much*.

1. Daniel has a lot of problems. → *Daniel has many problems.*
2. I don't have a lot of money.
3. I don't put a lot of sugar in my coffee.
4. I have a lot of questions to ask you.
5. Pietro and Mia have a small apartment. They don't have a lot of furniture.
6. Lara is lazy. She doesn't do a lot of work.
7. I don't drink a lot of coffee.
8. Do you send a lot of text messages?

*Part II.* Change *some* to *a few* or *a little*.

1. I need some paper. → *I need a little paper.*
2. I usually add some salt to my food.
3. I have some questions to ask you.
4. Robert needs some help. He has some problems. He needs some advice.
5. I need to buy some clothes.
6. I have some homework to do tonight.
7. When I'm hungry in the evening, I usually eat some dark chocolate.
8. We usually do some speaking exercises in class every day.

❑ **Exercise 32. Let's talk: pairwork.** (Chart 7-5)

Work with a partner. Take turns asking and answering questions. Use the words from your list. Remember, you can look at your book before you speak. When you speak, look at your partner. Use this model.

    Partner A: How **much/many** _____ would you like?
    Partner B: I'd like **a little/a few**, please. Thanks.

*Example:* chicken
PARTNER A: How **much chicken** would you like?
PARTNER B: I'd like **a little**, please. Thanks.
PARTNER A: Your turn now.

*Example:* pencil
PARTNER B: How **many pencils** would you like?
PARTNER A: I'd like **a few**, please.
PARTNER B: Your turn now.

| PARTNER A | PARTNER B |
|---|---|
| 1. pen | 1. salt |
| 2. tea | 2. banana |
| 3. book | 3. soup |
| 4. apple | 4. coffee |
| 5. money | 5. toy |
| 6. help | 6. cheese |

❑ **Exercise 33. Let's talk: small groups.** (Charts 7-1, 7-3, and 7-5)

Work in small groups. Imagine you are all famous chefs. Create a dessert using the ingredients below. Give your recipe a name (it can be funny or strange). Tell the class about your dessert. Begin with *We need a little / a few / a lot of / two / some*. OR *We don't need any*.

1. _____ salt
2. _____ flour
3. _____ honey
4. _____ sugar
5. _____ nuts
6. _____ coconut

7. _____ pieces of chocolate
8. _____ baking soda
9. _____ baking powder
10. _____ eggs
11. _____ cream
12. _____ butter

other ingredients: _____

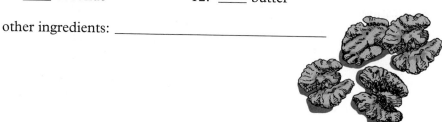

walnuts

❏ **Exercise 34. Warm-up.** (Chart 7-6)

Read the two conversations. In which conversation are Speaker A and Speaker B thinking about the same bedroom?

    1. A: Where are the kids?

       B: I think they're hiding in *a* bedroom.

    2. A: Where's Raymond?

       B: He's in *the* bedroom.

---

## 7-6 Using *The*

| | |
|---|---|
| (a) A: Where's Max?<br>    B: He's in *the kitchen*. | A speaker uses *the* when the speaker and the listener have the same thing or person in mind. *The* shows that a noun is specific (not general). |
| (b) A: I have two pieces of fruit for us, an apple and a banana. What would you like?<br>    B: I'd like *the apple*, please. | In (a): Both A and B have the same kitchen in mind.<br>In (b): When B says "the apple," both A and B have the same apple in mind. |
| (c) A: It's a nice summer day today. *The sky* is blue. *The sun* is hot.<br>    B: Yes, I really like summer. | In (c): Both A and B are thinking of the same sky (there is only one sky for them to think of) and the same sun (there is only one sun for them to think of). |
| (d) Nick has *a* pen and *a* pencil. *The* pen is blue. *The* pencil is yellow.<br><br>(e) Nick has *some* pens and pencils. *The* pens are blue. *The* pencils are yellow. | *The* is used with<br>  • singular count nouns, as in (d).<br>  • plural count nouns, as in (e).<br>  • noncount nouns, as in (f).<br>In other words, *the* is used with each of the three kinds of nouns. |
| (f) Nick has *some* rice and *some* cheese. *The* rice is white. *The* cheese is yellow. | Notice in the examples: The speaker is using *the* for the <u>second</u> mention of a noun. When the speaker mentions a noun for a second time, both the speaker and listener are now thinking about the same thing.<br>    First mention:     I have *a pen*.<br>    Second mention:  *The pen* is blue. |

---

❏ **Exercise 35. Looking at grammar.** (Chart 7-6)

Complete the sentences with *the* where necessary.

    1. Elizabeth is standing outside. It is midnight.

       a. She's looking up at _____ sky.

       b. She sees _____ moon.

       c. She doesn't see _____ sun.

       d. _____ stars are very bright.

       e. _____ planets are difficult to find.

2. Rick and Lucy are looking for an apartment to rent. Right now they are standing in an old apartment. The kitchen has a lot of problems.

a. _____ refrigerator is broken.

b. _____ faucet doesn't turn on.

c. _____ ceiling has a leak.     a faucet

d. _____ window doesn't open.

e. _____ floor has a hole in it.

❏ **Exercise 36. Looking at grammar.** (Chart 7-6)
Complete the sentences with **the** or **a/an**.

1. I have ___*a*___ notebook and _____ grammar book. _____ notebook is brown. _____ grammar book is red.

2. Right now Maurice is sitting in class. He's sitting between _____ woman and _____ man. _____ woman is Graciela. _____ man is Mustafa.

3. Hana is wearing _____ ring and _____ necklace. _____ ring is on her left hand.

4. Brad and Angela are waiting for their plane to leave. Brad is reading _____ magazine. Angela is reading _____ newspaper online. When Angela finishes _____ newspaper and Brad finishes _____ magazine, they will trade.

5. In the picture below, there are four figures: _____ circle, _____ triangle, _____ square, and _____ rectangle. _____ circle is next to _____ triangle. _____ square is between _____ triangle and _____ rectangle.

circle    triangle    square    rectangle

6. I gave my friend _____ card and _____ flower for her birthday. _____ card wished her "Happy Birthday." She liked both _____ card and _____ flower.

❏ **Exercise 37. Let's talk: pairwork.** (Chart 7-6)

Work with a partner. Read the conversation aloud using *the* or *a/an*. After you finish speaking, write the answers.

A: Look at the picture below. What do you see?

B: I see _____ chair, _____ table, _____ window, and _____ plant.
          1          2          3          4

A: Where is _____ chair?
            5

B: _____ chair is under _____ window.
      6           7

A: Where is _____ plant?
            8

B: _____ plant is beside _____ chair.
      9          10

*Change roles.*

A: Do you see any people?

B: Yes. I see _____ man and _____ woman. _____ man is standing.
            11          12          13

   _____ woman is sitting down.
      14

A: Do you see any animals?

B: Yes. I see _____ dog, _____ cat, and _____ bird in _____ cage.
            15          16          17          18

A: What is _____ dog doing?
            19

B: It's sleeping.

A: How about _____ cat?
            20

B: _____ cat is watching _____ bird.
      21          22

❑ **Exercise 38. Looking at grammar.** (Chart 7-6)

Complete the sentences with *the* or *a/an*.

1. A: I need to go shopping.  I need to buy _____ coat.

   B: I'll go with you.  I need to get _____ umbrella.

2. A: Hi!  Come in.

   B: Hi!  _____ weather is terrible today!  My umbrella is all wet.

   A: I'll take your umbrella and put it in _____ kitchen so it can dry.

3. A: Gloria has _____ great job.  She builds websites.  Her company gives her

   _____ new computer every year.

   B: Wow!  She's lucky.

4. A: How much longer do you need to use _____ computer?

   B: Just five more minutes, and then you can have it.

5. A: I need _____ stamp for this letter.  Do you have one?

   B: Right here.

6. A: Would you like _____ egg for breakfast?

   B: No thanks.  I'll just have _____ glass of juice and some toast.

   some toast

   a toaster

7. A: Do you see my pen?  I can't find it.

   B: There it is.  It's on _____ floor.

   A: Oh.  I see it.  Thanks.

8. A: Could you answer _____ phone?  Thanks.

   B: Hello?

❑ **Exercise 39. Game.** (Chart 7-6)

Work in teams.  Answer the questions.  One person on each team writes the answers.  You have five minutes.  The team with the most grammatically correct answers wins.

1. What's on the floor?

   _____ *Some desks, a piece of gum, some dirt, a garbage can, etc.* _____

2. What's on the ceiling?

3. What's out in the hallway?

4. What's outside the window?

5. What's on the board (chalkboard, whiteboard, or bulletin board)?

❑ **Exercise 40. Warm-up.** (Chart 7-7)

Which sentence (a. or b.) is true for each statement?

1. Bananas are expensive right now.
   a. Only some bananas are expensive.
   b. Bananas in general are expensive.

2. The bananas are green.
   a. A specific group of bananas is green.
   b. Bananas in general are green.

## 7-7 Using Ø (No Article) to Make Generalizations

| | |
|---|---|
| (a) **Ø** *Apples* are good for you.<br>(b) **Ø** *Students* use **Ø** *pens* and **Ø** *pencils.*<br>(c) I like to listen to **Ø** *music.*<br>(d) **Ø** *Rice* is good for you. | No article (symbolized by **Ø**) is used to make generalizations with<br>• plural count nouns, as in (a) and (b), and<br>• noncount nouns, as in (c) and (d). |
| (e) Tim and Jan ate some fruit.<br>***The*** *apples* were very good, but ***the*** *bananas* were too old.<br><br>(f) We went to a concert last night.<br>***The*** *music* was very good. | COMPARE: In (a), the word ***apples*** is general. It refers to all apples, any apples. No article (**Ø**) is used.<br>In (e), the word ***apples*** is specific, so ***the*** is used in front of it. It refers to the specific apples that Tim and Jan ate.<br><br>COMPARE: In (c), ***music*** is general. In (f), ***the music*** is specific. |

❑ **Exercise 41. Looking at grammar.** (Chart 7-7)

Decide if the words in **bold** are general or specific.

| | | |
|---|---|---|
| 1. The **eggs** are delicious. | general | specific |
| 2. Are **eggs** healthy? | general | specific |
| 3. Please pass the **salt**. | general | specific |
| 4. I love **salt**! | general | specific |
| 5. **Apples** have vitamin C. | general | specific |
| 6. The **apples** have brown spots. | general | specific |

❑ **Exercise 42. Looking at grammar.** (Chart 7-7)

Complete the sentences with ***the*** or **Ø** (no article).

1. Oranges are orange, and ____Ø____ bananas are yellow.

2. Everybody needs _____ food to live.

3. We ate at a good restaurant last night. _____ food was excellent.

4. _____ salt tastes salty, and _____ pepper tastes hot.

5. _____ coffee has caffeine.

6. _____ coffee in the pot is fresh.

7. _____ pages in this book are full of grammar exercises.

8. _____ books have _____ pages.

9. I like _____ fruit. I also like _____ vegetables.

lettuce

a tomato   broccoli

celery

vegetables

❑ **Exercise 43. Listening.** (Charts 7-6 and 7-7)

Listen to each sentence. Decide if the given noun has a general or a specific meaning.

1. vegetables            (general)    specific

2. cats                  general      specific

3. teacher               general      specific

4. bananas               general      specific

5. cars                  general      specific

6. car                   general      specific

7. computers             general      specific

8. park                  general      specific

❑ **Exercise 44. Let's talk.** (Charts 7-3, 7-6, and 7-7)

Work in small groups or as a class. Choose the sentence that is closest in meaning to the given situation. Discuss the differences.

1. Mark is at an electronics store. There are five tablets. He buys one.
   a. He buys a tablet.
   b. He buys the tablet.

2. Pat is at a music store. There is only one guitar on the shelf. She buys it.
   a. She buys a guitar.
   b. She buys the guitar.

a tablet computer

3. Martha is at the library. There is one book about Nelson Mandela.
   a. She checks out the book about Nelson Mandela.
   b. She checks out a book about Nelson Mandela.

4. Misako walks outside and looks up at the sky.
   a. She sees the sun.
   b. She sees a sun.

5. Horses are my favorite animals.
   a. I love the horses.
   b. I love horses.

6. There are fifty cars in a parking lot. Ten cars are white.
   a. The cars in the parking lot are white.
   b. Some cars in the parking lot are white.

**Exercise 45. Listening.** (Charts 7-1 → 7-7)

Listen to the sentences and write the words you hear. Use *a, an,* or *the.*

1. A: Do you have ____*a*____ pen?

   B: There's one on _____ counter in _____ kitchen.

2. A: Where are _____ keys to _____ car?

   B: I'm not sure. You can use mine.

3. A: Shh. I hear _____ noise.

   B: It's just _____ bird outside, probably _____ woodpecker.
   Don't worry.

4. A: Henry Jackson teaches at _____ university.

   B: I know. He's _____ English professor.

   A: He's also the head of _____ department.

5. A: Hurry! We're late.

   B: No, we're not. It's five o'clock, and we have _____ hour.

   A: No, we don't. It's six! Look at _____ clock.

   B: Oops. I need _____ new battery for my watch.

❑ **Exercise 46. Warm-up.** (Chart 7-8)

Which words can complete each sentence?

1. I have   some fruit / some oranges / any oranges.

2. I don't have   some fruit / any fruit / any oranges.

3. Do you have   some fruit / some oranges / any fruit / any oranges?

## 7-8 Using *Some* and *Any*

| AFFIRMATIVE | (a) Vera has **some** money. | Use **some** in affirmative statements. |
|---|---|---|
| NEGATIVE | (b) Vera doesn't have **any** money. | Use **any** in negative statements. |
| QUESTION | (c) Does Vera have **any** money?<br>(d) Does Vera have **some** money? | Use either **some** or **any** in a question. |
| (e) I don't have **any** money. (noncount noun)<br>(f) I don't have **any** matches. (plural count noun) | | **Any** is used with noncount nouns and plural count nouns. |

❑ **Exercise 47. Looking at grammar.** (Chart 7-8)
Complete the sentences with *some* or *any*.

1. Harry has ___some___ money.

2. I don't have ___any___ money.

3. Do you have ___some / any___ money?

4. Do you need _____ help?

5. No, thank you. I don't need _____ help.

6. Kalil needs _____ help.

7. Diana usually doesn't get _____ mail.

8. We don't have _____ fruit in the apartment. We don't have _____ apples, _____ bananas, or _____ oranges.

9. The house is empty. There aren't _____ people in the house.

10. I need _____ paper. Do you have _____ paper?

11. Heidi can't write a letter because she doesn't have _____ paper.

12. Sasha is getting along fine. He doesn't have _____ problems.

13. I need to go to the grocery store. I need to buy _____ food. Do you need to buy _____ groceries?

14. I'm not busy tonight. I don't have _____ homework to do.

15. I don't have _____ money in my wallet.

16. There are _____ beautiful flowers in my garden this year.


❑ **Exercise 48. Let's talk: interview.** (Chart 7-8)
Walk around the room. Interview your classmates. Use this model.
Student A: Do you have some/any ____?
Student B: Yes, I have some ____. OR No, I don't have any ____.

1. pencils with erasers
2. notebook paper
3. money in your pocket
4. children

5. stepchildren
6. pets
7. worries
8. advice for me

Now share some of your answers with the rest of the class.

❑ **Exercise 49. Let's talk: small groups.** (Chart 7-8)

Work in small groups. You are at a mall. You have a gift card for your group. The amount is equal to the cost of a new computer. What do you want to buy for your group? What don't you want to buy? Add two more suggestions to the list.

| | | | |
|---|---|---|---|
| camera | music CD | socks | video game |
| DVD | perfume | software | winter jacket |
| hat | pet | suitcase | _____ |
| jewelry | shoe | summer clothes | _____ |

1. We want to buy some / a lot of / two . . . .

2. We don't want to buy any . . . .

❑ **Exercise 50. Looking at grammar.** (Chapters 6 and 7)

Complete the sentences with these words. If necessary, use the plural form.

| | | | |
|---|---|---|---|
| bush | glass | ✓ match | strawberry |
| centimeter | homework | page | thief |
| dish | inch | paper | tray |
| edge | information | piece | valley |
| fish | knife | sex | weather |
| foot | leaf | size | woman |

1. I want to light a candle. I need some _____ *matches* _____ .

2. _____ fall from the trees in autumn.

3. The application asked for my name, address, and _____: male or female.

4. Some _____ , forks, and spoons are on the table.

5. I want to take the bus downtown, but I don't know the bus schedule. I need some _____ about the bus schedule.

6. I need to write a composition. I have a pen, but I need some _____.

7. Plates and bowls are called _____.

8. Married _____ are called wives.

9. There are a lot of trees and _____ in the park.

10. Ike is studying. He has a lot of _____ to do.

11. My dictionary has 437 _____.

12. This puzzle has 200 _____.

13. A piece of paper has four _____.

14. Mountains are high, and _____ are low.

15. When the temperature is around 35°C (77°F), I'm comfortable. But I don't like very hot _____.

16. _____ steal things: money, jewelry, cars, etc.

17. _____ are small, red, sweet, and delicious.

18. People carry their food on _____ at a cafeteria.

19. Sweaters in a store usually come in four _____: small, medium, large, and extra large.

20. In some countries, people usually use cups for their tea. In other countries, they use _____ for their tea.

21. Toshiro has five _____ in his aquarium.

22. There are 100 _____ in a meter.

23. There are 12 _____ in a foot.*

24. There are 3 _____ in a yard.*

❏ **Exercise 51. Check your knowledge.** (Chapter 7)
Correct the mistakes.

        *some*
1. I need ~~an~~ advice from you.

2. I don't like hot weathers.

3. I usually have a egg for breakfast.

4. Sun rises every morning.

5. The students in this class do a lot of homeworks every day.

6. How many language do you know?

7. I don't have many money.

8. Alexander and Carmen don't have some children.

9. A pictures are beautiful. You're a good photographer.

---

*1 inch = 2.54 centimeters; 1 foot = 30.48 centimeters; 1 yard = 0.91 meters

10. There isn't a traffic early in the morning.

11. I can't find any bowl for my soup.

❑ **Exercise 52. Let's talk.** (Chapter 7)

Imagine that a new shopping center is coming to your neighborhood. It will have a drugstore, a bank, and a grocery store. Decide what additional stores you want. Your teacher will help you with any vocabulary you don't know.

***Part I.*** Choose any six businesses from the list and write their names in any of the five available spaces on Blueprint #1 on this page.

| | | |
|---|---|---|
| ✓ a bank | ✓ a grocery store | a post office |
| a bookstore | an ice-cream shop | a shoe store |
| a camera shop | an Internet café | a sports equipment store |
| ✓ a drugstore | a laundromat | a vegetarian food store |
| a drycleaner's | a movie theater | a video rental store |
| an exercise gym | a music store | |
| a fast-food restaurant | a pet supply store | |

Blueprint #1
(your business locations)

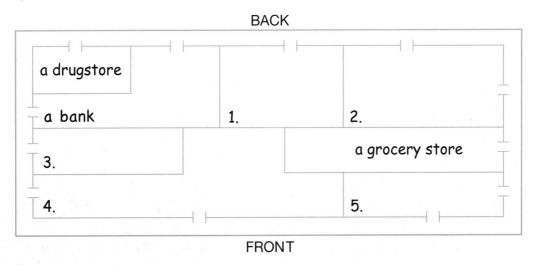

***Part II.*** Work with a partner, but do not look at each other's blueprints. Ask your partner about the location of his/her new businesses. Write your partner's answers on your copy of Blueprint #2 on p. 222. Use this pattern:

Partner A: Is there **a/an** . . . ?
Partner B: Yes, there is. / No, there isn't.
Partner A: Where is **the** . . . ?
Partner B: It's next to / beside / in back of / in front of **the** . . . .

*Example:*

PARTNER A: Is there **an** exercise gym?
PARTNER B: No, there isn't.
PARTNER A: Is there **a** bank?
PARTNER B: Yes, there is.
PARTNER A: Where is **the** bank?
PARTNER B: It's in front of **the** drugstore.

Blueprint #2
(your partner's business locations)

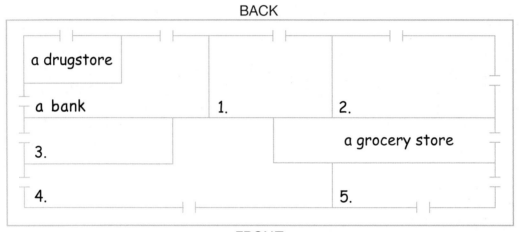

BACK

a drugstore

a bank 1. 2.

a grocery store

3.

4. 5.

FRONT

❑ **Exercise 53. Reading, grammar, and writing.** (Chapter 7)
***Part I.*** Read the story.

### A Day at the Park

It is a beautiful day. Some people are at a park. A woman is sitting on a blanket. She is having a picnic. A little girl nearby is smelling some flowers. An older man is standing near a pond. He is pointing at some toy boats. Two boys are riding their bikes. A man and a woman are sitting on a bench. The woman is knitting. The man is feeding some birds. Some ducks are swimming, and a cat wants to catch them. The cat is hungry.

**Part II.** Write *a, an,* or *some* in front of each word according to the paragraph. Is the article usage clear to you?

1. _____ beautiful day

2. _____ people

3. _____ park

4. _____ woman

5. _____ blanket

6. _____ picnic

7. _____ little girl

8. _____ flowers

9. _____ older man

10. _____ pond

11. _____ toy boats

12. _____ man and
     _____ woman

13. _____ bench

14. _____ woman

15. _____ man

16. _____ birds

17. _____ ducks

18. _____ cat

19. _____ cat

**Part III.** Describe the picture. Begin with *It is a* _____ *day*. Make sure to use *a, an,* and *some*.

**Part IV.** Editing check: Work individually or change papers with a partner. Check (✓) for the following:

1. ____ indented paragraph

2. ____ capital letter at the beginning of each sentence

3. ____ period at the end of each sentence

4. ____ a verb in every sentence

5. ____ correct use of *a, an, some*

6. ____ *-s/-es* endings for plural nouns

7. ____ correct spelling (use a dictionary or spell-check)

# Chapter **8**

# Expressing Past Time, Part 1

❑ **Exercise 1. Warm-up.** (Chart 8-1)
Read the statements and choose the answers.

1. I am tired now.                           yes     no

2. I was tired two hours ago.                yes     no

3. Some students are absent today.           yes     no

4. Some students were absent yesterday.      yes     no

## 8-1 Using *Be:* Past Time

| PRESENT TIME | PAST TIME |
|---|---|
| (a) I *am* in class *today*. | (d) I *was* in class *yesterday*. |
| (b) Alison *is* sick *today*. | (e) Alison *was* sick *yesterday*. |
| (c) My friends *are* at home *today*. | (f) My friends *were* at home *yesterday*. |

SIMPLE PAST TENSE OF *BE*

| SINGULAR | PLURAL |
|---|---|
| **I was** | **we were** |
| **you were** (one person) | **you were** (more than one person) |
| **she was** | **they were** |
| **he was** | |
| **it was** | |

I
she
he          } + *was*
it

we
you         } + *were*
they

❑ **Exercise 2. Looking at grammar.** (Chart 8-1)
Complete the sentences with *was* or *were*.

TODAY                                    YESTERDAY

1. You are at school.          You _____*were*_____ at home.

2. We are at school.           We _____ at home.

3. He is at school.            He _____ at home.

4. You and I are at school.  You and I _____ at home.

5. She is at school.  She _____ at home.

6. They are at school.  They _____ at home.

7. Brian and James are at school.  Brian and James _____ at home.

8. My parents are at school.  My parents _____ at home.

9. I am at school.  I _____ at home.

10. The teacher is at school.  The teacher _____ at home.

❏ **Exercise 3. Looking at grammar.** (Chart 8-1)
Change the sentences to past time.

1. Bashar is in class today. → *He was in class yesterday too.*

2. I'm in class today. → *I was in class yesterday too.*

3. Martina is at the library today.

4. We're in class today.

5. You're busy today.

6. I'm happy today.

7. The classroom is hot today.

8. Elise is in her office today.

9. Tony is in his office today.

10. Noor and Eli are in their offices today.

❏ **Exercise 4. Let's talk.** (Chart 8-1)
*Part I.* Think about yourself as a three-year-old child. Check (✓) the words that describe you best.

| ____ quiet | ____ loud | ____ afraid |
| ____ shy | ____ smart | ____ friendly |
| ____ funny | ____ curious | ____ a troublemaker |

*Part II.* Work with a partner. Tell your partner about yourself. Begin with *I was . . . .*

❑ **Exercise 5. Warm-up.** (Chart 8-2)
Choose the correct verb to make true sentences.

**The weather**

1. Last month, it    was / was not    nice.

2. The weekends    were / were not    sunny.

3. Yesterday, it    was / was not    hot.

---

## 8-2 Simple Past Tense of *Be:* Negative

| | |
|---|---|
| (a) I **was not** in class yesterday. <br> (b) I **wasn't** in class yesterday. | NEGATIVE CONTRACTIONS <br> **was** + **not** = **wasn't** <br> **were** + **not** = **weren't** |
| (c) They **were not** at home last night. <br> (d) They **weren't** at home last night. | I <br> she <br> he   } + wasn't     we <br> it            you } + weren't <br>            they |

---

❑ **Exercise 6. Looking at grammar.** (Chart 8-2)
Complete the sentences with **wasn't** or **weren't**.

*Joe and JoAnn went on a trip. They were very happy because . . .*

1. the airplane ride _____ *wasn't* _____ long.

2. the trains _____ slow.

3. the hotel _____ expensive.

4. the restaurants _____ expensive.

5. the tourist areas _____ crowded.

6. the language _____ difficult.

7. the weather _____ cold.

❑ **Exercise 7. Grammar and speaking.** (Chart 8-2)
Use the given words to make true sentences. Share some of your answers with the class.

*Yesterday at noon, I was/wasn't . . .*

1. hungry.
2. tired.
3. at home.
4. at school.
5. with my family.

6. sick.
7. in the hospital.
8. on an airplane.
9. outdoors.
10. at the movies.

**Exercise 8. Listening.** **(Charts 8-1 and 8-2)**

Listen to the sentences. Choose the verbs you hear.

*Example:* You will hear:    I was at school all day yesterday.

You will choose: (was)    wasn't

1. was        wasn't
2. was        wasn't
3. was        wasn't
4. was        wasn't
5. was        wasn't
6. was        wasn't
7. were       weren't
8. were       weren't
9. were       weren't
10. were      weren't

❏ **Exercise 9. Warm-up: pairwork.** **(Chart 8-3)**

Work with a partner. Ask these questions.

*Last night at midnight,*

1. were you asleep?
2. were you on the phone?
3. was it quiet at your home?

## 8-3 Past of *Be:* Questions

| YES/NO QUESTIONS | SHORT ANSWER | (LONG ANSWER) |
|---|---|---|
| (a) **Were** **you** in class yesterday?<br>*(be)* + *(subject)* | → **Yes, I was.**<br>→ **No, I wasn't.** | (I was in class yesterday.)<br>(I wasn't in class yesterday.) |
| (b) **Was** **Carlos** tired last night?<br>*(be)* + *(subject)* | → **Yes, he was.**<br>**No, he wasn't.** | (He was tired last night.)<br>(He wasn't tired last night.) |
| INFORMATION QUESTIONS | SHORT ANSWER | (LONG ANSWER) |
| (c) **Where** **were** **you** yesterday?<br>*Where* + *(be)* + *(subject)* | → **In class.** | (I was in class yesterday.) |
| (d) **When** **was** **Emily** sick?<br>*When* + *(be)* + *(subject)* | → **Last week.** | (She was sick last week.) |

Make questions and give short answers. Use the words from the box.

> at the airport      in Iceland
> at the dentist      in the hospital
> ✓ at the library

1. (*you \ at home \ last night*)

   A: _____*Were you at home last night?*_____

   B: No, _____*I wasn't.*_____

   A: Where _____*were you?*_____

   B: I _____*was at the library.*_____

2. (*Mr. Gupta \ at work \ last week*)

   A: _____

   B: No, _____

   A: Where _____

   B: He _____

3. (*Oscar and Anya \ at the train station \ at midnight*)

   A: _____

   B: No, _____

   A: Where _____

   B: They _____

4. (*Gabriella \ at the gym \ yesterday afternoon*)

   A: _____

   B: No, _____

   A: Where _____

   B: She _____

5. (*you and your family \ in Canada \ last year*)

A: _____

B: No, _____

A: Where _____

B: We _____

Iceland

❑ **Exercise 11. Let's talk: class activity.** (Chart 8-3)
Think about your first day in this class. Check (✓) the words that describe your feelings that day. Then answer your teacher's questions.

*Example:* happy
   TEACHER: Were you happy the first day of class?
STUDENT A: Yes, I was happy.
STUDENT B: No, I wasn't happy.
   TEACHER: (*to Student C*) Tell me about (*Student A*) and (*Student B*).
STUDENT C: (*Student A*) was happy. (*Student B*) wasn't happy.

1. ____ excited

2. ____ scared/afraid

3. ____ nervous

4. ____ relaxed (not nervous)

5. ____ quiet

6. ____ talkative

❑ **Exercise 12. Let's talk: pairwork.** (Chart 8-3)
Work with a partner. Take turns making questions orally. After you finish, write the verbs.

SITUATION: You went on a roller coaster ride with a friend yesterday.

1. _____*Was*_____ it fun?

2. _____ it scary?

3. _____ you afraid?

4. _____ the ride long?

5. _____ you sick afterwards?

6. _____ your friend sick?

7. _____ you nervous?

8. _____ your friend nervous?

9. _____ the ride safe?

10. _____ you tired?

❏ **Exercise 13. Looking at grammar.** (Chapter 2 and Chart 8-3)
Make questions and give short answers.

1. (*you \ in class \ yesterday*)

   A: _____Were you in class yesterday?_____

   B: Yes, _____I was._____

2. (*Claire \ in class \ today*)

   A: _____Is Claire in class today?_____

   B: No, _____she isn't._____ She's absent.

3. (*you \ tired \ last night*)

   A: _____

   B: Yes, _____ I went to bed early.

4. (*you \ hungry \ right now*)

   A: _____

   B: No, _____, but I'm thirsty.

5. (*the weather \ hot in New York City \ last summer*)

   A: _____

   B: Yes, _____ It was very hot.

6. (*the weather \ cold in Alaska \ in the winter*)

   A: _____

   B: Yes, _____ It's very cold.

7. (*Astrid and Mohammed \ here \ yesterday afternoon*)

   A: _____

   B: Yes, _____

8. (*the students \ in this class \ intelligent*)

   A: _____

   B: Of course _____ They are very intelligent!

9. (*Mr. Tok \ absent \ today*)

   A: _____

   B: Yes, _____

   A: Where _____

   B: _____

10. (*Tony and Benito \ at the party \ last night*)

A: _____

B: No, _____

A: Where _____

B: _____

11. (*Amy \ out of town \ last week*)

A: _____

B: Yes, _____

A: Where _____

B: _____

12. (*Mr. and Mrs. Sanchez \ in town \ this week*)

A: _____

B: No, _____ They're out of town.

A: Oh?  Where _____

B: _____

❏ **Exercise 14.  Let's talk: find someone who . . . .** (Charts 8-2 and 8-3)
Interview your classmates about their days in elementary school.  Make questions with
**was/were.**  Find people who can answer *yes* to your questions.  Write down their names.

*Example:* you \ shy
STUDENT A:  Were you shy?
STUDENT B:  No, I wasn't.
STUDENT A:  (*to Student C*) Were you shy?
STUDENT C:  Yes, I was.

| | FIRST NAME | | FIRST NAME |
|---|---|---|---|
| 1. you \ shy | | 7. you \ noisy | |
| 2. you \ outgoing★ | | 8. you \ athletic | |
| 3. you \ talkative | | 9. you \ active | |
| 4. you \ happy | | 10. you \ well-behaved | |
| 5. you \ hardworking | | 11. you \ a serious student | |
| 6. you \ quiet | | 12. you \ artistic | |

★*outgoing* = not shy

**Exercise 15. Warm-up.** (Chart 8-4)
Check (✓) your activities this morning.  What do you notice about the verb endings?

*Earlier today, I . . .*

1. _____ washed my face.

2. _____ brushed my teeth.

3. _____ combed my hair.

4. _____ shaved.

## 8-4 Simple Past Tense: Using *-ed*

| | | | | | | verb + *-ed* = simple past tense |
|---|---|---|---|---|---|---|
| SIMPLE PRESENT | (a) I | *walk* | to school | *every day*. | | |
| SIMPLE PAST* | (b) I | *walked* | to school | *yesterday*. | I you she he it we they | + walked (verb + *-ed*) |
| SIMPLE PRESENT | (c) Ann | *walks* | to school | *every day*. | | |
| SIMPLE PAST | (d) Ann | *walked* | to school | *yesterday*. | | |

*For pronunciation of the simple past tense, see Appendix Chart A5-3, p. 488.

❑ **Exercise 16. Looking at grammar.** (Chart 8-4)
Complete the sentences orally.  Use the simple past.  Then write the answers.

1. Every day I walk to work.  Yesterday I _____ *walked* _____ to work.

2. Every day I work.  Yesterday I _____.

3. Every day Nabeel shaves.  Yesterday Nabeel _____.

4. Every night Paula watches TV.  Last night she _____ TV.

5. Every day you exercise.  Last night you _____.

6. Every day people smile.  Yesterday they _____.

7. Every week it rains.  Last week it _____.

8. Every day we ask questions.  Yesterday we _____ questions.

9. Every day I talk on the phone.  Yesterday I _____ on the phone.

10. Every day Tomo listens to music.  Yesterday he _____ to music.

❏ **Exercise 17. Let's talk: pairwork.** (Chart 8-4)
Work with a partner. Check (✓) all your activities yesterday. Tell your partner about
them. Begin with *Yesterday I . . . .* Share a few of your partner's answers with the class.

1. ____ ask the teacher a question

2. ____ cook dinner

3. ____ wash some clothes

4. ____ listen to music on the radio

5. ____ use a computer

6. ____ stay home in the evening

7. ____ walk in a park

8. ____ watch TV

9. ____ work at my desk

10. ____ wait for a bus

11. ____ smile at several people

12. ____ talk on a cell phone

13. ____ dream in English

14. ____ dream in my language

❏ **Exercise 18. Looking at grammar.** (Chart 8-4)
Complete the sentences. Use the simple present or the simple past of the verbs from
the box.

| | | | |
|---|---|---|---|
| ask | erase | smile | walk |
| cook | ✓ rain | stay | watch |
| dream | shave | wait | work |

1. It often _____ *rains* _____ in the morning. It _____ *rained* _____
   yesterday.

2. I _____ to school every morning. I _____
   to school yesterday morning.

3. Sara often _____ questions. She _____
   a question in class yesterday.

4. I _____ a movie on television last night. I usually
   _____ TV in the evening because I want to improve my English.

5. Mario _____ his own dinner yesterday evening. He
   _____ his own dinner every evening.

6. I usually _____ home at night because I have to study.
   I _____ home last night.

7. I have a job at the library. I _____ at the library every evening.
   I _____ there yesterday evening.

8. When I am asleep, I often _____. I _____ about

   my family last night.*

9. Linda usually _____ for the bus at a bus stop in front of her

   apartment building. She _____ for the bus there yesterday

   morning.

10. The teacher _____ some words from the board a couple of minutes

    ago. He used his hand instead of an eraser.

11. Our teacher is a warm, friendly person. She often _____ when she

    talks to us.

12. Rick doesn't have a beard anymore. He _____ it five days ago.

    Now he _____ every morning.

❏ **Exercise 19. Vocabulary and listening.** (Chapter 3 and Chart 8-4)
   The simple past tense ending can be difficult to hear. Listen to each sentence and choose
   the verb you hear. Look at new vocabulary with your teacher first.

   *Example:* You will hear:     Jeremy loves soccer.

           You will choose:  love     (loves)     loved

   **A soccer coach**

   | | | |
   |---|---|---|
   | 1. work | works | worked |
   | 2. play | plays | played |
   | 3. play | plays | played |
   | 4. score | scores | scored |
   | 5. help | helps | helped |
   | 6. learn | learns | learned |
   | 7. watch | watches | watched |
   | 8. like | likes | liked |
   | 9. work | works | worked |
   | 10. work | works | worked |

   > **Do you know these words?**
   >
   > coach
   > tournament
   > score
   > goals

   ---

   *The past of *dream* can be *dreamed* or *dreamt*.

❑ **Exercise 20. Warm-up.** *(Chart 8-5)*
Choose the correct time words to make true sentences.

1. I was at home   yesterday morning / one hour ago / yesterday evening.

2. I watched TV   last weekend / last night / yesterday afternoon.

3. I talked to someone in my family   last month / last week / an hour ago.

## 8-5 Past Time Words: *Yesterday, Last,* and *Ago*

| PRESENT | | PAST | Note the changes in time expressions from present to past. |
|---|---|---|---|
| today | → | yesterday | |
| this morning | → | yesterday morning | |
| this afternoon | → | yesterday afternoon | |
| this evening | → | yesterday evening | |
| tonight | → | last night | |
| this week | → | last week | |

**REFERENCE LIST: TIME EXPRESSIONS**

| *YESTERDAY* | *LAST* | *AGO* |
|---|---|---|
| (a) Bob was here . . .<br>*yesterday.*<br>*yesterday morning.*<br>*yesterday afternoon.*<br>*yesterday evening.* | (b) Sue was here . . .<br>*last night.*<br>*last week.*<br>*last weekend.*<br>*last month.*<br>*last year.*<br><br>*last spring.*<br>*last summer.*<br>*last fall.*<br>*last winter.*<br><br>*last Monday.*<br>*last Tuesday.*<br>*last Wednesday.*<br>etc. | (c) Tom was here . . .<br>*five minutes ago.*<br>*two hours ago.*<br>*three days ago.*<br>*a (one) week ago.*<br>*six months ago.*<br>*a (one) year ago.* |

NOTICE

In (a): *yesterday* is used with *morning, afternoon,* and *evening.*

In (b): *last* is used with *night,* with long periods of time (*week, month, year*), with seasons (*spring, summer,* etc.), and with days of the week.

In (c): *ago* means "in the past." It follows specific lengths of time (e.g., *two minutes + ago, five years + ago*).

❏ **Exercise 21. Looking at grammar.** (Chart 8-5)
Complete the sentences with *yesterday* or *last*.

1. *I worked in the university bookstore . . .*

    a. _____ *last* _____ Friday.

    b. _____ week.

    c. _____ fall.

    d. _____ month.

    e. _____ year.

    f. _____ summer.

2. *I visited my cousins . . .*

    a. _____ night.

    b. _____ evening.

    c. _____ morning.

    d. _____ afternoon.

    e. _____ Sunday.

    f. _____ spring.


❏ **Exercise 22. Looking at grammar.** (Chart 8-5)
Complete the sentences. Use a past time expression and *wasn't* or *weren't*.

1. I'm at home tonight, but _____ *I wasn't at home last night.* _____

2. I am here today, but _____

3. Kaya is busy today, but _____

4. Mack and Carly are at work this afternoon, but _____

5. Ben is at the library tonight, but _____

6. You're here today, but _____

7. Dr. Ruckman is in her office this morning, but _____

8. It's cold this week, but _____

9. We're tired this evening, but _____

❑ **Exercise 23. Looking at grammar.** (Chart 8-5)
Use the information in the calendar to complete the sentences about Ken's activities.
Use a time expression from Chart 8-5.

| JUNE | | | | | | |
|---|---|---|---|---|---|---|
| **Sunday** | **Monday** | **Tuesday** | **Wednesday** | **Thursday** | **Friday** | **Saturday** |
| | | | | | | 1 |
| 2 | 3 | 4 | 5 | 6<br>*3:00 p.m.*<br>*doctor/Dad* | 7 | 8 |
| 9 | 10 | 11 | 12 | 13<br>*London* | 14 | 15 |
| 16<br>*Paris* | 17<br>*home* | 18<br>*dance*<br>*class/Ava* | 19<br>*10:00*<br>*a.m. dentist*<br>*movie/Sam* | 20<br>TODAY | 21 | 22 |
| 23 | 24 | 25 | 26 | 27 | 28 | 29 |
| 30 | | | | | | |

**Today is the 20th.**

1. ___*Three days ago*___, Ken ___*was*___ at home.

2. _____, he _____ in Paris.

3. _____, he _____ in London.

4. _____, he _____ at the dentist.

5. _____, Ken and his dad _____ at the doctor.

6. _____, Ken and Sam _____ at a movie.

7. _____, Ken and Ava _____ at a dance class.

**Exercise 24. Looking at grammar.** (Chart 8-5)
Complete the sentences with your own words. Use **ago**.

1. I'm in class now, but I was at home _____ *ten minutes ago / two hours ago / etc.* _____

2. I'm in class today, but I was absent from class _____

3. I'm in this country now, but I was in my country _____

4. I was in (*name of a city*) _____

5. I was in elementary school _____

6. I arrived in this city _____

7. There is a nice park in this city. I was at the park _____

8. We finished Exercise 16 _____

9. I was home in bed _____

10. It rained in this city _____

❏ **Exercise 25. Listening.** (Chart 8-5)
*Part I.* Write the date.

Today's date is _____ .

Listen to the questions. Write the dates.

1. _____     5. _____

2. _____     6. _____

3. _____     7. _____

4. _____

*Part II.* Write the time.

Right now the time is _____ .

Listen to the questions. Write the times.

1. _____

2. _____

3. _____

□ **Exercise 26. Warm-up.** (Chart 8-6)
Read the information about Jerry. Complete the sentences. Change the verbs in red to present time.

**Last Night**

Last night, Jerry ate dinner at 7:00. Then he did his homework for two hours. At 10:00, he went to bed.

**Every Night**

Every night, Jerry _____ dinner at 7:00. Then he _____
                          1                                              2

his homework for two hours. At 10:00, he _____ to bed.
                                                  3

## 8-6 Simple Past Tense: Irregular Verbs (Group 1)

Some verbs do not have **-ed** forms. Their past forms are irregular.

| PRESENT | | SIMPLE PAST | |
|---|---|---|---|
| come | – | came | (a) I **come** to class *every day*. |
| do | – | did | (b) I **came** to class *yesterday*. |
| eat | – | ate | |
| get | – | got | (c) I **do** my homework *every day*. |
| go | – | went | (d) I **did** my homework *yesterday*. |
| have | – | had | |
| put | – | put | (e) Meg **eats** breakfast *every morning*. |
| see | – | saw | (f) Meg **ate** breakfast *yesterday morning*. |
| sit | – | sat | |
| sleep | – | slept | |
| stand | – | stood | |
| write | – | wrote | |

□ **Exercise 27. Vocabulary and speaking.** (Chart 8-6)
Practice using irregular verbs. Close your book for this activity.

*Example:* **come–came**
   TEACHER: come–came. I come to class every day. I came to class yesterday.
            What did I do yesterday?
   STUDENTS: (*repeat*) come–came. You came to class yesterday.

1. **do–did**   We do exercises in class every day. We did exercises yesterday. What did we do yesterday?

2. **eat–ate**   I eat lunch at 12:00 every day. Yesterday I ate lunch at 12:00. What did I do at 12:00 yesterday?

3. ***get–got*** I get up early every day. I got up early yesterday. What did I do yesterday? Did you get up early yesterday? What time did you get up?

4. ***go–went*** I go downtown every day. I went downtown yesterday. What did I do yesterday? Did you go downtown? Where did you go?

5. ***have–had*** I have breakfast every morning. I had breakfast yesterday morning. I had toast and fruit. What did I have yesterday morning? What did you have for breakfast yesterday morning?

6. ***put–put*** I like hats. I put on a hat every day. I put on a hat yesterday. What did I do yesterday?

7. ***see–saw*** I see my best friend every day. Yesterday I saw my best friend. What did I do yesterday? Did you see your best friend? Who did you see?

8. ***sit–sat*** I usually sit at my desk in the mornings. I sat at my desk yesterday morning. What did I do yesterday morning?

9. ***sleep–slept*** Sometimes I sleep for a long time at night. I slept for 10 hours last night. What did I do last night? Did you sleep for 10 hours last night? How many hours did you sleep last night?

10. ***stand–stood*** I stand at the bus stop every day. I stood at the bus stop yesterday. What did I do yesterday?

11. ***write–wrote*** I usually write in my journal every day. I wrote in my journal yesterday. What did I do yesterday? Did you write in your journal? What did you write about?

❑ **Exercise 28. Let's talk: pairwork.** (Chart 8-6)
Work with a partner. Take turns changing the sentences from the present to the past.

*Example:* I have class every day.
PARTNER A: I have class every day. I had class yesterday. Your turn now.

*Example:* Orlando gets mail from home every week.
PARTNER B: Orlando gets mail from home every week. Orlando got mail from home last week. Your turn now.

| PARTNER A | PARTNER B |
|---|---|
| 1. Lara gets some mail every day. | 1. We have lunch every day. |
| 2. They go to work every day. | 2. I write emails to my parents every week. |
| 3. The students stand in line at the cafeteria every day. | 3. Jin comes to class late every day. |
| | 4. I do my homework every day. |
| 4. I see my friends every day. | 5. I eat breakfast every morning. |
| 5. Hamid sits in the front row every day. | 6. Carlos puts his books in his briefcase every day. |
| 6. I sleep for eight hours every night. | |

❑ **Exercise 29. Looking at grammar.** (Charts 8-4 and 8-6)
Complete the sentences. Change the words in parentheses to the simple present, the present progressive, or the simple past. Pay attention to the spelling.

1. I (*get*) _____*got*_____ up at eight o'clock yesterday morning.

2. Ellie (*talk*) _____ to Barack on the phone last night.

3. Ellie (*talk*) _____ to Barack on the phone right now.

4. Ellie (*talk*) _____ to Barack on the phone every day.

5. Jim and I (*eat*) _____ lunch in the cafeteria two hours ago.

6. We (*eat*) _____ lunch in the cafeteria every day.

7. I (*go*) _____ to bed early last night.

8. My roommate (*study*) _____ Spanish last year.

9. Kate (*write*) _____ an email to her parents yesterday.

10. Kate (*write*) _____ an email to her parents every week.

11. Kate is in her room right now. She (*sit*) _____ at her desk.

12. Hanna (*do*) _____ her homework last night.

13. Yesterday I (*see*) _____ Fumiko at the library.

14. I (*have*) _____ a dream last night. I (*dream*)

_____ about my friends. I (*sleep*) _____

_____ for eight hours.

15. A strange thing (*happen*) _____ to me yesterday. I couldn't

remember my own telephone number.

16. My wife (*come*) _____ home around five every day.

17. Yesterday, she (*come*) _____ home at 5:15.

18. Our teacher (*stand*) _____ in the middle of the room right now.

19. Our teacher (*stand*) _____ in the front of the room yesterday.

20. Devon (*put*) _____ the butter in the refrigerator yesterday.

21. He (*put*) _____ the milk in the refrigerator every day.

22. Antonio usually (*sit*) _____ in the back of the room, but yesterday he (*sit*) _____ in the front row. Today, he (*be*) _____ absent. He (*be*) _____ absent two days ago too.

❏ **Exercise 30. Listening.** (Chart 8-6)

Listen to the beginning of each sentence. Choose the correct completion(s). There may be more than one correct answer.

*Example:* You will hear:　He did . . .

You will choose:　(a.) his homework.　(b.) a good job.　c. absent.

1. a. a chair.　　　　b. some rice.　　　　c. some numbers.

2. a. on the floor.　　b. a man.　　　　　c. together.

3. a. late.　　　　　b. yesterday.　　　　c. car.

4. a. an answer.　　　b. pretty.　　　　　c. a book.

5. a. a good grade.　　b. last month.　　　c. a new truck.

6. a. a watch.　　　　b. next to my parents.　c. at the bus stop.

❏ **Exercise 31. Warm-up.** (Chart 8-7)

Choose the verbs to make true sentences.

*When my grandparents were in high school, they . . .*

1. had / didn't have　computers.

2. ate / didn't eat　　fast food.

## 8-7 Simple Past Tense: Negative

| | | | | | |
|---|---|---|---|---|---|
| | SUBJECT + | *DID* + | *NOT* + | MAIN VERB | |
| (a) | I | **did** | **not** | **walk** | to school yesterday. |
| (b) | You | **did** | **not** | **walk** | to school yesterday. |
| (c) | Tim | **did** | **not** | **eat** | lunch yesterday. |
| (d) | They | **did** | **not** | **come** | to class yesterday. |

INCORRECT: *I did not walked to school yesterday.*
INCORRECT: *Tim did not ate lunch yesterday.*

I
you
she
he     } + **did not** + main verb*
it
we
they

Notice: The base form of the main verb is used with **did not**.

(e) I **didn't walk** to school yesterday.
(f) Tim **didn't eat** lunch yesterday.

NEGATIVE CONTRACTION
**did** + **not** = **didn't**

*EXCEPTION: **did** is NOT used when the main verb is **be**. See Charts 8-2 and 8-3.
   CORRECT: Dan *wasn't* here yesterday.
INCORRECT: *Dan didn't be here yesterday.*

❏ **Exercise 32. Looking at grammar.** (Chart 8-7)
Complete the sentences. Use **not**.

| TWO DAYS AGO | YESTERDAY |
|---|---|
| 1. I got to school late. | I _____ *didn't get* _____ to school late. |
| 2. You got to school late. | You _____ school late. |
| 3. She got to school late. | She _____ to school late. |
| 4. They stayed home. | They _____ home. |
| 5. We stayed home. | We _____ home. |
| 6. She did her homework. | She _____ her homework. |
| 7. You did your homework. | You _____ your homework. |
| 8. We did our homework. | We _____ our homework. |
| 9. I was sick. | I _____ sick. |
| 10. They were sick. | They _____ sick. |

❏ **Exercise 33. Let's talk: pairwork.** (Chart 8-7)
Work with a partner. Take turns using *I don't . . . every day* and *I didn't . . .
yesterday*.

*Example:* walk to school
PARTNER A:  I don't walk to school every day.  I didn't walk to school yesterday.
            Your turn now.

*Example:* listen to the radio
PARTNER B:  I don't listen to the radio every day.  I didn't listen to the radio yesterday.
            Your turn now.

| PARTNER A | PARTNER B |
|---|---|
| 1.  eat breakfast | 1.  go to the library |
| 2.  watch TV | 2.  visit my friends |
| 3.  go shopping | 3.  see (*name of a person*) |
| 4.  read a newspaper | 4.  do my homework |
| 5.  study | 5.  get on the Internet |

❏ **Exercise 34. Looking at grammar.** (Chart 8-7)
Complete the sentences.  Change the words in parentheses to the simple present, present
progressive, or simple past.

1.  Jasmin (*come, not*) _____ *didn't come* _____ to the meeting yesterday.  She (*stay*)
    _____ *stayed* _____ in her office.

2.  I (*go*) _____ to a movie last night, but I (*enjoy, not*)

    _____ it.  It (*be, not*) _____ very good.

3.  Kay (*read*) _____ a magazine right now.  She (*watch, not*)

    _____ TV.  She (*like, not*) _____ to

    watch TV during the day.

4.  A: (*Be*) _____ you sick yesterday?

    B: No, but my daughter (*feel, not*) _____ good, so I stayed

       home with her.  She's fine now.

5.  Toshi is a busy student.  Sometimes he (*eat, not*) _____ lunch

    because he (*have, not*) _____ enough time between classes.

    Yesterday he (*have, not*) _____ time for lunch.  He (*get*)

    _____ hungry during his afternoon class.

□ **Exercise 35. Let's talk: game.** (Chart 8-7)

Work in groups of six to eight students. Tell your group things you didn't do yesterday.
Repeat the information from the other students in your group. The last person in the
group repeats all the sentences.

*Example:* go

STUDENT A: I didn't go to the zoo yesterday.
STUDENT B: (*Student A*) didn't go to the zoo yesterday. I didn't have lunch in Beijing
yesterday.
STUDENT C: (*Student A*) didn't go to the zoo yesterday. (*Student B*) didn't have lunch in
Beijing yesterday. I didn't swim in the Pacific Ocean yesterday.
Etc.

*Suggestions:*

| | | | |
|---|---|---|---|
| drive to | wake up | wear | talk to |
| walk to | swim | buy | use |
| eat | sing | study | fly to |

□ **Exercise 36. Reading and grammar.** (Chart 8-7)

Read the story about Matt's morning. Then read the sentences that follow. If a sentence is
true, do not change it. If it is not true, write a negative statement.

### My Early Morning

Yesterday, my alarm clock didn't go off. I jumped out of bed and looked at the clock.
I was late for work. I hurried to the kitchen and quickly prepared breakfast. I had some
juice and toast. After breakfast, I put the dishes in the sink. I didn't have time to wash
them. Then I quickly got dressed. Soon, I was ready. I walked to the bus. At the bus
stop, I didn't recognize anyone. Then I looked at my watch. I was two hours early! I was
half asleep when I jumped out of bed earlier and misread* the time on my clock.

1. Matt's alarm clock went off. _____*Matt's alarm clock didn't go off.*_____

2. He got out of bed quickly. _____*(no change)*_____

3. He cooked a big breakfast. _____

4. He washed the dishes. _____

5. He got dressed in a hurry. _____

6. He saw his friends at the bus stop. _____

7. He was late for work. _____

8. It was time for work. _____

---

*misread = read incorrectly

❏ **Exercise 37. Warm-up.** (Chart 8-8)
Answer the questions.

1. a. Do you wake up early every day?
   b. Did you wake up early today?

2. a. Do you eat breakfast every morning?
   b. Did you eat breakfast this morning?

## 8-8 Simple Past Tense: Yes/No Questions

| *DID* + SUBJECT + MAIN VERB | | | | SHORT ANSWER | (LONG ANSWER) |
|---|---|---|---|---|---|
| (a) *Did* | *Tess* | *walk* | to school? → | **Yes, she did.** | (She walked to school.) |
| | | | → | **No, she didn't.** | (She didn't walk to school.) |
| (b) *Did* | *you* | *come* | to class? → | **Yes, I did.** | (I came to class.) |
| | | | → | **No, I didn't.** | (I didn't come to class.) |

❏ **Exercise 38. Let's talk: class activity.** (Chart 8-8)
Answer the simple past tense questions. Close your book for this activity.

*Example:*
   TEACHER: Did you work late last night?
STUDENT A: No, I didn't.
   TEACHER: (*Student A*), ask another student the same question.
STUDENT A: Did you work late last night?
STUDENT B: Yes, I did.
   TEACHER: (*Student B*), ask another student the same question.

Continue to the next question after three to five students have answered.

1. Did you walk home yesterday?
2. Did you come to class late today?
3. Did you wake up early today?
4. Did you eat meat for breakfast?
5. Did you drink coffee this morning?
6. Did you exercise today?
7. Did you play video games yesterday?
8. Did you text someone before 7:00 A.M.?
9. Did you make your bed this morning?
10. Did you wash the dishes this morning?

❑ **Exercise 39. Looking at grammar.** (Chart 8-8)

Make questions and give short answers.

1. A: _____*Did you walk downtown yesterday?*_____

   B: _____*Yes, I did.*_____ (I walked downtown yesterday.)

2. A: _____*Did it rain last week?*_____

   B: _____*No, it didn't.*_____ (It didn't rain last week.)

3. A: _____

   B: _____ (I ate lunch at the cafeteria.)

4. A: _____

   B: _____ (Mr. Kwan didn't go out of town last week.)

5. A: _____

   B: _____ (I had a cup of tea this morning.)

6. A: _____

   B: _____ (Ricardo and I went to a dance last night.)

7. A: _____

   B: _____ (Galina studied English in high school.)

8. A: _____

   B: _____ (Kirsten and Ali didn't do their homework.)

9. A: _____

   B: _____ (I saw Gina at dinner last night.)

10. A: _____

    B: _____ (I didn't dream in English last night.)

❏ **Exercise 40. Listening.** (Chart 8-8)

Listen to the questions. Write the words you hear.

*Example:* You will hear: Did you have your test already?

You will write: ____*Did you*____ have your test already?

1. _____ do well on the test?

2. _____ finish the assignment?

3. _____ make sense?

4. _____ answer your question?

5. _____ need more help?

6. _____ understand the homework?

7. _____ explain the project?

8. _____ complete the project?

9. _____ do well?

10. _____ pass the class?

❏ **Exercise 41. Let's talk: find someone who . . . .** (Chart 8-8)

Interview your classmates. Make simple past questions with the given words. Find people who can answer *yes* and write their names.

*Example:* eat ice cream \ yesterday?
STUDENT A: Did you eat ice cream yesterday?
STUDENT B: No, I didn't. I didn't eat ice cream yesterday.
STUDENT A: (*Ask another student.*) Did you eat ice cream yesterday?
STUDENT C: Yes, I did. I ate ice cream yesterday. (*Write Student C's name.*)

| ACTIVITY | FIRST NAME |
|---|---|
| 1. eat rice \ yesterday? | |
| 2. do homework \ last night? | |
| 3. get an email \ yesterday? | |
| 4. go shopping \ yesterday? | |
| 5. sleep well \ last night? | |
| 6. a. have coffee for breakfast \ this morning? <br> b. put sugar in your coffee \ this morning? | |
| 7. see a good movie \ last week? | |
| 8. write in English \ today? | |
| 9. sit on the floor \ yesterday? | |
| 10. stand in line for something \ last week? | |

❑ **Exercise 42. Listening.** **(Chart 8-8)**

In spoken English, speakers sometimes change or drop sounds. In questions, *did* and the pronoun that follows it can change.

*Part I.* Listen to the examples.

1. **Did you** ("dih-juh") see the news this morning?

2. A: Jim called.
   B: **Did he** ("dih-de") leave a message?

3. A: Julia called.
   B: **Did she** ("dih-she") leave a message?

4. **Did it** ("dih-dit") rain yesterday?

5. A: The kids are watching TV.
   B: **Did they** ("dih-they") finish their homework?

6. My keys aren't here. **Did I** ("dih-di") leave them in the car?


*Part II.* You will hear questions with *did* + *a pronoun*. Write the full forms.

*Examples:* You will hear: "Dih-dit" rain yesterday?
   You will write: _____*Did it*_____ rain yesterday?

   You will hear: "Dih-juh" come to class yesterday?
   You will write: _____*Did you*_____ come to class yesterday?


1. _____ finish the homework assignment?

2. _____ take a long time?

3. _____ hear my question?

4. _____ hear my question?

5. _____ speak loud enough?

6. _____ understand the information?

7. _____ understand the information?

8. _____ want more help?

9. _____ explain it okay?

10. _____ do a good job?

❏   **Exercise 43. Reading and grammar.** **(Chart 8-8)**
Read the story.  Then write the questions the doctor asked Kevin and give Kevin's answers.

### Kevin's Unhealthy Habits

   Kevin didn't feel well.  He went to see Dr. Benson.  Dr. Benson checked him and asked him about his lifestyle.  Kevin had several unhealthy habits:  he slept very little, he didn't exercise, he ate unhealthy foods, and he smoked.  He needed to change these habits. Kevin listened to the doctor, but he didn't change any habits.  He went back to the doctor a month later.  The doctor asked him several questions.

1.  Dr. Benson: *you \ continue*

   _____*Did you continue*_____ to smoke last month?  Kevin: _____*Yes, I did.*_____

2.  Dr. Benson: *you \ change*

   _____ your eating habits?  Kevin: _____

3.  Dr. Benson: *you \ exercise*

   _____? Kevin: _____

4.  Dr. Benson: *you \ sleep*

   _____ more?  Kevin: _____

5.  Dr. Benson: *you \ think*

   _____ my advice was a joke?  Kevin: _____

**Exercise 44. Warm-up.** (Chart 8-9)

Which sentences are true for you?

1. ____ I sometimes drink water with dinner.

2. ____ I drank water with dinner last night.

3. ____ I think about my family every day.

4. ____ I thought about my family at midnight last night.

---

## 8-9 Simple Past Tense: Irregular Verbs (Group 2)

| | | |
|---|---|---|
| bring – brought | drive – drove | run – ran |
| buy – bought | read – read* | teach – taught |
| catch – caught | ride – rode | think – thought |
| drink – drank | | |

*The simple past form of *read* is pronounced the same as the color *red*.

---

❏ **Exercise 45. Vocabulary and speaking.** (Chart 8-9)

Practice using irregular verbs. Close your book for this activity.

*Example:* ***teach–taught***

TEACHER:   teach–taught. I teach class every day. I taught class yesterday. What did I do
yesterday?

STUDENTS:   (*repeat*) teach–taught. You taught class yesterday.

1. ***bring–brought***   I bring my book to class every day. I brought my book to class
yesterday. What did I do yesterday?

2. ***buy–bought***   I buy apps for my phone. Yesterday, I bought an app for my phone.
What did I do yesterday?

3. ***catch–caught***   On weekends, I go fishing. Sometimes, I catch fish. I caught a fish
last week. Sometimes I catch a cold. Last week, I caught a bad cold. What did I do
last week?

4. ***think–thought***   I often think about my family. I thought about my family yesterday.
What did I do yesterday?

5. **REVIEW:**   What did I bring to class yesterday? What did you bring yesterday? What
did I buy yesterday? What did I catch last week? What did I think about yesterday?
What did you think about yesterday?

6. ***run–ran***   Sometimes I'm late for class, so I run. Yesterday I was late, so I ran. What
did I do yesterday?

7. ***read–read***   I like to read books. I read every day. Yesterday I read a book. What
did I do yesterday? What did you read yesterday?

8. ***drink–drank***   I usually drink a cup of coffee in the morning. I drank a cup of
coffee this morning. What did I do this morning? Did you drink a cup of coffee this
morning? What do you usually drink in the morning? Do you drink the same thing
every morning?

9. ***drive–drove*** I usually drive my car to school. I drove my car to school this morning. What did I do this morning? Who has a car? Did you drive to school this morning?

10. ***ride–rode*** Sometimes I ride the bus to school. I rode the bus yesterday morning. What did I do yesterday morning? Who rode the bus to school this morning?

11. REVIEW: I was late for class yesterday morning, so what did I do? What did I read yesterday? What did you read yesterday? Did you read a newspaper this morning? What did I drink this morning? What did you drink this morning? I have a car. Did I drive to school this morning? Did you? Did you ride the bus?

❏ **Exercise 46. Looking at grammar.** (Chart 8-9)
Complete each sentence with the correct form of the word in parentheses.

1. A: Why are you out of breath?

   B: I (*run*) _____ to class because I was late.

2. A: I (*ride*) _____ the bus to school yesterday. How did you get to school?

   B: I (*drive*) _____ my car.

3. A: Did you decide to change schools?

   B: I (*think*) _____ about it, but then I decided to stay here.

4. A: (*you, go*) _____ shopping yesterday?

   B: Yes. I (*buy*) _____ a new pair of shoes.

5. A: (*you, study*) _____ last night?

   B: No, I didn't. I was tired. I (*read*) _____ the news online and then

   (*go*) _____ to bed early.

6. A: Do you like milk?

   B: No. I (*drink*) _____ milk when I (*be*) _____ a child, but I don't like milk now.

7. A: Did you leave your dictionary at home?

   B: No. I (*bring*) _____ it to class with me.

8. Yesterday Sasha (*teach*) _____ us how to say "thank you" in Japanese. Kim (*teach*) _____ us how to say "I love you" in Korean.

9. A: Did you enjoy your fishing trip?

   B: I had a wonderful time! I (*catch*) _____ a lot of fish.

**Exercise 47. Let's talk: pairwork.** (Chart 8-9)

Work with a partner. Take turns asking and answering simple past tense questions.

*Example:* think
PARTNER A: Did you think about me last night?
PARTNER B: Yes, I did. I thought about you last night. OR
No, I didn't. I didn't think about you last night.

| PARTNER A | PARTNER B |
|-----------|-----------|
| 1. drive  | 1. think  |
| 2. ride   | 2. drink  |
| 3. catch  | 3. read   |
| 4. teach  | 4. buy    |
| 5. bring  | 5. run    |

❑ **Exercise 48. Listening.** (Chart 8-9)

Listen to the beginning of each sentence. Choose the correct completion(s). There may be more than one correct answer.

*Example:* You will hear:    He drank . . .
You will choose: (a.) some tea.    b. bread.    (c.) water.

| | | |
|---|---|---|
| 1. a. last week. | b. a fish. | c. happy. |
| 2. a. very fast | b. a house. | c. to the store. |
| 3. a. books. | b. the kids. | c. the newspaper. |
| 4. a. a story. | b. a bike. | c. a horse. |
| 5. a. good. | b. some food. | c. a doctor. |
| 6. a. people. | b. into town. | c. home. |

❑ **Exercise 49. Writing.** (Charts 8-1 → 8-9)

Use the expressions from the list to write sentences about yourself. When did you do these things in the past? Use the simple past tense and past time expressions (*yesterday, two days ago, last week, etc.*) in all of your sentences. Use your own paper.

*Example:* go downtown with (*someone*)
*Possible sentence:* I went downtown with Marco two days ago.

1. arrive in (*this city*)
2. eat at a restaurant
3. buy (*something*)
4. have a cold
5. be in elementary school
6. drink a cup of coffee
7. talk to (*someone*) on the phone
8. study arithmetic
9. read a newspaper
10. play (soccer, a pinball machine, etc.)
11. see (*someone* or *something*)
12. think about (*someone* or *something*)
13. be born

## Exercise 50. Warm-up. (Chart 8-10)

Which sentences are true for you?

1. _____ I sing in the shower every morning.

2. _____ I sang in the shower yesterday morning.

3. _____ I sometimes speak English in my dreams.

4. _____ I spoke English in my last dream.

---

### 8-10 Simple Past Tense: Irregular Verbs (Group 3)

| | | |
|---|---|---|
| break – broke | meet – met | sing – sang |
| fly – flew | pay – paid | speak – spoke |
| hear – heard | ring – rang | take – took |
| leave – left | send – sent | wake up – woke up |

---

## Exercise 51. Vocabulary and speaking. (Chart 8-10)

Practice using irregular verbs. Close your book for this activity.

*Example:* **break–broke**

TEACHER: break–broke. Sometimes a person breaks an arm or a leg.
I broke my arm five years ago. What happened five years ago?

STUDENTS: (*repeat*) break–broke. You broke your arm.

TEACHER: (*to Student A*) Did you ever* break a bone?

STUDENT A: Yes. I broke my leg ten years ago.

1. ***fly–flew*** Sometimes I fly home in an airplane. I flew home in an airplane last month. What did I do last month? Did you fly to this city? When?

2. ***hear–heard*** I hear birds singing every morning. I heard birds singing yesterday. What did I hear yesterday? What did you hear when you woke up this morning?

3. ***pay–paid*** I pay the rent every month. I paid the rent last month. What did I do last month? Did you pay your rent last month?

4. ***send–sent*** I send my mom a gift every year on her birthday. I sent my mom a gift last year on her birthday. What did I do last year? When did you send a gift to someone?

5. ***leave–left*** I leave for school at 8:00 every morning. I left for school yesterday at 8:00 A.M. What did I do at 8:00 A.M. yesterday? What time did you leave for class this morning?

6. ***meet–met*** I sometimes meet friends for lunch. Last month I met some friends for lunch. What did I do last month? Do you sometimes meet friends for lunch?

7. ***take–took*** I take my younger brother to the movies every month. I took my younger brother to the movies last month. What did I do last month? Who has a younger brother or sister? Where and when did you take him/her someplace?

---

*ever = at any time

8. *wake–woke*   I usually wake up at six. This morning I woke up at six-thirty. What time did I wake up this morning? What time did you wake up this morning?

9. *speak–spoke*   I speak to many students every day. Before class today, I spoke to ( . . . ). Who did I speak to? Who did you speak to before class today?

10. *ring–rang*   I didn't turn my cell phone off when I went to bed last night. This morning, it rang at six-thirty and woke me up. What happened at six-thirty this morning? Who had a phone call this morning? What time did the phone ring?

11. *sing–sang*   I sing in the shower every morning. I sang in the shower yesterday. What did I do yesterday? Do you ever sing in the shower? When was the last time?

12. *break–broke*   Sometimes I break things. This morning I dropped a glass on the floor, and it broke. What happened this morning? When did you break something?

❑ **Exercise 52. Looking at grammar.** (Chart 8-10)
Complete the conversations. Use the correct form of the verbs from the box.

| break | leave | ring | speak |
|-------|-------|------|-------|
| fly   | meet  | send | take  |
| hear  | pay   | sing | wake  |

1. A: What happened to your finger?

   B: I _____ it in a soccer game.

2. A: Who did you talk to at the director's office?

   B: I _____ to the secretary.

3. A: When did Jessica leave for Europe?

   B: She _____ for Europe five days ago.

4. A: Did you write Ted an email?

   B: No, but I _____ him a text.

5. A: Do you know Meg Adams?

   B: Yes. I _____ her a couple of weeks ago.

6. A: Why did you call the police?

   B: Because I _____ a burglar!

7. A: Where did you go yesterday?

   B: I _____ my son and daughter to the zoo.

8. A: What time did you get up this morning?

   B: 6:15.

   A: Why did you get up so early?

   B: The phone _____.

9. A: Did you enjoy the party?

   B: Yes, I had a good time. We _____ songs and danced. It was fun.

10. A: You look sleepy.

    B: I am. I _____ up before dawn this morning and never went back to sleep.

11. A: Did you give the painter a check?

    B: No. I _____ him in cash.

12. A: A bird _____ into our apartment yesterday through an open window.

    B: Really? What did you do?

    A: I caught it and took it outside.

❑ **Exercise 53. Let's talk: pairwork.** (Chart 8-10)
Work with a partner. Take turns asking and answering simple past tense questions.

*Example:* fly
PARTNER A: Did you fly to Paris last week?
PARTNER B: Yes, I did. I flew to Paris last week. OR
          No, I didn't. I didn't fly to Paris last week.

| PARTNER A | PARTNER B |
|-----------|-----------|
| 1. hear | 1. fly |
| 2. break | 2. leave |
| 3. take | 3. speak |
| 4. sing | 4. wake up |
| 5. ring | 5. send |
| 6. pay | 6. meet |

**Exercise 54. Listening.** (Chart 8-10)

Listen to the story. Then read each sentence and choose the correct answer.

**A doctor's appointment**

| | |
|---|---|
| 1. The man was at the doctor's office. | yes no |
| 2. He took some medicine. | yes no |
| 3. He was in bed for a short time. | yes no |
| 4. The man spoke to the nurse. | yes no |
| 5. He is feeling okay now. | yes no |

□ **Exercise 55. Warm-up.** (Chart 8-11)

Which sentences are true for you?

1. _____ I sometimes lose my keys.

2. _____ I lost my keys last week.

3. _____ I often wear jeans.

4. _____ I wore jeans yesterday.

## 8-11 Simple Past Tense: Irregular Verbs (Group 4)

| | | |
|---|---|---|
| begin – began | say – said | tell – told |
| find – found | sell – sold | tear – tore |
| lose – lost | steal – stole | wear – wore |
| hang – hung | | |

□ **Exercise 56. Vocabulary and speaking.** (Chart 8-11)

Practice using irregular verbs. Close your book for this activity.

*Example:* **begin–began**

TEACHER: begin–began. Our class begins at (9:00) every day. Class began at (9:00 this morning). When did class begin (this morning)?

STUDENTS: (*repeat*) begin–began. Class began at (9:00 this morning).

1. **lose–lost**   Sometimes I lose things. Yesterday I lost my keys. What did I lose yesterday?

2. **find–found**   Sometimes I lose things. And then I find them. Yesterday I lost my keys, but then I found them in my jacket pocket. What did I do yesterday?

3. **tear–tore**   If I make a mistake when I write a check, I tear the check up. Yesterday, I made a mistake when I wrote a check, so I tore it up and wrote a new check. What did I do yesterday?

4. **sell–sold**   People sell things that they don't need anymore. My friend has a new bike, so she sold her old bike. What did she do?

5. **hang–hung**  I like to hang pictures on my walls. This morning I hung a new picture in my bedroom. What did I do this morning?

6. **tell–told**  The kindergarten teacher likes to tell stories to her students. Yesterday she told a story about a little red train. What did the teacher do yesterday?

7. **wear–wore**  I wear a sweater to class every evening. Last night I also wore a jacket. What did I wear last night?

8. **steal–stole**  Thieves steal money and other things. Last month a thief stole my aunt's wallet. What did a thief do last month?

9. **say–said**  People usually say "hello" when they answer a phone. When my friend answered his phone this morning, he said "hello." What did he do this morning?

❑ **Exercise 57. Looking at grammar.** (Chart 8-11)
Complete the sentences with the correct form of the verbs from the box.

| begin | hang | say | steal | tell |
|-------|------|-----|-------|------|
| find  | lose | sell | tear | wear |

1. A: Did you go to the park yesterday?
   B: No. We stayed home because it _____ to rain.
   A: Oh, that's too bad.

2. A: Susie is in trouble.
   B: Why?
   A: She _____ a lie. Her mom and dad are upset.
   B: I'm sure she's sorry.

3. A: Did you find your sunglasses?
   B: No. I _____ them at the soccer game. I need to get some new ones.

4. A: Where's my coat?
   B: I _____ it up in the closet for you.

5. A: Where did you get that pretty shell?
   B: I _____ it on the beach.

   shells

6. A: Do you still have your bike?
   B: No. I _____ it because I needed some extra money.

7. A: It's hot in here.

B: Excuse me? What did you say?

A: I _____, "It's hot in here."

8. A: Why did you take the bus to work this morning? Why didn't you drive?

B: Because somebody _____ my car last night.

A: Did you call the police?

B: Of course I did.

9. A: Did you wear your blue jeans to the job interview?

B: Of course not! I _____ a suit.

10. A: I wrote the wrong amount on the check, so I had to write a new check.

B: What did you do with the first check?

A: I _____ it into pieces.

❑ **Exercise 58. Let's talk: pairwork.** (Chart 8-11)
Work with a partner. Take turns asking and answering simple past tense questions.

*Example:* wear
PARTNER A: Did you wear slippers last night?
PARTNER B: Yes, I did. I wore slippers last night. OR
           No, I didn't. I didn't wear slippers last night.

| PARTNER A | PARTNER B |
|-----------|-----------|
| 1. hang   | 1. find   |
| 2. steal  | 2. sell   |
| 3. wear   | 3. lose   |
| 4. say    | 4. tell   |
| 5. begin  | 5. tear   |

**Exercise 59. Listening.** (Chart 8-11)

Listen to the story. Then read each sentence and choose the correct answer.

**A wedding ring**

| | | |
|---|---|---|
| 1. The woman lost her mother's ring. | yes | no |
| 2. Someone stole the ring. | yes | no |
| 3. Her dog found the ring in the garden. | yes | no |
| 4. Her mother wore the ring for a while. | yes | no |
| 5. The woman was happy at the end of the story. | yes | no |

❏ **Exercise 60. Looking at grammar.** (Chapter 8)

You went to a birthday party last night. A friend is asking you questions about it. Complete the sentences with *did*, *was*, or *were*.

1. _____ you go with a friend?

2. _____ your friends at the party?

3. _____ the party fun?

4. _____ many people there?

5. _____ you have a good time?

6. _____ there a birthday cake?

7. _____ you eat a piece of birthday cake?

8. _____ everyone sing "Happy Birthday"?

9. _____ you hungry?

10. _____ you bring a present?

*a present*

❏ **Exercise 61. Looking at grammar.** (Chapter 8)

Complete the sentences with *did*, *was*, or *were*.

1. I ____*did*____ not go to work yesterday. I ____*was*____ sick, so I stayed home.

2. Ray _____ not in his office yesterday. He _____ not go to work.

3. A: _____ Mr. Chan in his office yesterday?

   B: Yes.

   A: _____ you see him about your problem?

   B: Yes. He answered all my questions. He _____ very helpful.

4. A: _____ you at the meeting yesterday?

   B: Yes.

   A: _____ I miss anything?

   B: No. It _____ really short. The fire alarm went off right after it started.

      We _____ outside for the rest of the hour.

5. A: Where _____ you yesterday?

   B: I _____ at the zoo.

   A: _____ you enjoy it?

   B: Yes, but the weather _____ very hot. I tried to stay out of the sun.

      Most of the animals _____ in their houses or in the shade. The sun

      _____ too hot for them too. They _____ not want to be outside.


❑ **Exercise 62. Looking at grammar.** (Chapter 8)
Make questions.

**A bad experience**

1. A: _____*Do you live in an apartment?*_____

   B: Yes, I do. (I live in an apartment.)

2. A: _____*Do you have a roommate?*_____

   B: No, I don't. (I don't have a roommate.)

3. A: _____

   B: No, I don't. (I don't want a roommate.)

4. A: _____

   B: Yes, I did. (I had a roommate last year.)

5. A: _____

   B: No, it wasn't. (It wasn't a good experience.)

6. A: _____

   B: Yes, he was. (He was messy.)

      For example, he never picked up his dirty clothes. He never washed his dirty

      dishes. He was always late with his part of the rent.

7. A: _____

   B: No, he didn't. (He didn't help me clean.)

8. A: _____

   B: Yes, I was. (I was glad when he left.)

❏ **Exercise 63. Let's talk.** (Chapter 8)
Work in pairs or small groups. Read the facts about four people: Lara, Josh, Max, and
Kira. They live in an apartment building on the same floor. Which apartment does each
person live in? Use the clues to find out.

*Clues:*

1. Lara painted her door yellow.
2. Josh and Lara lived in the same neighborhood as children. Now they are next-door
   neighbors.
3. Max loves music. He works at a music store. His parents were musicians in a band.
4. Kira isn't very social. She didn't want neighbors on both sides, so she rented an end
   unit.
5. Lara moved into her apartment last year.
6. The first time Max played loud music, both Kira and Josh knocked on the walls. They
   told him to turn it down.

| APARTMENT NUMBER | 1 | 2 | 3 | 4 |
|---|---|---|---|---|
| NAME | | | | |

Correct the mistakes.

                    *stole*                 *s*

1. Someone ~~stealed~~ my bike two day ago.

2. Did you went to the party yesterday weekend?

3. I hear an interesting story yesterday.

4. The teacher not ready for class yesterday.

5. Did came Dennis to work last week?

6. Yesterday night I staied home and work on my science project.

7. A few students wasn't on time for the final exam yesterday.

8. Your fax came before ten minutes.  Did you got it?

9. Did you the movie watch?

10. The store no have yellow bananas.  I get some green ones.

11. Did you nervous about your test last week?

12. I didn't saw you at the party.  Did was you there?

❏  **Exercise 65. Reading and writing.** (Chapter 8)
*Part I.* Read the story.

### An Embarrassing Week

Andy did some embarrassing things last week.  For example, on Monday, he wore his slippers to work.  He got on the bus and looked down at his feet.  He felt very stupid and wanted to hide his feet.

That night, he typed an email to his girlfriend.  He told her he loved her.  But he hit the wrong button and he sent the message to his boss.  His girlfriend and his boss have the same first name.  He didn't know until the next morning when she greeted him at work. She didn't look very happy.

On Friday, he went to a nice restaurant with co-workers for lunch and ate a salad. After lunch he had a meeting.  He talked a lot at the meeting.  People gave him strange looks, but Andy didn't know why.  Later he found out the reason.  He had lettuce on his front teeth.

Andy is hoping for a better week this week.  He hid his slippers under the bed and put a mirror in his desk drawer.  But he didn't tell his girlfriend about the email because he is still very embarrassed.

***Part II.*** Write about something embarrassing that you did or something embarrassing that happened to you. Your title can be "An Embarrassing Week," "An Embarrassing Day," "An Embarrassing Night," "An Embarrassing Experience," etc. If you can't think of things, write about a family member or a friend.

1. First, write single sentences about one or more embarrassing things you or someone else did. Use simple past tense verbs.

2. Add details to make the story interesting. Answer these questions:

    Where and/or when did it happen?

    What did you think?

    How did you feel?

    What did you do next?

    Did you need to find a solution?

3. Put this information into one or more paragraphs.

***Part III.*** Editing check: Work individually or change papers with a partner. Check (✓) for the following:

1. _____ indented paragraph

2. _____ capital letter at the beginning of each sentence

3. _____ period at the end of each sentence

4. _____ correct use of the simple past for a completed activity

5. _____ correct use of ***didn't*** and ***wasn't*** for simple past negatives

6. _____ correct spelling (use a dictionary or computer spell-check)

# Appendix 1
## English Handwriting

| English Handwriting | |
|---|---|
| PRINTING | CURSIVE |
| Aa    Jj    Ss <br> Bb    Kk    Tt <br> Cc    Ll    Uu <br> Dd    Mm    Vv <br> Ee    Nn    Ww <br> Ff    Oo    Xx <br> Gg    Pp    Yy <br> Hh    Qq    Zz <br> Ii    Rr | Aa    Jj    Ss <br> Bb    Kk    Tt <br> Cc    Ll    Uu <br> Dd    Mm    Vv <br> Ee    Nn    Ww <br> Ff    Oo    Xx <br> Gg    Pp    Yy <br> Hh    Qq    Zz <br> Ii    Rr |

Vowels = *a, e, i, o, u*

Consonants = *b, c, d, f, g, h, j, k, l, m, n, p, q, r, s, t, v, w, x, y, z*\*

---

\*The letter **z** is pronounced "zee" in American English and "zed" in British English.

# Appendix 2
## Numbers

| CARDINAL NUMBERS | | ORDINAL NUMBERS | |
|---|---|---|---|
| 1 | one | 1st | first |
| 2 | two | 2nd | second |
| 3 | three | 3rd | third |
| 4 | four | 4th | fourth |
| 5 | five | 5th | fifth |
| 6 | six | 6th | sixth |
| 7 | seven | 7th | seventh |
| 8 | eight | 8th | eighth |
| 9 | nine | 9th | ninth |
| 10 | ten | 10th | tenth |
| 11 | eleven | 11th | eleventh |
| 12 | twelve | 12th | twelfth |
| 13 | thirteen | 13th | thirteenth |
| 14 | fourteen | 14th | fourteenth |
| 15 | fifteen | 15th | fifteenth |
| 16 | sixteen | 16th | sixteenth |
| 17 | seventeen | 17th | seventeenth |
| 18 | eighteen | 18th | eighteenth |
| 19 | nineteen | 19th | nineteenth |
| 20 | twenty | 20th | twentieth |
| 21 | twenty-one | 21st | twenty-first |
| 22 | twenty-two | 22nd | twenty-second |
| 23 | twenty-three | 23rd | twenty-third |
| 24 | twenty-four | 24th | twenty-fourth |
| 25 | twenty-five | 25th | twenty-fifth |
| 26 | twenty-six | 26th | twenty-sixth |
| 27 | twenty-seven | 27th | twenty-seventh |
| 28 | twenty-eight | 28th | twenty-eighth |
| 29 | twenty-nine | 29th | twenty-ninth |
| 30 | thirty | 30th | thirtieth |
| 40 | forty | 40th | fortieth |
| 50 | fifty | 50th | fiftieth |
| 60 | sixty | 60th | sixtieth |
| 70 | seventy | 70th | seventieth |
| 80 | eighty | 80th | eightieth |
| 90 | ninety | 90th | ninetieth |
| 100 | one hundred | 100th | one hundredth |
| 200 | two hundred | 200th | two hundredth |
| 1,000 | one thousand | 1,000th | one thousandth |
| 10,000 | ten thousand | 10,000th | ten thousandth |
| 100,000 | one hundred thousand | 100,000th | one hundred thousandth |
| 1,000,000 | one million | 1,000,000th | one millionth |

# Appendix 3
## Ways of Saying Time

9:00   It's nine o'clock.
       It's nine.

9:05   It's nine-oh-five.
       It's five (minutes) after nine.
       It's five (minutes) past nine.

9:10   It's nine-ten.
       It's ten (minutes) after nine.
       It's ten (minutes) past nine.

9:15   It's nine-fifteen.
       It's a quarter after nine.
       It's a quarter past nine.

9:30   It's nine-thirty.
       It's half past nine.

9:45   It's nine-forty-five.
       It's a quarter to ten.
       It's a quarter of ten.

9:50   It's nine-fifty.
       It's ten (minutes) to ten.
       It's ten (minutes) of ten.

12:00  It's noon.
       It's midnight.

A.M. = morning:  It's nine A.M.
P.M. = afternoon/evening/night:  It's nine P.M.

# Appendix 4
## *Days/Months/Seasons*

| DAYS | ABBREVIATION | MONTHS | ABBREVIATION | SEASONS* |
|---|---|---|---|---|
| Monday | Mon. | January | Jan. | winter |
| Tuesday | Tues. | February | Feb. | spring |
| Wednesday | Wed. | March | Mar. | summer |
| Thursday | Thurs. | April | Apr. | fall or autumn |
| Friday | Fri. | May | May | |
| Saturday | Sat. | June | Jun. | |
| Sunday | Sun. | July | Jul. | |
| | | August | Aug. | |
| | | September | Sept. | |
| | | October | Oct. | |
| | | November | Nov. | |
| | | December | Dec. | |

*Seasons of the year are only capitalized when they begin a sentence.

**WRITING DATES:**

### Month/Day/Year

    10/31/41  =  October 31, 1941
    4/15/98   =  April 15, 1998
    7/4/1906  =  July 4, 1906
    7/4/07    =  July 4, 2007

**SAYING DATES:**

| Usual Written Form | Usual Spoken Form |
|---|---|
| January 1 | January first / the first of January |
| March 2 | March second / the second of March |
| May 3 | May third / the third of May |
| June 4 | June fourth / the fourth of June |
| August 5 | August fifth / the fifth of August |
| October 10 | October tenth / the tenth of October |
| November 27 | November twenty-seventh / the twenty-seventh of November |

# Appendix 5
## Supplementary Charts

## A5-1 Basic Capitalization Rules

| | Use a capital letter for: |
|---|---|
| (a) Joan and I are friends. | the pronoun "I" |
| (b) They are late. | the first word of a sentence |
| (c) Sam Bond and Tom Adams are here. | names of people |
| (d) Mrs. Peterson<br>Professor Jones<br>Dr. Costa | titles of people* |
| (e) Monday, Tuesday, Wednesday | the days of the week |
| (f) April, May, June | the months of the year |
| (g) New Year's Day | holidays |
| (h) Los Angeles<br>Florida, Ontario<br>Germany<br>Lake Baikal<br>Amazon River<br>Pacific Ocean<br>Mount Everest<br>Broadway, Fifth Avenue | names of places: cities, states and provinces, countries, lakes, rivers, oceans, mountains, streets |
| (i) German, Chinese, Swedish | languages and nationalities |
| (j) Pirates of the Caribbean<br>Romeo and Juliet | the first word of a title, for example, in a book or movie. Capitalize the other words, but not: articles (*the, a, an*), short prepositions (*with, in, at*, etc.), and these words: *and, but, or*. |
| (k) Buddhism, Christianity, Hinduism, Islam, Judaism | religions |

\* *Mrs.* = woman: married  *Miss* = woman: unmarried
  *Ms.* = woman: married or unmarried *Mr.* = man: married or unmarried

## A5-2 Voiceless and Voiced Sounds for -s Endings on Verbs

| Voiceless | Voiced | |
|---|---|---|
| (a) /p/ sleep<br>/t/ write<br>/f/ laugh | (b) /b/ rub<br>/d/ ride<br>/v/ drive<br><br>*I can feel my voice box. It vibrates.* | Some sounds are "voiceless." You don't use your voice box. You push air through your teeth and lips. For example, the sound /p/ comes from air through your lips. The final sounds in (a) are voiceless. Common voiceless sounds are **f, k, p, t, sh, ch**, and voiceless **th**. |
| | | Some sounds are "voiced." You use your voice box to make voiced sounds. For example, the sound /b/ comes from your voice box. The final sounds in (b) are voiced. Common voiced sounds are **b, d, g, j, l, m, n, r, v**, and voiced **th**. |
| (c) sleeps = *sleep*/s/<br>writes = *write*/s/<br>laughs = *laugh*/s/ | (d) rubs = *rub*/z/<br>rides = *ride*/z/<br>drives = *drive*/z/ | Final **-s** is pronounced /s/ after voiceless sounds, as in (c).<br>Final **-s** is pronounced /z/ after voiced sounds, as in (d). |

## A5-3 Final -ed Pronunciation for Simple Past Verbs

Final **-ed** has three pronunciations: /t/, /d/, and /əd/.

| End of Verb | Base Form | Simple Past | Pronunciation | |
|---|---|---|---|---|
| VOICELESS | (a) help<br>laugh<br>wash | helped<br>laughed<br>washed | *help*/t/<br>*laugh*/t/<br>*wash*/t/ | Final **-ed** is pronounced /t/ if a verb ends in a voiceless sound, as in (a). |
| VOICED | (b) rub<br>live<br>smile | rubbed<br>lived<br>smiled | *rub*/d/<br>*live*/d/<br>*smile*/d/ | Final **-ed** is pronounced /d/ if a verb ends in a voiced sound, as in (b). |
| **-d** OR **-t** | (c) need<br>want | needed<br>wanted | *need*/əd/<br>*want*/əd/ | Final **-ed** is pronounced /əd/ if a verb ends in the letters **d** or **t**, as in (c). |

# Listening Script

NOTE: You may want to pause the audio after each item or in longer passages so that there is enough time to complete each task.

## Chapter 1: Using *Be*

### Exercise 20, p. 11.
A: Hi. My name is Mrs. Smith. I'm the substitute teacher.
B: Hi. I'm Franco.
C: Hi. I'm Lisa. We're in your class.
A: It's nice to meet you.
B: We're glad to meet you too.

### Exercise 24, p. 12.
A: Hello. I'm Mrs. Brown. I'm the substitute teacher.
B: Hi. I'm Paulo, and this is Marie. We're in your class.
A: It's nice to meet you.
B: We're happy to meet you too.
A: It's time for class. Please take a seat.

### Exercise 28, p. 14.
1. Andrew isn't a child.
2. Isabelle is an aunt.
3. Marie is a mom.
4. David isn't a dad.
5. Billy and Janey are brother and sister.
6. Marie and Andrew are adults.
7. Billy and Janey aren't parents.
8. David and Andrew aren't daughters.

### Exercise 41, p. 23.

*The First Day of Class*

Paulo is a student from Brazil. Marie is a student from France. They're in the classroom. Today is an exciting day. It's the first day of school, but they aren't nervous. They're happy to be here. Mrs. Brown is the teacher. She isn't in the classroom right now. She's late today.

### Exercise 44, p. 25.
1. Grammar's easy.
2. My name's Josh.

3. My books're on the table.
4. My brother's 21 years old.
5. The weather's cold today.
6. The windows're open.
7. My money's in my wallet.
8. Mr. Smith's a teacher.
9. My parents're at work now.
10. The food's good.
11. Tom's sick today.
12. My roommates're from Chicago.
13. My sister's a student in high school.

## Chapter 2: Using *Be* and *Have*

### Exercise 4, p. 29.
A: Elena's absent today.
B: Is she sick?
A: No.
B: Is her husband sick?
A: No.
B: Are her children sick?
A: No.
B: Is she homesick?
A: No.
B: So? What's the matter?
A: Her turtle is sick!
B: Are you serious? That's crazy!

### Exercise 25, p. 43.

*Anna's clothes*

1. Her boots have zippers.
2. She has a raincoat.
3. Her raincoat has buttons.
4. They are small.
5. Her sweater has long sleeves.
6. She has earrings on her ears.
7. They are silver.
8. She has on jeans.
9. Her jeans have pockets.

### Exercise 36, p. 52.

*In the kitchen*

1. That is my coffee cup.
2. This is your dessert.
3. Those are our plates.
4. Those sponges are wet.
5. These dishcloths are dry.
6. That frying pan is dirty.
7. This frying pan is clean.
8. That salt shaker is empty.

## Chapter 3: Using the Simple Present

### Exercise 4, p. 61.

1. I wake up early every day.
2. My brother wakes up late.
3. He gets up at 11:00.
4. I go to school at 8:00.
5. My mother does exercises every morning.
6. My little sister watches TV in the morning.
7. I take the bus to school.
8. My brother takes the bus to school.
9. My friends take the bus too.
10. We talk about our day.

### Exercise 15, p. 66.

1. eat
2. eats
3. push
4. pushes
5. sleeps
6. fixes

### Exercise 17, p. 68.

1. Mrs. Miller teaches English on Saturdays.
2. Mr. and Mrs. Hanson teach English in the evenings.
3. Chang fixes cars.
4. His son fixes cars too.
5. Carlos and Chris watch DVDs on weekends.
6. Their daughter watches TV shows on her computer.
7. I brush my hair every morning.
8. Jimmy seldom brushes his hair.
9. The Nelsons wash their car every weekend.
10. Jada rarely washes her car.

### Exercise 24, p. 71.

Marco is a student. He has an unusual schedule. All of his classes are at night. His first class is at 6:00 P.M. every day. He takes a break from 7:30 to 8:00. Then he has classes from 8:00 to 10:00.

He leaves school and goes home at 10:00. After he has dinner, he watches TV. Then he does his homework from midnight to 3:00 or 4:00 in the morning.

Marco has his own computer at home. When he finishes his homework, he usually goes on the Internet.

He often stays at his computer until the sun comes up. Then he does a few exercises, has breakfast, and goes to bed. He sleeps all day. Marco thinks his schedule is great, but his friends think it is strange.

## Chapter 4: Using the Present Progressive

### Exercise 7, p. 99.

1. Tony is sitting in the cafeteria.
2. He is sitting alone.
3. He is wearing a hat.
4. He is eating lunch.
5. He is reading his grammar book.
6. He is holding a cup.
7. He is studying hard.
8. He is smiling.
9. He is listening to the radio.
10. He is waving to his friends.

### Exercise 24, p. 111.

1. I write in my grammar book . . .
2. I am writing in my grammar book . . .
3. It is raining outside . . .
4. It doesn't rain . . .
5. My cell phone rings . . .
6. My cell phone isn't ringing . . .
7. My friends and I listen to music in the car . . .
8. We're not listening to music . . .

### Exercise 28, p. 114.

A: What are you doing? Are you working on your English paper?
B: No, I'm not. I'm writing an email to my sister.
A: Do you write to her often?
B: Yes, but I don't write a lot of emails to anyone else.
A: Does she write to you often?
B: No, but she texts me a lot.

## Chapter 5: Talking About the Present

### Exercise 6, p. 129.

1. I have class in the morning. I was born in July. I was born in 1990. Who am I?
2. My birthday is in June. I was born on June 24th. I have class every day at 1:00 o'clock. Who am I?
3. I was born in 1997. My birthday is July 7th. I go to class at night. Who am I?
4. I have class at 7:00 o'clock. I go to class in the morning. I was born in 1992. Who am I?

## Exercise 16, p. 134.

1. There're ten students in the classroom.
2. There's a new teacher today.
3. There're two new math teachers this year.
4. There's a piece of gum on the floor.
5. There's some information on the bulletin board.
6. There're some spelling mistakes on this paper.
7. There's a grammar mistake in this sentence.
8. There're two writing assignments for tonight.

## Exercise 32, p. 145.

1. There are trees behind the train.
2. A bird is under the picnic table.
3. There are butterflies near the flowers.
4. There is a knife on top of the table.
5. There is a fishing pole on the boat.
6. A boat is under the water.
7. The bridge is below the water.
8. There are clouds above the mountains.
9. There are flowers beside the river.
10. There are flowers next to the river.
11. A guitar is in back of the table.
12. Two bikes are under the tree.
13. A fish is in the water.
14. The table is between the tree and the river.
15. The boots are far from the picnic bench.

## Exercise 41, p. 151.

1. I'd like a hamburger for dinner.
2. We like to eat at fast-food restaurants.
3. Bob'd like to go to the gym now.
4. He likes to exercise after work.
5. The teacher'd like to speak with you.
6. The teacher likes your work.
7. We like to ride our bikes on weekends.
8. We'd like to ride in a race.
9. Bill and Kay like jazz music.
10. They'd like to go to a concert next week.

## Chapter 6: Nouns and Pronouns

## Exercise 18, p. 168.

1. Renata knows Oscar. She knows him very well.
2. Where does Shelley live? Do you have her address?
3. There's Vince. Let's go talk to him.
4. There are Dave and Lois. Let's go talk to them.
5. I'm looking online for JoAnne's phone number. What's her last name again?
6. I need to see our airline tickets. Do you have them?

## Exercise 19, p. 169.

1. A: Mika and I are going downtown this afternoon. Do you want to come with us?
   B: I don't think so, but thanks anyway. Chris and I are going to the library. We need to study for our test.

2. A: Hi, Abby. How do you like your new apartment?
   B: It's great. I have a new roommate too. She's very nice.
   A: What's her name?
   B: Rita Lopez. Do you know her?
   A: No, but I know her brother. He's in my math class.

3. A: Do you see Mike and George very much?
   B: Yes, I see them often. We play video games at my house.
   A: Who usually wins?
   B: Mike. We never beat him!

## Exercise 22, p. 172.

1. toys
2. table
3. face
4. hats
5. offices
6. boxes
7. package
8. chairs
9. edge
10. tops

## Exercise 23, p. 173.

1. The desks in the classroom are new.
2. I like to visit new places.
3. Luke wants a sandwich for lunch.
4. The teacher is correcting sentences with a red pen.
5. This apple is delicious.
6. The students are finishing a writing exercise in class.
7. I need two pieces of paper.
8. Roses are beautiful flowers.
9. Your rose bush is beautiful.
10. The college has many scholarships for students.

## Exercise 40, p. 184.

1. Mack's parents live in Singapore.
2. Mack has two brothers and one sister.
3. My teacher's apartment is near mine.
4. My teacher is very funny.
5. What is your friend saying?
6. My friend's birthday is today.
7. The store manager's name is Dean.
8. My cousin studies engineering.

## Exercise 45, p. 186.

1. Who's that?
2. Whose glasses are on the floor?
3. Who's coming?
4. Who's next?
5. Whose homework is this?
6. Whose car is outside?
7. Who's ready to begin?
8. Whose turn is it?
9. Whose work is ready?
10. Who's absent?

## Chapter 7: Count and Noncount Nouns

### Exercise 10, p. 197.
1. I live in an apartment.
2. It's a small apartment.
3. My biology class lasts an hour.
4. It's an interesting class.
5. We have a fun teacher.
6. My mother has an office downtown.
7. It's an insurance office.
8. My father is a nurse.
9. He works at a hospital.
10. He has a busy job.

### Exercise 43, p. 216.
1. Vegetables have vitamins.
2. Cats make nice pets.
3. The teacher is absent.
4. I love bananas.
5. Cars are expensive.
6. I need the keys to the car.
7. Are the computers in your office working?
8. Let's take a walk in the park.

### Exercise 45, p. 217.
1. A: Do you have a pen?
   B: There's one on the counter in the kitchen.

2. A: Where are the keys to the car?
   B: I'm not sure. You can use mine.

3. A: Shh. I hear a noise.
   B: It's just a bird outside, probably a woodpecker. Don't worry.

4. A: Henry Jackson teaches at the university.
   B: I know. He's an English professor.
   A: He's also the head of the department.

5. A: Hurry! We're late.
   B: No, we're not. It's five o'clock, and we have an hour.
   A: No, we don't. It's six! Look at the clock.
   B: Oops. I need a new battery for my watch.

## Chapter 8: Expressing Past Time, Part 1

### Exercise 8, p. 227.
1. I wasn't at home last night.
2. I was at the library.
3. Our teacher was sick yesterday.
4. He wasn't at school.
5. There was a substitute teacher.
6. She was friendly and funny.
7. Many students were absent.
8. They weren't at school for several days.
9. My friends and I were nervous on the first day of school.
10. You weren't nervous.

### Exercise 19, p. 234.
*A soccer coach*

1. Jeremy works as a soccer coach.
2. His team plays many games.
3. His team played in a tournament.
4. Yesterday, they scored five goals.
5. Jeremy helped the players a lot.
6. They learned about the other team.
7. They watched movies of the other team.
8. The players like Jeremy.
9. All year, they worked very hard.
10. Every practice, each player works very hard.

### Exercise 25, p. 238.
*Part I.*
1. What day was it two days ago?
2. What day was it five days ago?
3. What day was it yesterday?
4. What month was it last month?
5. What year was it ten years ago?
6. What year was it last year?
7. What year was it one year ago?

*Part II.*
1. What time was it one hour ago?
2. What time was it five minutes ago?
3. What time was it one minute ago?

### Exercise 30, p. 242.
1. I ate . . .
2. We sat . . .
3. They came . . .
4. She had . . .
5. He got . . .
6. I stood . . .

### Exercise 40, p. 248.
1. Did we do well on the test?
2. Did you finish the assignment?
3. Did it make sense?
4. Did I answer your question?
5. Did they need more help?
6. Did he understand the homework?
7. Did she explain the project?
8. Did they complete the project?
9. Did you do well?
10. Did she pass the class?

## Exercise 42, p. 249.

### Part I.

1. Did you see the news this morning?
2. A: Jim called.
   B: Did he leave a message?
3. A: Julia called.
   B: Did she leave a message?
4. Did it rain yesterday?
5. A: The kids are watching TV.
   B: Did they finish their homework?
6. My keys aren't here. Did I leave them in the car?

### Part II.

1. Did you finish the homework assignment?
2. Did it take a long time?
3. Did you hear my question?
4. Did they hear my question?
5. Did I speak loud enough?
6. Did he understand the information?
7. Did she understand the information?
8. Did you want more help?
9. Did I explain it okay?
10. Did he do a good job?

## Exercise 48, p. 253.

1. She caught . . .
2. They drove . . .
3. We read . . .
4. I rode . . .
5. He bought . . .
6. We ran . . .

## Exercise 54, p. 257.

*A doctor's appointment*

I woke up with a headache this morning. I took some medicine and went back to bed. I slept all day. The phone rang. I heard it, but I was very tired. I didn't answer it. I listened to the answering machine. It was the doctor's office. The nurse said I missed my appointment. Now my headache is really bad!

## Exercise 59, p. 260.

*A wedding ring*

My mother called me early this morning. She had wonderful news for me. She had my wedding ring. I lost it last year during a party at her house. She told me she was outside in her vegetable garden with her dog. The dog found my ring under some vegetables. My mom said she immediately put it on her finger and wore it. She didn't want to lose it. I was so happy. I hung up the phone and began to laugh and cry at the same time.

# Let's Talk: Answers

## Chapter 3, Exercise 33, p. 75.

1. No.  [They like to look for food at night.]
2. Yes.
3. Yes.
4. Yes.
5. Yes.
6. No.  [Only female mosquitoes bite.]
7. Yes.

## Chapter 3, Exercise 53, p. 88.

| Name | Where does she/he live? | What does he/she do? | Where does she/he work? | What pets does he/she have? |
|---|---|---|---|---|
| ANTONIO | (on a boat) | catches fish | on his boat | a turtle |
| LENA | in a cabin in the mountains | (teaches skiing) | at a ski school | ten fish |
| KANE | in an apartment in the city | makes jewelry | (at a jewelry store) | three cats |
| LISA | in a beach cabin on an island | surfs and swims | has no job | (a snake) |
| JACK | in a house in the country | designs web pages | at home | a horse |

## Chapter 4, Exercise 18, p. 106.

**PARTNER B**

1  
2  
3  
4  
5  
6

## Chapter 5, Exercise 20, p. 136.

|  | a swimming pool | a beach | hiking trails | horses | ocean-view rooms |
|---|---|---|---|---|---|
| HOTEL 1 | (yes) | yes | yes | no | yes |
| HOTEL 2 | yes | (yes) | yes | yes | no |
| HOTEL 3 | yes | yes | (yes) | yes | yes |
| HOTEL 4 | yes | yes | no | (yes) | yes |
| HOTEL 5 | no | yes | yes | yes | (yes) |

## Chapter 7, Exercise 17, p. 201.

**Partner B**

1. an apple
2. some apples
3. some childen
4. an old man
5. some men
6. a word
7. some music
8. some rice
9. an hour
10. an island

**Partner A**

11. an animal
12. some animals
13. some people
14. some fruit
15. an egg
16. a university
17. an uncle
18. some bananas
19. some bread
20. some vocabulary

## Chapter 7, Exercise 26, p. 207.

**Partner B's answers:**

1. a. some food.
   b. an apple.
   c. a sandwich.
   d. a bowl of soup.
2. a. a glass of milk.
   b. some water.
   c. a cup of tea.
3. a. some medicine.
   b. an ambulance.
4. a. a coat.
   b. a hat.
   c. some warm clothes.
   d. some heat.
5. a. some sleep.
   b. a break.
   c. a relaxing vacation.

**Partner A's answers:**

6. a. a snack.
   b. some fruit.
   c. an orange.
   d. a piece of chicken.
7. a. some juice.
   b. a bottle of water.
   c. a glass of iced tea.
8. a. a doctor.
   b. some help.
9. a. some boots.
   b. a blanket.
   c. a hot bath.
   d. some gloves.
10. a. some strong coffee.
    b. a break.
    c. a vacation.
    d. a nap.

# Index

| | |
|---|---|
| ***A/an***, 6, 8, 196<br>(*Look on pages 6, 8, and 196.*) | The numbers following the words listed in the index refer to page numbers in the text. |
| Capital letters, 159*fn.*<br>(*Look at the footnote on page 159.*) | The letters *fn.* mean "footnote." Footnotes are at the bottom of a chart or the bottom of a page. |

# NOTES

# NOTES

# NOTES

# NOTES

# NOTES

# NOTES

# NOTES

# NOTES